Justice in America

The Separate Realities of Blacks and Whites

As reactions to the O. J. Simpson verdict, the Rodney King beating, and the Amadou Diallo killing make clear, Whites and African Americans in the United States inhabit two different perceptual worlds, with the former seeing the justice system as largely fair and color-blind and the latter believing it to be replete with bias and discrimination. Drawing on data from a nationwide survey of both races, Mark Peffley and Jon Hurwitz tackle two important questions in this book: what explains the widely differing perceptions, and why do such differences matter? They attribute much of the racial chasm to the relatively common personal confrontations that many Blacks have with law enforcement – confrontations seldom experienced by Whites. And more importantly, the authors demonstrate that this racial chasm is consequential: it leads African Americans to react much more cynically to incidents of police brutality and racial profiling, and also to be far more skeptical of punitive anticrime policies ranging from the death penalty to the three-strikes laws.

Mark Peffley is a Professor of Political Science at the University of Kentucky.

Jon Hurwitz is a Professor of Political Science at the University of Pittsburgh.

They are the coeditors of *Perception and Prejudice: Race and Politics in the U.S.* (1998) and the journal *Political Behavior*. Their articles have appeared in numerous journals, including *American Political Science Review*, *American Journal of Political Science*, *Journal of Politics*, *International Studies Quarterly*, and *Political Psychology*.

CAMBRIDGE STUDIES IN PUBLIC OPINION AND POLITICAL PSYCHOLOGY

Series Editors

Cambridge Studies in Public Opinion and Political Psychology publishes innovative research from a variety of theoretical and methodological perspectives on the mass public foundations of politics and society. Research in the series focuses on the origins and influence of mass opinion; the dynamics of information and deliberation; and the emotional, normative, and instrumental bases of political choice. In addition to examining psychological processes, the series explores the organization of groups, the association between individual and collective preferences, and the impact of institutions on beliefs and behavior.

Cambridge Studies in Public Opinion and Political Psychology is dedicated to furthering theoretical and empirical research on the relationship between the political system and the attitudes and actions of citizens.

Books in the series are listed on the page following the Index.

Justice in America

The Separate Realities of Blacks and Whites

MARK PEFFLEY
University of Kentucky
JON HURWITZ
University of Pittsburgh

CAMBRIDGE
UNIVERSITY PRESS

CAMBRIDGE UNIVERSITY PRESS
Cambridge, New York, Melbourne, Madrid, Cape Town, Singapore,
São Paulo, Delhi, Dubai, Tokyo, Mexico City

Cambridge University Press
32 Avenue of the Americas, New York, NY 10013-2473, USA

www.cambridge.org
Information on this title: www.cambridge.org/9780521134750

First published 2010

Printed in the United States of America

A catalog record for this publication is available from the British Library.

Library of Congress Cataloging in Publication data
Peffley, Mark.
Justice in America : the separate realities of blacks and whites / Mark Peffley, Jon Hurwitz.
p. cm. – (Cambridge studies in public opinion and political psychology)
Includes bibliographical references and index.
ISBN 978-0-521-11925-2
1. Discrimination in criminal justice administration – United States – Public opinion. 2. Discrimination in law enforcement – United States. I. Hurwitz, Jon. II. Title. III. Series.
KF9223.P44 2010
345.73'05–dc22 2010007238

ISBN 978-0-521-11925-2 Hardback
ISBN 978-0-521-13475-0 Paperback

Contents

Tables

Figures

Acknowledgments

This, of course, is a project for which we owe many people much gratitude. The National Race and Crime Survey (NRCS), which provides the data for the analyses that follow, was funded by the National Science Foundation (NSF Grant # 9906346). We are particularly grateful to Doris Marie Provine, former director of the Law and Society Division of the NSF, for her assistance with this grant. The School of Arts and Sciences at the University of Pittsburgh provided a generous subsidy for this project. For this we are indebted to Peter Koehler, the former dean of the School of Arts and Sciences, and Ray Owen, the former chair of the Department of Political Science. We are also grateful for support from a Research Committee Grant from the Office of Research and Graduate Studies at the University of Kentucky. We also wish to acknowledge support from the Richard D. and Mary Jane Edwards Endowed Publication Fund.

The NRCS was conducted by the Survey Research Program (SRP) at the University of Pittsburgh, under the auspices of the University Center for Social and Urban Research (UCSUR). Scott Beach, the program director at the SRP, was enormously helpful through all phases of the data collection process; he was ably assisted by Mike Bridges, the senior survey research specialist, and Laurel Person, the fieldwork supervisor for CATI Operations. We are also grateful to Director Richard Schultz at UCSUR, who continued this project to fruition – long after we had run out of money. Finally, we wish to convey our thanks, and our thoughts, to the family of Steve Manners, the program director at the SRP when we began this project who was monumentally helpful, encouraging, and optimistic. Unfortunately, he passed away far too early in life.

Numerous colleagues, friends, and anonymous reviewers have read, and provided invaluable comments on, various portions of this manuscript. Our ideas and interpretations benefited immeasurably from several opportunities to present our research to keen scholars at invited talks at the University of Minnesota Symposium on Political Psychology, Washington University, the Chicago Political Behavior Workshop at Northwestern University, the New York Political Psychology Workshop at Columbia University, the Conference on "Race, Inequality, and Incarceration" at Stanford University, the University of Nebraska, Vanderbilt University, the Netherlands Institute for Advanced Study, and the "Diversity and Democratic Politics Workshop" at Queens University. In particular, we are thankful for the comments of Darren Davis, Martin Gilens, John Sullivan, James Gibson, James Druckman, Benjamin Page, Paul Brewer, Leonie Huddy, Stanley Feldman, Rick Lau, Devon Johnson, Lawrence Bobo, Jennifer Eberhardt, Robert Weisberg, Elizabeth Theiss-Morse, John Hibbing, Joe Soss, Charles Taber, Michael Dawson, Tom Nelson, Michael Cobb, Dietlind Stolle, Allison Harrell, and Devah Pager.

Our colleagues and friends who provided a constant sounding board of encouragement and advice deserve special mention: Robert Rohrschneider, Richard Fording, Stephen D. Voss, Matt Gabel, and Margo Monteith, as well as David Barker, Marc Hetherington, Jennifer Victor, and Barry Ames.

Lee Sigelman provided sage advice on our NSF proposal, and we were often guided by his work in the area. Lee's wonderful wit, friendship, and mentorship will be sorely missed.

We are especially grateful for the advice and assistance from the editors of this series: Dennis Chong, who was extremely helpful at every turn, and Jim Kuklinski.

Several graduate students provided important contributions to this project while authoring excellent dissertations. James (Mac) Avery worked for two years as a research assistant using his insight and skill to prepare the survey data, write statistical code, and perform statistical analysis. Jeff Fine supervised a small crew of undergraduate research assistants to download and "geocode" the contextual data, which was merged with the survey data. Stephanie McLean conducted research and data analysis and, additionally, served as a sounding board for numerous ideas central to this project.

We also are indebted to a number of graduate students who have provided a great deal of research assistance. At the risk of omitting anyone, this list includes Kristen Coopie, Brent Dupay, Marc Hutchison, Jason Kehrberg, Terra Miskovich, Stephanie Muraca, Ramesh Sharma, Sam Weiser, Becky Zajdel, and Lawrence Zigarell.

Paul Sniderman deserves special mention – for his mentoring, intellectual insights, and friendship. Paul has done far more than his share to stimulate discussion, debate, and research within the community of scholars who study political persuasion and racial politics. He has shown patience with, and support for, this project, providing invaluable help from start to finish. It is not an exaggeration to claim that this book would be far less interesting and far less thoughtful without his assistance. For all of his help and kindness, we are deeply appreciative.

Our greatest gratitude must go to our immediate families: Kathy Kalias and Rebecca Peffley, and Rebecca Dick-Hurwitz and Joanna Hurwitz. They have not seen much of us while this book has been in process. We will leave it up to them as to whether this is good or bad. Finally, we would be remiss if we did not mention the support we received from Kevin Peffley and Louise Peffley, and Sidney and Rhoda Hurwitz.

Note: Portions of Chapter 4 are based on "Explaining the Great Racial Divide: Perceptions of Fairness in the U.S. Criminal Justice System," *Journal of Politics* 67 (3) (2005): 762–83. Copyright © Southern Political Science Association 2005. Reprinted with the permission of Cambridge University Press.

Portions of Chapter 5 are based on "Persuasion and Resistance: Race and the Death Penalty in America," *American Journal of Political Science* 51 (4) (2007): 996–1012. Copyright © Midwest Political Science Association 2007. Reprinted with the permission of Wiley-Blackwell.

1

Introduction

> This case has been portrayed by the news media as being about race. But the case is not, and never has been, about race. It is about finding justice for an innocent victim and holding people accountable for their actions.
>
> Jena, Louisiana, District Attorney Reed Walters, explaining his decision to charge six African-American high school students with attempted murder after they beat a White student but declining to charge White students, who hung nooses from a school yard tree, with hate crimes[1]

> If you can figure out how to make a school yard fight into an attempted murder charge, I'm sure you can figure out how to make stringing nooses into a hate crime.
>
> Latese Brown, protesting District Attorney Walter's decisions in Jena[2]

On August 9, 1997, Abner Louima, a Haitian immigrant, was arrested outside of the Rendez-Vous Club in Flatbush, Brooklyn, where police arrived to break up a fight. On the way to the police station, the officers beat Louima. Unfortunately, this treatment became far more sadistic when, upon arrival at the 70th Precinct Police Station, one officer (Justin Volpe) sodomized him with a toilet plunger rod.

[1] Taken from http://cnn.com/video/#/video/us/2007/09/19/jena.6.da.press.conference.cnn (accessed September 21, 2007).

[2] "Protest in Louisiana Case Echoes the Civil Rights Era," *New York Times*, September 21, 2007, A15.

Although Volpe is currently serving a thirty-year sentence, the other three officers had their convictions overturned in February 2002 by a federal appeals court for lack of evidence. Louima later settled with the city of New York for $8.7 million.[3]

Less than two years after the Louima episode, four New York policemen searching for a rape suspect knocked on the door of Amadou Diallo in order to question him. When Diallo reached inside his jacket, the police shot him forty-one times, hitting him with nineteen bullets – at least some of which were fired postmortem. Although the officers feared that Diallo was reaching for a gun, it turned out to be his wallet.

As reported in the *Washington Post*, "The four White New York City police officers charged with murder for shooting down an unarmed Black man in a hail of 41 bullets were acquitted today on all counts *in a case that has become a rallying cry for racial justice*."[4] In remarks to guests at a Democratic National Committee dinner shortly thereafter, President Bill Clinton denounced the racial overtones of the incident, claiming "... I know most people in America of all races believe that if it had been a young White man in a young all-White neighborhood, it probably wouldn't have happened."[5]

Despite the president's claim, there is considerable evidence that "people in America of all races" do *not* look at such incidents identically. Several years earlier on the west coast, for example, racial divisions in response to a series of high-profile criminal incidents were unmistakable. On April 29, 1992, a mainly White jury in Simi Valley, California, voted to acquit four White police officers charged with the beating of Rodney King, an African American. The response in nearby Los Angeles was swift and intense, as massive rioting broke out in the north-central section of the city, resulting in hundreds

[3] In addition, two police officers and a former colleague were found guilty of conspiring to obstruct justice for lying about the colleague's role in the torture of Abner Louima (*Washington Post*, March 7, 2000, A03).

[4] Duke, Lynne. February 26, 2000. "Jury Acquits 4 N.Y. Officers; Panel Rules Police Acted Reasonably in Slaying of Amadou Diallo," *Washington Post*, A01 (emphasis added).

[5] Remarks by President Clinton to the Democratic National Committee, San Francisco, March 3, 2000. Amadou Diallo's parents later sued the New York City police department for $81 million, or $1 million for each of 41 shots fired and $40 million for pain and suffering.

of injuries and millions of dollars of property damage. One of the casualties was Reginald Denny, a White truck driver who was pulled from his vehicle by angry rioters and severely beaten. On October 18, a mostly African-American jury acquitted the two Blacks accused of beating Denny on virtually all counts. Racial divisions over this verdict were stark: a *Los Angeles Times* poll found Whites almost twice as likely to disagree with the verdict as Blacks (67% vs. 38%), with Whites more than twice as likely to express "anger" over the outcome (48% vs. 19%).[6]

These differential racial responses should have, but did not, adequately prepare the nation for the extraordinary responses to the 1995 O. J. Simpson jury decision, in which a jury composed predominantly of African Americans acquitted the defendant of two counts of homicide. News coverage that evening inevitably consisted of contrasts between reactions of mainly joyous Blacks and mainly appalled Whites – the former believing the system to have (finally) served justice, the latter perceiving a system unable to handle racial disputes in a fair fashion.

A more recent reminder culminated in an estimated 15,000 to 20,000 civil rights sympathizers converging from across the country on the tiny town of Jena, Louisiana. On September 20, 2007, they arrived to protest the charges brought against six African-American students who allegedly beat Justin Barker, a White student who was treated for multiple injuries at a local hospital and released the same day. Parents of the six students claimed they were provoked by Barker's use of racial epithets – a charge that Barker denied.

But this case was about far more than a school yard incident. It began in September 2006 when several Black students at the predominantly White Jena High School asked permission from the vice principal to sit under an oak tree on school property where Whites typically

[6] The 1992 riots led the city of Los Angeles to empanel a commission to make reform recommendations. Ten years after the commission issued its recommendations, most of them had still not been fully implemented, prompting the city to recruit and hire the police commissioner of New York City, William Bratton. As the police chief of Los Angeles, Bratton has successfully implemented many, but not all, of the remaining recommendations. Unfortunately, as an indication of the prevalence of these problems, Chief Bratton assumed responsibilities after the 2005 incident in which a Los Angeles police officer shot and killed Devin Brown, an unarmed 13-year-old African American who was joyriding in a stolen automobile (Murr 2005).

gathered. The next day, three nooses were found hanging from the tree. Even though the principal recommended expulsion for the White students found responsible for the noose incident, the school district subsequently overruled the expulsion and, instead, ordered brief suspensions.

Shortly after the December 4 beating of Barker, District Attorney Reed Walters formally charged the six Black students with attempted murder and conspiracy to commit murder – charges that many believed to be far too draconian in nature. Mychal Bell was the first to be convicted (on a reduced charge of aggravated battery) and served eighteen months in prison.[7]

The Barker incident was only one element of a much broader pattern – a pattern either ignored or unrecognized by many Whites and increasingly infuriating to many Blacks, even to the degree that they (accompanied by many Whites) came from across the entire country to protest. Consider the comments of Jena resident Terry Adams: "We are not a racial town. We get along with each other. We get along fine. This is something that got out of proportion. It really has." Or the explanation by Jonny Fryar, a member of the LaSalle Parish School Board who supported suspension rather than expulsion, of the White students who hung the nooses: "I hate to see people label us something we are not. Because we have black students and white students playing football together. They shake hands, get along."[8] As if in thorough agreement with District Attorney Walters, such Whites find it inconceivable that race factored into any of the decisions pertaining to these incidents.

Needless to say, Blacks interpreted the incidents through starkly different lenses, essentially as if Jena is nothing less than a microcosm of all instances of racial injustice bundled into a brief period of history. Reverend Jesse Jackson, one of the organizers of the protest, derided Walter's actions as "that's not prosecution, that's persecution."

[7] Two years after the incident, the other five defendants pleaded to a charge of simple battery, with seven days of unsupervised probation, a $500 fine, and restitution to Justin Barker. Through their attorney, they also had to acknowledge that Barker had done nothing to provoke the attack, express sympathy for Barker, and admit that the prosecutors had enough evidence for a conviction.

[8] Quotes taken from "Thousands 'March for Justice' in Jena, Court Orders Hearing on Teen." http://www.cnn.com/2007/us/law/09/20/jena.six/index.html (accessed December 23, 2009).

Interviews with African Americans were replete with references to pre–civil rights movement discrimination, chronic unfairness in the criminal justice system, and pervasive bigotry among police officers, judges, and prosecutors.[9]

These incidents served to expose an enormous racial chasm in responses toward the U.S. criminal justice system – a chasm that dwarfs the divisions typically uncovered in the analysis of public opinion data.[10] The historical origins of this "race gap" are long-standing, clearly predating our ability to measure it. Undeniably, African Americans have had fundamentally different experiences with the justice system during the entirety of their existence in the United States, having to submit to the brutalities of slavery and to witness the "blind eye of the law" in regard to White-on-Black vigilantism and lynchings (Kennedy 1997). In more recent years, discrimination against racial minorities has continued, with African Americans being far more likely to be apprehended, incarcerated, subjected to vehicular stops, and more.

To generalize only slightly, most of what we know about the reactions of Whites and Blacks to racial matters comes from one of two sources. The first is media coverage. The second is scholarly studies. The strength of the first is the weakness of the second; the strength of the second, the weakness of the first. Media coverage has thrown a spotlight on the enormous divide between Black and White

[9] What is most revealing, from our perspective, are the wildly varying interpretations of such events on the part of citizens and leaders – from and outside of Jena. It is essential to keep in mind that the Barker beating, and the subsequent charges brought against the "Jena 6," constituted only one part of the unfolding story. Although it is impossible to recap everything that transpired, certain incidents are essential elements in the drama. Approximately 2.5 months after the beating, e.g., the main academic high school building was torched – an action widely assumed to be racially motivated. One week later, Justin Sloan, a 22-year-old White man, broke a bottle of beer over the head of a 17-year-old Black student. Sloan received only a probationary sentence. Very shortly thereafter, a White high school student encountered three Black students in the parking lot of a Jena convenience store; claiming fear of the students, he went to his car to retrieve a shotgun, which was wrested from him by the three. Although no charges were ever brought against the White student, the Black teenagers were charged with aggravated battery, assault, disturbing the peace, and theft of the weapon.

[10] Differences between men and women (the "gender gap") regarding issues pertaining to certain defense and social (e.g., abortion) policies are often cited as examples of large demographic splits in public opinion. Compared to interracial differences on many issues, however, gender differences appear almost trivial.

Americans. It has documented that at the heart of this "race gap" lays the profound belief of many African Americans that the criminal justice system is, to its core, profoundly unfair – a belief that is, to say the least, not shared by many Whites.

Although journalistic surveys have been invaluable for underscoring the depth of the racial cleavage, they are also severely limited in two important respects. First, by highlighting the cleavage between Blacks and Whites in the foreground, they have obscured the differences of views *within* both Black and White communities. We know, for example, that Whites display substantially more favorable views of the justice system (relative to African Americans), but very little is known about the diversity of judgments among individuals of either race, particularly among Blacks. The tendency among pollsters has been to assume that the political opinions of African Americans constitute an undifferentiated and monolithic mass. However, a variety of academic surveys has uncovered important differences of opinion within the Black community regarding a range of racial and economic issues.[11]

Second, the journalistic work tells us very little about the *genesis* of distrust among African Americans (or, for that matter, about the genesis of the more sanguine beliefs held by Whites). Media surveys, for the most part, are highly focused and extremely limited in terms of the quantity and breadth of questions that are included. As a result, they are not useful for the purpose of investigating either the sources or the consequences of these beliefs. From these journalistic surveys, we cannot understand either why African Americans differ from Whites in their views toward the justice system or why these differential views matter.

Scholarly literature provides a much richer and more nuanced picture of the variety of views of the justice system within the White and the Black communities. Much of the work in criminology and sociology, for example, has documented the extraordinarily high levels of discontent and cynicism prevalent among many African Americans.[12]

[11] See, e.g., Allen et al. 1989; Sigelman and Welch 1991; Dawson 1994; Hochschild 1995; Kinder and Sanders 1996; Bobo 1997; Schuman et al. 1998; Gay 2002; Tate 2003.

[12] E.g., Curran 1977; Peek et al. 1981; Hagan and Albonetti 1982; Hawkins 1986; Parker, Onyekwuluje, and Murtry 1995; Sampson and Bartusch 1998.

In contrast, the relatively rare studies in political science exploring race and crime have focused largely on Whites. A particularly germane strand of this work has examined the link between racial prejudice and crime, examining the degree to which real prejudice bolsters support for "get tough" policies on crime. Implicit in this work is the question: how much is the demand for more punitive solutions to crime really a demand for getting tough with Blacks?[13]

Although these, and a handful of other studies in political science, may be useful in their ability to shed light on the antecedents and consequences of Whites' views of crime and punishment, they are severely limited in two important respects. First, and most obviously, they have focused almost exclusively on the attitudes of Whites (cf. Dawson 1994). Second, they do not tell us anything about why Blacks and Whites differ in their judgments of the justice system, nor do they tell us anything about the meaning of these differential judgments. Comparatively few broad, systematic investigations of public thinking regarding criminal justice issues exist.[14]

The "state of our knowledge," then, primarily consists of a number of journalistic accounts whose strength lies in the documentation of division between White and Black Americans regarding their orientation toward the justice system, but whose weakness is in its inability to explore anything intraracial in nature, or from the scholarly literature, which presents a mirror image – that is, its strength and weakness tend to be its ability to explore intraracial differences and its inability to explore interracial differences, respectively.

Our primary purpose in this book is to delve into interracial differences in Americans' experiences with, perceptions of, and beliefs about the U.S. criminal justice system. Using responses from a national probability survey of approximately six hundred White and six hundred African-American respondents, we examine how individuals of both races see the system – whether they believe it has treated them fairly, whether they believe it treats both races

[13] E.g., Soss et al. 2003; Peffley and Hurwitz 2007.

[14] Aside from a widely cited national survey study by Stinchcombe et al. (1980) and a handful of recent in-depth interviews with a small number of subjects (Gaubatz 1993; Sasson 1995), there have been comparatively few comprehensive efforts to study what drives Americans' attitudes toward crime (see Roberts and Stalans [1997] for a review of this literature).

equitably, and what they see as the strengths and weaknesses of the system. We also ask respondents about their policy beliefs in regard to issues ranging from the death penalty to the three-strikes laws to racial profiling. In the end, we believe that we have a reasonably complete picture of the racial differences in the criminal justice domain.

But merely documenting these differences between Whites and Blacks is the easy part of our job. The challenge is to understand the differences between them. Paradoxically, in order to understand why Blacks and Whites differ, it is necessary to understand why Blacks and Whites differ among themselves. We need to know the reasons why some citizens (both Black and White) evaluate the justice system so much more favorably than others. We need to appreciate the reasons why some Blacks distrust the police more than other Blacks, and why some Whites support capital punishment more than other Whites. Only when we understand the antecedents of individuals' beliefs – that is, what drives our beliefs – can we begin to understand why Whites and African Americans see the U.S. criminal justice system in such profoundly different ways. Although our primary focus may be on interracial differences, we will explore intraracial differences intensively, as well.

One reason for undertaking this study is to correct popular misconceptions about the racial divide in the justice domain. Because public impressions are based primarily on sensationalized news coverage of high-profile events (e.g., the O. J. Simpson verdict, the Los Angeles riots, and controversial incidents of police shootings and beatings), Blacks and Whites often view each others' reactions as being motivated by a reflexive form of in-group favoritism and out-group prejudice. Without appreciating the broader context of an incident, many Whites view Blacks as simply wanting to "protect their own," with little regard for the police, with little regard for the rule of law and punishing lawbreakers, and as unwilling to punish Black offenders. Many Blacks view Whites' unwillingness to acknowledge, let alone redress, a blatantly biased justice system as being motivated by racism. Perhaps inevitably, African Americans wonder why else Whites would use their control of the justice system to continue to intimidate, demean, and imprison so many in the Black community.

Our study shows that one cannot fully understand the differences in the way Whites and Blacks view the justice system by focusing on racial prejudice alone. We gain much greater insight into how the races respond to events and policies in the justice domain by focusing on how they view the *fairness* of the justice system. We understand more of how the races *use* their fairness beliefs to guide their responses by using survey experiments to randomly assign respondents to different question wording groups, asking them, for example, about a Black *or* a White police-brutality victim. What emerges from our study is not just the insight that Blacks view the justice system as unfair and Whites do not, but also that Blacks, understandably, do not typically think about questions of fairness without considering race, and that Whites almost never think about fairness by taking race into account. The racial cleavage in views of fairness that we uncover is profound, consequential, and disturbing, but it is not as simplistic as popular conceptions lead one to believe.

THE IMPORTANCE OF BELIEFS ABOUT CRIME AND THE JUSTICE SYSTEM

We have emphasized the vacuum of knowledge. Scholars, particularly in political science, have paid little attention to public opinion in the criminal justice domain. Often the explanation for such neglect can be found in the subject – a subject that is alleged to be neither terribly interesting nor terribly consequential. On one level, justice-related beliefs *are* inconsequential, at least in a way that is often defined by political scientists: with only rare exceptions, the vote choice, and therefore electoral outcomes, is seldom influenced by how citizens feel about crime and punishment. Crime is a valence issue in the sense that everyone is opposed to it. Candidates, therefore, cannot possibly diverge in their positions in a way that is necessary for citizens to base their votes on such a criterion.

But this is an exceedingly narrow definition of *consequence*, if for no other reason than that candidates *do* differ in the *emphasis* that they place on law and order, as evidenced during the 1988 presidential campaign when Democratic Party candidate Michael Dukakis was constantly criticized for a stance that some felt was insufficiently "tough" on crime or, in 1968 when Richard Nixon (as well as third-party candidate George Wallace) based much of his campaign on law and order appeals.[15]

But even while ignoring any electoral implications, public opinion about the criminal justice system matters in ways that are often subtle yet enormously powerful. Given the nature of the issue, it would be surprising to learn that these opinions are irrelevant. Carmines and Stimson (1980) would classify crime-related attitudes as "easy" in the sense that the topic is easy to comprehend and constantly on the agenda. As such, these attitudes should be, and are, unusually crystallized and salient in the minds of the mass public (Roberts and Stalans 1997). In almost every year since Gallup first asked the questions, the percentage of Americans who thought that there was "more crime in the U.S. than a year ago" outnumbered those who felt there was less crime (1989–2009), and a majority of the public described crime in the United States as either a "very" or "extremely" important problem (2000–7).[16] From 1994 to 1998, "crime/violence" ranked as the single "most important problem" in the Gallup survey, with between 20 and 37 percent of respondents selecting it among all other issues.[17] When asked about the "biggest problems facing public schools," "fighting violence/gangs" is consistently mentioned as a chief concern. When combined with those who mention drug use in schools, crime in schools almost always trumps any other issue as the most substantial problem faced in the educational system, surpassing funding, discipline, overcrowding, and teacher quality.[18] Quite clearly, Americans have a concern with crime that makes the issue hypersalient – at least in recent years.

[15] On the importance of crime in the 1968 election, see Asher 1980. Among others, Pomper et al. 1989 and Abramson et al. 1991 address the issue in the 1988 election.

[16] With the exception of 2002, when approximately equal proportions of Americans thought there was "more crime" vs. "less crime" than a year ago, far more respondents felt there was "more crime" in every other year the question has been asked. Jeffrey M. Jones. "Americans Perceive Increased Crime in U.S." http://www.gallup.com/poll/123644/Americans-Perceive-Increased-Crime.aspx (accessed December 29, 2009).

[17] In 1999 "crime/violence" was barely edged out by "ethics, moral, family decline" as the most important problem, and in 2000 it came in a close fourth to "ethics, moral, family decline," education, and "high cost of living." See http://www.albany.edu/sourcebook/pdf/t212008.pdf (accessed January 2, 2010).

[18] See Gallup surveys from 1988 to 2002 reported in *Sourcebook of Criminal Justice Statistics Online*. http://www.albany.edu/sourcebook/pdf/t242008.pdf (accessed January 2, 2010). After 2002, issues such as funding and overcrowding began to take on more salience.

Moreover, even irrespective of heightened salience to the public, elected officials appear to be unusually cognizant of, and responsive to, citizens' attitudes toward crime. Since the late 1960s, there seems to have been something approaching a crisis of confidence in the justice system, or at least policy makers have assumed this to be the case. As expressions of public fears began to escalate into the 1980s and 1990s, the federal government (along with many state governments) responded with enormous increases in prison construction expenditures and ever more punitive approaches to law violation – for example, three-strikes laws, the restoration of prison chain gangs, and far more punitive sentencing guidelines. The prison population, in consequence, has tripled during the past twenty-five years, even while *actual* crime rates were decreasing (Caplow and Simon 1999). Although it is impossible to determine whether policy makers responded to public opinion or vice versa, it is highly suggestive that polls showed very strong support for the more punitive approaches that were being taken (Johnson 2001). Polls also charted widespread support for mandatory sentencing, as if the public were openly expressing its lack of faith in judges to mete out justice. In sum, even if crime-related attitudes cannot often be linked to the vote choice, it seems quite clear that public opinion in this domain "counts" as a major influence over public policy, and that elected officials behave *as if* they believe their constituents judge them closely on this issue.

Tellingly, the impact of these decisions is neither temporary nor episodic. The decisions made by elected officials in the 1990s – to inflate the prison populations through mandatory sentencing and the application of tougher penalties to previously overlooked crimes (e.g., marijuana possession) – continue to impose substantial costs on state and municipal budgets today. Budgets that are already strained now have to pay for prison construction and additional funding for judicial personnel, ranging from parole officers to district attorneys to magistrate judges.

Presidents and legislators are not the only ones who seem to be motivated by the concerns of the public. Additionally, the link between citizen attitudes in the crime domain and judicial response has been well documented in the literature, particularly regarding such salient issues as capital punishment. According to McGarrell and Sandys (1996), the U.S. Supreme Court has used public support for the death penalty as its barometer of "evolving standards of decency," a criterion the Court in turn uses to settle the "cruel and unusual" question (Soss 2003, 398). The decisions of state jurists, as well, have been found to be influenced by public opinion on this issue. For example, Brace and colleagues (Brace and Hall 1997; Brace and Boyea 2008) determined that, in states with citizens supportive of capital punishment, supreme court justices are significantly more likely to uphold the death sentence (or less likely to dissent from a prodeath majority) when they face "competitive electoral conditions" (e.g., they are close to the end of a judicial term or won by narrow margins).

Finally, when they serve as citizen jurists, individuals have been empowered to render decisions as a form of direct democracy that is lacking in virtually any other domain of public policy. It is in this capacity that the beliefs of Americans are most directly translated into meaningful behaviors because they determine the guilt and the severity of punishment, often in ways that are driven by their attitudes toward crime and, more broadly, the entire criminal justice system.

Our concern with individuals' judgments of the justice system extends beyond our assumption that such attitudes are salient and potentially consequential to the political process. More broadly, we argue that attitudes about the justice system, particularly whether it is fair, color citizens' views of much of the rest of the political system. A good deal of research demonstrates that people who believe the justice system to be unfair tend to evaluate the government more harshly and are more likely to judge the entire system to be illegitimate (Lind and Tyler 1988). One need only recall the overtly political role played by the U.S. Supreme Court in helping to determine the outcome of the 2000 presidential election, and the resultant (for many) disgust with the broader electoral process, in order to appreciate the importance of the judiciary to our view of the broader system. Simply put, the justice system, as perhaps represented by the neighborhood cop or a summons to jury duty, is as close as many individuals come to an experience with the government; thus, low levels of confidence in the justice system clearly have the potential to generate a more negative view of the broader government.

The consequences of cynicism toward the criminal justice system, however, are more pernicious than a sour taste toward the U.S. political system. For those who judge the justice system to be grossly unfair, the potential for disaffection and disobedience is high (Tyler 1990). Given Tyler's conclusion that citizens are substantially more likely to comply with the law when they believe legal authorities to be fair and legitimate, it is therefore not surprising to find that civil disobedience is often located in areas plagued by widespread feelings of injustice. In their careful analysis of public opinion before and after the Los Angeles riots of 1992, Bobo et al. (1994) found that 56 percent of Blacks (compared to 21% of Whites) expressed "not much" confidence in the Los Angeles police, and that 80 percent of Blacks agreed with the statement that "Blacks usually don't get fair treatment in the courts and criminal justice system" (compared to 39% of Whites). Because of the design of their study, Bobo and his colleagues cannot tie these cynical sentiments disproportionately to African Americans who participated in the rioting. However, a study of an earlier Los Angeles riot (Sears and McConahay 1982, Chapter 6) can: Black participants in the Watts riots of 1965 were found to be far more likely than Black nonparticipants to hold grievances against the police because of perceived brutality. Although legitimate explanations of civil disobedience are manifestly complex, it is clear that the distrust of the justice system found among many African Americans is at least an important contributor.

RACE AND THE CRIMINAL JUSTICE SYSTEM

As the title of this book makes clear, this is an analysis of the U.S. criminal justice system and how it is perceived – and experienced – differently across races. It has become common to categorize studies of race in America into diverse, and conflicting, camps. In *Racialized Politics* (2000), for example, Sears et al. trichotomize the literature into "sociopsychological models" that begin with the assumption that racial beliefs stem from one or more forms of prejudice (e.g., Kinder and Sears 1981; McConahay 1986; Sears et al. 1997); "social structural theories" that emphasize the importance of racial group identity and a consequent tendency for Whites to adopt attitudes that perpetuate the hegemony of their group (e.g., Sidanius 1993; Bobo et al. 1997); and a "politics-centered" perspective mostly associated with Paul Sniderman (e.g., Sniderman and Piazza 1993; Sniderman and Carmines 1997) and based on the assumption that racial policy beliefs stem more from political values (e.g., equal treatment) than from racial animus.

Although codification of rival explanations can be helpful, we are more concerned with questions that unify them, not questions that distinguish them: to what degree do Whites and African Americans judge the justice system to be just? How fair is it, in their eyes? What are the consequences of believing that it is either fair or not?

The answers to these questions illuminate much that divides Black and White Americans. But they also bring out what unites them – their mutual fear of victimization. In response to a 2003 Gallup survey asking about precautions individuals take in order to avoid victimization, fully 47 percent of Whites and 62 percent of African Americans indicated that they "avoid going to certain places or neighborhoods [they] might otherwise want to go."[19] (As will be shown, Blacks are consistently more apprehensive about crime than are Whites.) The concern seems to have little to do with reality. In the same 2003 survey, after a year of falling crime rates,[20] 57 percent and 84 percent of Whites and Blacks, respectively, responded that "there is more crime in the U.S. than there was a year ago."[21]

Although the anxiety level of Whites is palpable, the anxiety level of African Americans is even more pronounced, for two fundamental reasons. First, Blacks are disproportionately victimized by crime (Walker et al. 2004, Chapter 2) and, consequently, far more fearful of it. The aforementioned Gallup survey clearly documents that African Americans are substantially more likely to take precautions against crime (e.g., installing burglar alarms, carrying mace or pepper spray, or carrying guns for defensive purposes), and substantially more concerned about falling prey to crimes ranging from burglary, assault,

[19] *Sourcebook of Criminal Justice Statistics Online.* http://www.albany.edu/sourcebook/pdf/t240.pdf (accessed July 23, 2007).

[20] According to the National Crime Victimization Survey (2004, 3), personal crimes decreased by 14.3% from 2000–1 to 2002–3, while property crimes decreased by 6.6% during this same period.

[21] *Sourcebook of Criminal Justice Statistics Online.* http://www.albany.edu/sourcebook/pdf/t2342008.pdf (accessed January 2, 2010).

mugging, and murder to sexual assault and having a child physically harmed while in school.

Second, African Americans are also significantly more suspicious of the system to which they look for the protection that they so badly need (Hurwitz and Peffley 2005). The 2003 Gallup survey found that 62 percent of Whites and 32 percent of Blacks rate the "honesty and ethical standards of police" as "very high" or "high"; that 27 percent of Whites and 56 percent of Blacks believe that the police "treat one or more groups unfairly"; and that 16 percent of Whites and 42 percent of Blacks report being "sometimes afraid that the police will stop and arrest [me] when [I am] completely innocent."

Thus, African Americans (and some other minorities) are trapped in what some (e.g., Meares 1997) have labeled the "joint frustration" syndrome: African Americans, who are far more often the victims of crime, are simultaneously the most dependent upon and the most distrustful of the justice system. Perceptions of unfairness, therefore, can easily become magnified in the minds of many who look to the system for protection rather than mistreatment.

Distrust of justice is poisonous. Heightened cynicism among African Americans may well be responsible for some fundamental changes in our legal institutions and procedures. For example, a growing number of attorneys defending Black defendants are encouraging the practice of race-based jury nullification, whereby Black jurors use their powers to correct perceived social injustices, despite compelling evidence implicating defendants of the same color (see Butler 1995, 1997 for the intellectual justification for this movement). During the past decade, at least twenty-five state legislatures have debated Fully Informed Jury Acts (FIJA), which would require judges to inform juries in criminal cases of their right to nullify the law (John 1997). Although none of the states has, to date, enacted the FIJA, and although it is impossible to determine the frequency with which Black jurors are exercising their powers of nullification, it seems clear that "a growing number of jurors are coming to trial with at least some awareness of their power to nullify" (Dilworth 1996, 12).

There are other consequences of distrust that have been injurious to the legal system. It is likely that perceptions of injustice among African Americans have even served to worsen crime problems. At a minimum, we know that Blacks are significantly less likely to testify in court, provide information to the police, or even report crimes against them, largely because of a pervasive distrust of the system (Neville and Pugh 1997). Without such information, authorities are at a disadvantage to investigate crimes and/or prosecute criminals.

This problem has become increasingly pernicious in recent years, even taking on a label – the "stop snitchin' code" – in many inner-city neighborhoods. As reported by Anderson Cooper on the CBS newsmagazine *60 Minutes*, the prohibition against cooperating with law enforcement in predominantly minority areas has become part of the popular culture. It is now a staple of songs, videos, and other merchandise (e.g., t-shirts) issued by popular rap artists. Rappers remain adamant about promoting the stop snitchin' campaign, mainly because they strive for the "street cred" necessary to sell themselves. When asked by Cooper whether he would report a serial killer living next door, for example, rapper Cameron Giles (whose artistic names are Cam'ron and Killa Cam) responded: "No, I wouldn't call and tell anybody on him. But I'd probably move.... But I'm not gona call and be like, you know, 'The serial killer's in 4E.' "

But it is more than merchandising that drives this trend. According to Professor David Kennedy of The John Jay College of Criminal Justice, who was interviewed for the *60 Minutes* report, "the root cause ... is a long-standing belief that law enforcement is the enemy." The sentiment is heightened dramatically in minority neighborhoods. In response to a question from Cooper about whether he trusts the police, one of the teenagers interviewed replied: "No ... 'cause there's been numerous times I've been walking, just being a regular American citizen and getting stopped for no reason."[22]

Thus, the consequences are pernicious whether referred to as distrust, cynicism, or a perception of unfairness. Although Whites and African Americans may be united in their fear of crime, they are sharply divided in the degree to which they perceive the U.S. justice system as fair. Although we will cast our net broadly and our study of race and the justice system will be far reaching, the cornerstone of this book must, by necessity, be the concept of fairness, and not merely

[22] Daniel Schorn. "Stop Snitchin'." http://www.cbsnews.com/stories/2007/04/19/60minutes/main2704565.shtml (accessed December 23, 2000).

because of the enormous interracial differences in fairness judgments that we will subsequently document.

Quite obviously, we are not the first to study perceived fairness. To the contrary, there is a rich, albeit rather small, literature on fairness judgments, mostly focusing on such beliefs in the economic sector (see, e.g., Schlozman and Verba 1979; Hochschild 1981; and Kluegel and Smith 1986 for some seminal works). Without exception – and without question – these works have found consistently that individuals typically formulate their evaluations of the economy and the economic system on the basis of the degree to which they perceive it as fair.

Tyler and his associates have made an analogous argument about the role of fairness judgments and the justice system, focusing on the concept of procedural justice. According to Tyler (1990; 2000; Tyler and Folger 1980), it is the *process*, rather than the *outcome*, that has the capacity to shape judgments of the system. In one study (Tyler and Folger 1980), the authors found that when citizens are stopped by police officers or call the police for assistance, it is their perception of the fairness with which they were treated, rather than the outcome (i.e., whether the police cited the citizen or solved the problem about which the citizen called), that determined individuals' senses of satisfaction with the encounter. Perceived fairness of process can serve as a buffer against unpopular outcomes.

Continuing in this tradition, our purpose in this book is to explore the role of fairness judgments – their antecedents and consequences – in the criminal justice domain and, more specifically, to analyze how such judgments differ both within and across the races. It is our intention to examine the way that personal experiences with the justice system give rise to differential assessments of fairness by the races, and then to identify how fairness judgments influence the way Whites and Blacks respond to controversial incidents (e.g., of police brutality) as well as a host of policy attitudes, ranging from capital punishment to three-strikes laws.

The study of fairness and the study of race are manifestly intertwined in such a way that it makes little sense to examine either in isolation to the other. Just as we need to understand views of justice in order to understand Black-White differences regarding matters of law and order, we also need to appreciate Black-White differences in order to understand the nature of fairness beliefs. To truly understand how a belief in the inherent fairness of the system biases (Whites') judgments, one needs also to study an oppressed group (in this instance, Blacks) that views the system as inherently unjust. Solely focusing on individuals who think the system is fair provides a drastically truncated view of the justice system. By extending the analysis to include African Americans, we simultaneously introduce critical variation into the pool and, with our ability to make comparisons across racial groups, gain a greater ability to understand the biases of Whites.

THE BOUNDARIES OF THE ANALYSIS

This book is about race, but a reasonable question pertains to the narrowness of our focus: why do we confine ourselves to an analysis of differential views of Whites and Blacks in their beliefs about justice and the law? Certainly, the United States is a more variegated, more ethnically complex nation today than it was fifty or one hundred years ago, let alone twenty years ago. The often-cited prediction that non-Hispanic Whites will no longer have majority status in this country by the year 2050 is only one of numerous monumental demographic shifts. In many ways, the immigration of Latinos into the United States is an even more impressive phenomenon, at least in recent years. According to Kochar, Suro, and Tafoya (2005), in the ten years beginning in 1990, the percentage of this group increased by 48 percent – a trend that is dwarfed by the massive influx of Latinos into the southern states (e.g., the percentages of Latinos increased by 394% in North Carolina, by 337% in Arkansas, and by 300% in Georgia between 1990 and 2000.)

Examinations of ethnic variations in crime patterns are nothing new, clearly predating modern demographic shifts. Shaun L. Gabbidon and Helen Taylor Green (2005, 110), for example, note that "In the 1931 Wickersham Commission Report on Crime and the Foreign Born, three chapters specifically address the Mexican American immigrant. The focus is primarily on arrests, although there is some information on discriminatory treatment by the police." With the mass immigration of Latinos in recent years, research on this group has become increasingly common (e.g., Martinez 2003; Riedel 2003).

As the nation becomes increasingly diverse, we have noticed even more complex patterns of crime – in terms of commission, victimization, and punishment. Youth gangs, for example, typically form around particular racial and ethnic groups, resulting in gangs that are almost exclusively African American, Native American, Asian, Latino, or White (Walker, Spohn, and DeLone 2004). It is no longer sufficient to merely examine how these groups differ from Whites. To the contrary, intergroup relations have become extremely complex (see, e.g., McClain, et al.'s [2006] analysis of Latino immigrants' views of African Americans).

Why, then, do we cast our net narrowly, spotlighting just two groups? We have already provided one response to this question – that is, the sheer and overwhelming complexity of the subject. As will become apparent in the pages to follow, an exploration of Black-White differences (not to mention, differences that are intraracial) is sufficiently challenging that we could not possibly tackle the far greater task of introducing other ethnic groups into the analysis, no matter how important those groups are to the American criminal justice fabric.

But we have a second reason. Although Asians, Latinos, and (most obviously) Native Americans have lived in the United States for more than a century, often in great numbers, the deepest and widest fault line in America has always been racial in nature. No matter how offensive or prevalent the inequities suffered by other groups and no matter how much their patterns of criminal involvement differed from those of Whites, such differences have paled in comparison to the interracial chasm in the United States. To be sure, other groups have faced discrimination in the criminal justice system, and other groups have developed perceptions of the law that differ from those held by Whites. But African Americans have endured sufficiently unique experiences with the law, for a sufficiently long time, and in sufficiently large numbers to put them in a unique position. Consequently, without denying the substantive or historical importance of criminal justice patterns for other groups in the United States, we have chosen to focus on African Americans, and only African Americans.

THE NATIONAL RACE AND CRIME SURVEY

To examine race and crime, both inter- and intraracially, we designed and administered the National Race and Crime Survey (NRCS) – a nationwide telephone survey of approximately six hundred (non-Hispanic) Whites and six hundred African Americans in the forty-eight contiguous states. White respondents were selected through a variant of random-digit dialing procedures, along with a stratified oversample of Black respondents. (See Appendix A for a technical description of sampling procedures.) Professional interviewers at the Survey Research Center at the University Center for Social and Urban Research at the University of Pittsburgh spoke with respondents for an average of thirty minutes between October 19, 2000 and March 1, 2001. Although the questionnaire contains the usual assortment of demographic and nonracial attitudinal questions, the vast majority of questions in our survey focus on race and/or crime. Although we will have much more to say about items in subsequent chapters, we note that respondents were asked about various anticrime policies (e.g., the death penalty, three-strikes laws, and building prisons), perceptions of whether the justice system is fair (at various levels of abstraction), personal experiences with legal authorities, stereotypes of both Whites and Blacks, and more generic views of crime and punishment.

To a large extent, the analytical leverage in the NRCS is provided by a series of survey experiments, made possible through Computer Assisted Telephone Interviewing (CATI), a methodology that enables the researcher to embed an almost infinite number and variety of experimental manipulations in an otherwise standard instrument. Respondents can be randomly assigned to various experimental treatment groups, with each assignment essentially independent of the rest. Most common are the question-wording experiments, in which some respondents are (randomly) asked one variant of a question while others are asked other variations. Because of the random assignments, any differences between groups can *only* be attributable to the differential wording from group to group – an attribution that is vital for purposes of establishing cause-and-effect relationships and a degree of internal validity that traditional cross-sectional surveys are notoriously unable to deliver. Moreover, randomized selection of respondents (quite aside from random assignment to treatments) underwrites the vastly superior generalizability (i.e., external validity) of public opinion surveys relative to studies of, say, undergraduate college students that are common in psychology. CATI studies, of the type we utilize for the NRCS, provide the best of both worlds, offering large numbers of cases that represent a cross-section of the American public along with the type of experimental manipulation that has been successfully employed in the laboratory for decades as the preferred method in psychology.

On the NRCS, survey experiments serve a particularly important purpose: to disentangle the role of race from the role of other considerations with which race may be associated. A single example will suffice for present purposes. We will, in Chapter 5, examine crime-policy attitudes and, in particular, any role that racial attitudes may play. We know that a large majority of Americans – especially White Americans – are advocates of capital punishment, but we do not know whether such support is, at some level, associated with racial animosity coupled with the understanding that a disproportionate number of convicted murderers are Black. In an exceedingly simple way – doing nothing more than informing a randomly selected group of respondents that "some people" argue that the death penalty is administered in a racially discriminatory fashion, we are able to determine the degree to which Whites are sympathetic to or antagonistic to arguments that a particular policy might be fraught with racial bias. Simultaneously, we are able to evaluate nonracial explanations of attitudes toward the death penalty.

We also incorporate experimental procedures into a series of "vignettes" – questions in which we describe all-too-common encounters in the criminal justice system, usually involving some kind of citizen-police interaction. In Chapter 4 we present respondents with descriptions of police brutality and men who are stopped and searched for illegal drugs (presented as factual incidents). Subsequently we ask them a series of questions designed to assess whether the respondent is more sympathetic toward the police officer or the brutalized/searched citizen – the citizen who is experimentally manipulated to be either White or African American. These vignettes are deliberately written in an ambiguous way, providing respondents with a kind of Rorschach test in which either the officer or the civilian can be seen as culpable, enabling us to examine how Blacks and Whites respond differently from each other and the degree to which they are influenced by the race of the civilian in the vignette.

Although the majority of the analyses in the forthcoming chapters focuses on the individual-level data collected through the NRCS, we incorporate the crime rate in a respondent's county, the racial composition of his/her Zip Code, and the size of his/her metropolitan area in order to put people into their social contexts. This enables us to assess the role of the environment along with the individual differences between respondents. Such environmental characteristics are especially important in understanding, say, whether support for punitive measures to reduce crime is higher among those living in areas with high crime rates.

Questionnaire Construction

We have emphasized that our study design and the unique nature of our data help expose the roots of beliefs about justice in America. One other point is worthy of mention: we devoted an enormous amount of attention to the survey construction process, in large part because so little is known about the degree to which Whites and Blacks respond comparably (or differentially) to survey questions. By this we do not just mean that they have different attitudes. Rather, we mean that they are likely to *interpret* survey questions differently and that, due to the scarcity of interracial research, such differences are not well understood.[23]

With this uncertainty in mind, we took two important precautions prior to the field interviews, the second and more standard being the pretest of fifty cases (equally divided between Black and White respondents).[24] The first, and perhaps more important, was the use of *cognitive interviewing*, a methodology first developed during the 1980s through a multidisciplinary collaboration of survey researchers and psychologists that has become increasingly recognized and utilized within the survey research community. In large part, the methodology is helpful precisely because survey researchers do not always (or even usually) understand the response patterns and options in the minds of the respondents. We may, for instance,

[23] Additionally, as Caucasian researchers we felt an obligation to take precautions to help us better understand the survey response among African Americans.

[24] Pretesting was employed for the usual purposes: to check for unreliable scale items, heavily skewed items, items generating an inordinate number of missing data, and so forth. As a result of this process, the questionnaire was reduced by approximately 40%.

offer the respondent options A, B, C, and D, while, in actuality, they think in terms of W, X, Y, and Z. There is also reason to wonder if the question is appropriate for a given group of respondents. We have, for example, extensively studied the stereotypes that Whites hold toward African Americans (Hurwitz and Peffley 1997; Hurwitz and Peffley 2005; Peffley, Hurwitz, and Sniderman 1997), and have determined with relative certainty the most important descriptors that Whites use. But we do not know if Blacks use these same descriptors when stereotyping Whites, or even when stereotyping other African Americans. It is possible for Whites to use one set of adjectives when stereotyping Blacks, while Blacks use a different set to stereotype Whites. To deal with this problem, we had an African-American interviewer administer a preliminary survey to ten paid Black respondents, one at a time. Prior to the beginning of the interview, all individuals were instructed to call attention to any survey item that was confusing, misleading, or offensive. Throughout the process, the interviewer would interrupt the conversation, asking if the response options were sufficient and comprehensive, or whether certain options were irrelevant. They were also asked for alternative options and alternative questions. Essentially, the process enabled us to construct a survey instrument that is far more appropriate and relevant to African-American respondents.

THE PLAN OF THE BOOK

The core concept of this book is fairness or, more precisely, perceptions of fairness. These perceptions are rooted to a substantial degree in reality. The vital point is that people base their actions on the way they believe the world to be, not the way it is. In Chapter 2, we examine the lessons from the voluminous behavioral science literatures regarding discrimination in the criminal justice system. Not surprisingly, the preponderance of evidence points to a system that is fraught with bias at all stages, including arrest, detention, conviction, and sentencing. But the accumulation of this evidence is not the only source of information available to citizens. Additionally, they have personal experience with law enforcement and often interpret these experiences as race related and discriminatory. Even if individuals have not, personally, been victims of discriminatory treatment by legal authorities, they often develop a sense about the extent to which such bias exists in their neighborhoods.

The analysis in Chapter 2 is mainly devoted to the antecedents and consequences of personal experiences with law enforcement – at least those experiences that are seen as racially based. To be expected, African Americans are far more likely to report these experiences than are Whites. But, we ask, which African Americans are *most* likely to experience discriminatory treatment? What are the consequences of such contacts with the legal system? We learn, quite clearly, that Blacks generalize their personal experiences to the neighborhood level, often adopting the perception that the police and courts in their area are racially biased and unfair. This perception of discrimination is doubly unfortunate because, as we shall argue, the very people who are most vulnerable to crime (i.e., African Americans) and who are most dependent on the legal system for help are also most convinced that the system, at least in their neighborhood, is stacked against them.

In Chapter 3 we expand our analysis of fairness judgments beyond personal experiences and neighborhood conditions, examining more global evaluations of the criminal justice system. We begin this chapter with an analysis of the concept of fairness, focusing on the importance of both procedural and distributive justice to an individual's assessment of the legal system. We shall show that citizens can be strongly influenced by their perceptions of the procedures used by legal authorities and by their perceptions of the outcomes of legal decisions.

The empirical heart of Chapter 3 begins with an introduction of two measures of fairness – measures that we exploit throughout this book. When individuals assess the inherent fairness of a legal system, they can do so with at least three different referents. They can, first, focus the degree to which the system has treated them, personally, in an equitable way – the central topic of Chapter 2. Second, they can evaluate the most general systemic attributes – that is, whether they see the criminal justice system, in its most abstract form, as inherently fair or unfair. Accordingly, our measure of *system fairness* is stripped of any references to specific actors (e.g., the police or African Americans) and to any specific activities (e.g., profiling or the death penalty). Respondents are quite simply asked about their most general impressions of whether the system is fair. Third, citizens can assess the justice system with respect to how it treats certain groups – in this case, Blacks. Indisputably, African Americans are arrested and incarcerated in numbers far in excess of their numbers in the general population. But are these phenomena attributable to certain characteristics – say, inherently violent temperaments – of African Americans (which would be the explanation of respondents who believe the system is fair) or, instead, to bias within the system? Our measure of *explanations of Black punishment*, consequently, is designed to assess the degree to which respondents blame the justice system, rather than African Americans, for the disparities in racial outcomes. Appraisals of both types of fairness – system fairness and explanations of Black punishment – could not be more polarized, with Blacks' rating justice as fundamentally unfair and Whites taking the opposite view. We devote the remainder of the chapter to an analysis of the antecedents of fairness judgments, focusing especially on the role played by the personal experiences discussed in Chapter 2.

Chapters 4 and 5, in turn, are devoted to the consequences of fairness judgments. We described, in the preceding text, a series of vignettes placed on the NRCS – vignettes in which respondents are asked to respond to an ambiguous scenario in which the lead role is sometimes played by a White and sometimes by a Black. In one vignette, there are allegations of police brutality against a (White or Black) motorist, and in another there are suspicions of police misconduct when officers search two men (again randomized by race) walking near a known drug supply house. What is most revealing about responses to these scenarios is not just whether fundamental fairness beliefs detailed in Chapter 3 underlie perceptions of police behavior (they do) but also when and how fairness matters for the races. Our basic finding is that not only do Blacks and Whites diverge sharply in the content of their beliefs about the fairness of the justice system, but also that these beliefs influence the interpretation of police misconduct quite differently for Blacks and Whites, suggesting that "fairness" often takes on a radically different meaning for the races.

Chapter 5 examines another consequence of fairness judgments – albeit one that is more concrete: anticrime-policy attitudes. As we have argued, citizens' beliefs about crime policies are politically consequential, even if they don't often factor into the vote choice. Such policy beliefs clearly influence elected and unelected government decision makers and even translate directly into tangible outcomes when citizens render decisions in the jury box. In this chapter, we first focus on the degree to which Blacks and Whites differ in their opinions regarding the most important crime policies on the public agenda: the death penalty, the degree to which crime should be addressed through punishment rather than through tackling underlying social and economic problems, three-strikes laws, racial profiling, and juvenile justice. We then focus on the ease with which Blacks and Whites become even more polarized in their policy preferences and the conditions under which such polarization is likely to occur. Underlying the entire discussion, once again, are citizens' judgments of fairness, examining, for example, whether attitudes toward the death penalty rest on assessments of whether the justice system is, for the most part, racially fair.

Chapter 6 is devoted to some of the broader implications of the analyses. We begin with a brief overview of our key findings, returning consistently to the two main themes permeating the book. First, we underscore how the two perceptual realities of the races are based on the degree to which Whites and Blacks believe the justice system is equitable – to themselves, each race, and the society at large. Second, partly because Blacks and Whites begin with such discrepant judgments of fairness, they end up at fundamentally different positions in their views of the police, the courts, and the best policies to employ in order to deal with pervasive problems of crime in America.

We then turn to a discussion of how our study fits into the contemporary political climate. There is enormous fluidity in the criminal justice domain – fluidity caused by the changing salience of crime to the political environment (including the elites who formulate anticrime policies), and much more. We argue that even in a period of falling crime rates, in which issues such as terrorism and recession are pushing crime to the back burner, and with the election of an African-American president and democratically controlled Congress, there are real reasons to believe the races will remain polarized, largely because the punitive anticrime policies enacted during the 1980s and 1990s have created staggering rates of Black incarceration. We end with an exploration of various possible scenarios for bridging the racial divide.

Each chapter aims at a specific topic but they are united in their concern. All hinge on the concept of fairness – at the individual level, group level, or systemic level. All speak to the racial chasm in the United States. Above all, all address the question of whether America can have a justice system in which its citizens can have equal confidence in the face of racial polarization.

2

Racial Bias in the Justice System

Reality and Perception

In the last chapter, we defined the central role that fairness judgments will play in our analysis. To understand the huge race gap in public reactions to events (e.g., police brutality) and policies (e.g., racial profiling, or even ostensibly race-neutral policies such as the death penalty or three-strikes laws) in the justice system, it is essential to examine the races' diverging views of the fairness of the system. In subsequent chapters, we take a close look at the content, sources, and consequences of global views of the fairness of the justice system among Blacks and Whites. In this chapter, we confront several preliminary and altogether crucial questions in our analysis. Lurking behind any study of public perceptions of political objects is the question of whether these perceptions bear any resemblance to political and social reality. Accordingly, we begin this chapter with an assessment of whether the justice system in the United States is fair. More specifically, we ask: to what degree, and under what circumstances, is the justice system racially biased? As we will see in the discussion in the following text, this is not an easy question to answer. Determining whether racial disparities in arrests, sentencing, incarceration, and police misconduct are due to characteristics of offenders (who are disproportionately Black) or discrimination by agents of the system (e.g., police or prosecutors) is a difficult task. Sorting through the huge volume of evidence points to a justice system that is not only riddled with racial bias but that also defies any facile characterization.

The accumulation of social science evidence is not the only (or even primary) source of information available to citizens when forming evaluations of the fairness of the system. Additionally, they have personal experiences with law enforcement and often interpret these experiences as race related and discriminatory. Even if individuals have not, personally, been victims of discriminatory treatment by legal authorities, they often develop a sense about the extent to which such bias exists in their neighborhoods. As we eventually show in this chapter and the next, racially polarized evaluations of the criminal justice system are based, at least in part, on the radically different experiences of Blacks and Whites with police and the courts – experiences that can be either personal or vicarious. In the following text, we pinpoint the characteristics of individuals (and their social environments) that make personal experiences with discriminatory treatment more likely and that lead people, especially Blacks, to generalize such personal incidents to perceptions of discrimination in the broader environment.

ASSESSING RACIAL BIAS IN THE JUSTICE SYSTEM

In the criminal justice system, experience is, to a large degree, defined in terms of process. As reported in Chapter 1, citizens seem to define their experiences as a product of their level of satisfaction with the process, not the outcome (see, e.g., Tyler and Folger 1980; Tyler 2000). If the process is perceived as fair, the experience is, by definition, a positive one – though we will have much more to say about this in the following chapter.

The logical question, then, is: under what circumstances do individuals perceive the process as a fair one? Easily the richest literature examining procedural justice and fairness has been developed by Tyler and his associates. In studies that are particularly relevant to an understanding of intergroup differences in perceptions of fairness (Tyler et al. 1996; Lind et al. 1997), Tyler bases his arguments on a group values model, which proposes that fair procedures are crucial because they convey several symbolic messages to group members, namely that an individual is a respected member of his/her group and that she/he can feel pride in the group as a whole. For these messages to be communicated, according to Tyler, the procedure must be marked by "neutrality, trustworthiness, and status recognition." When the justice system is perceived as unfair, untrustworthy, or as failing to respect an individual's group membership, therefore, it will be seen as inadequate and violative of the rights of the group to which an individual belongs.

It is essential, therefore, to begin any discussion of the antecedents of perceived racial injustice in the criminal justice system by focusing on the degree to which the judicial process is neutral, trustworthy, and fair with respect to racial groupings, in reality and in perception. By now there is an enormous literature examining the racial bias in the justice system – a literature that, despite its inherent controversies, generally documents at least large pockets of discrimination.

But what constitutes discrimination? Studies of decisions to imprison are replete with evidence of a race effect. Not only are African Americans significantly more likely to be prosecuted (Crawford et al. 1998), but they are also sentenced disproportionately to prison terms (Perry 1980; Blumstein 1982; Crutchfield et al. 1994), especially for drug-related crimes (Mauer 1999). Racial disparities in incarceration are staggering and, since the mid-1980s, have been more severe than at any time in recent American history (Tonry 1995; Yates and Fording 2005). In his searing study of racial inequalities in imprisonment, Bruce Western (2006) finds that although 3 out of 200 young Whites were incarcerated in 2000, the rate for young Blacks was one in nine. By the time they reach their mid-thirties, an astonishing 60 percent of Black high school dropouts are prisoners or exconvicts, versus 11 percent for White dropouts. A significant portion of racial disparities in imprisonment are accounted for by higher arrest rates of Black men for drug offenses, even though Blacks are no more likely to use drugs than Whites.[1] To put this into the starkest possible language, in 2000, despite accounting for only 12 percent of the U.S. population, 27.9 percent of all arrests, 32.9 percent of all index crime arrests, and 37.8 percent of all violent crime arrests were of Blacks (Walker, Spohn, and DeLone 2004, 94). In 2003, almost 40 percent

[1] Western also reveals that racial disparities in imprisonment have severe but little noticed economic and social consequences for Black communities. By locking up so many Black men, the prison boom of the 1990s risked destroying the neighborhoods it sought to save by destabilizing families and reducing their employment and earnings prospects for years to come.

of jail inmates were African Americans (U.S. Department of Justice 2003, 8). By any standard, these racial disparities in arrests and incarceration are sobering. Nonetheless, there is considerable controversy regarding the question of whether such differential outcomes stem from a discriminatory justice system.

In large measure, according to Cureton (2001, 65), the controversy hinges on the "various theories [that] have been formulated to explain Black-to-White arrest differentials." Consensus theory (sometimes labeled the nondiscrimination thesis) "contends that the law will be more or less equally imposed on minorities and majorities so that any differences in application will be in response to actual criminal behavior" and that "criminal justice decisions are nondiscriminatory because decisions will be based on offensive conduct and/or relevant legal variables." In support of the consensus theory, numerous studies (most of which are older) have concluded that the disproportionate African-American arrest and incarceration rates are a consequence of higher levels of involvement in criminal activity and/or involvement in more serious crimes (e.g., Skolnick 1966; Wilson 1968; Black and Reiss 1970; Hindelang 1978; Williams and Drake 1980; Liska and Chamlin 1984). Taking this consensus theory to an extreme, Wilbanks (1987) even refers to allegations of racism in the U.S. criminal justice system as a "myth."

Conflict theory "posits that the law will be differentially enforced against minorities and that this differential enforcement will vary in magnitude with the degree of threat posed (or perceived to be posed) to the elite positions by minorities" (Cureton 2001, 65). Conflict theory is exemplified by one of the earliest studies to examine and find strong evidence for the linkage between disproportionate rates of African-American arrest and levels of bigotry among the arresting officers (Wilson 1968). It is this differential enforcement – quite often the consequence of prejudice – that is at the heart of perceptions of unfairness, largely because of the climate created in which African Americans experience, typically vicariously, injustice.

Both theories recognize enormous differences in outcomes: African Americans are more often arrested, convicted, and incarcerated (e.g., Liska and Chamlin 1984); are less often released on recognizance (Bridges 1997); are less often offered plea bargains (Maxfield and Kramer 1998); are more often subject to abusive treatment from police officers; and are more often profiled (Bureau of Justice Statistics 2001). But the theories part ways in their *explanations* of these disparities. Consensus theorists argue that differential outcomes stem from the propensities of the African-American population to engage in behavior that is criminal, and that a fair and equitable justice system responds with punishments that are appropriate for individuals who violate the law. Conflict theorists argue that differential outcomes stem mainly from the discrimination that exists within the criminal justice system, which (for a variety of reasons) treats African Americans more punitively than other populations. Because the two theories differ primarily in the degree to which racial disparities are felt to arise from discrimination, the following discussion focuses on discrimination rather than the mere documentation of differential outcomes.

Distinguishing True Discrimination

The first thing to note about explaining, rather than merely documenting, differential outcomes is that it is a far more controversial and subjective exercise. Although the controversies and subjectivities are complex, much of the debate centers on the definition and employment of "legally relevant variables," such as prior criminal record, that need to be taken into account before concluding that racial disparities in apprehension and punitiveness are due to discrimination. If African-American offenders are treated more punitively than White offenders principally because they have more prior convictions, it can be argued that the justice system simply treats all offenders the same without discriminating against Blacks.

The lethal force debate provides just one example. Blacks are shot and killed by police officers by a ratio of 4:1 compared to Whites – seemingly clear evidence of racial discrimination. However, most shooting victims are in one or more "at risk" categories (e.g., using a weapon in a street crime). In their study of shootings by the Chicago police, Geller and Karales (1981) found that, controlling for at risk status (e.g., weapons), African Americans are actually shot at a somewhat lower rate than are Whites. Other apparent race effects also dissipate with the introduction of legally relevant variables. Despite the assumption of many, for instance, there is no consistent evidence that the death penalty is administered disproportionately to African Americans, because the proportion of Blacks who have been found guilty of a capital offense who are executed does not exceed that of Whites (Pasternoster 1991; Lauritsen and Sampson 1998), once aggravating and mitigating circumstances are held constant (but see following text).

Such research is often quite controversial because scholars frequently disagree about the variables that should be considered "legally relevant." In a police-civilian encounter, the officer has considerable discretion in deciding whether to arrest the civilian. As noted earlier, African Americans are more frequently put under arrest relative to Whites. Even after considering factors assumed to be legally relevant, Smith, Visher, and Davidson (1984) found Blacks to be arrested more frequently, and Petersilia (1983) found them to be arrested on the basis of less stringent evidence. However, Black (1980) determined that African Americans are arrested more frequently, but mainly because they are more often disrespectful to the officers. It is legitimate to ask, however, whether disrespect is an appropriate criterion by which to place a civilian under arrest. Not only is demeanor defined almost entirely subjectively by the arresting officer, but one also can question the degree to which it bears on the legality of the civilian behavior.

EVIDENCE OF DISCRIMINATION

Many of the race effects remain, even after considering legal relevance. Even though the scholarly literature may be somewhat mixed in the degree to which it adopts the consensus versus the conflict theory, the bottom line, according to Lauritsen and Sampson, is that scholars have by now shifted away from the nondiscrimination thesis to the belief "that there is some discrimination, some of the time, in some places" (1998, 73). Even scholars have paid far less attention to crimes committed by Whites than by crimes committed by Blacks (Delgado 1994).

Some of these "times" and "places" are subtle and beyond the radar of most citizens. In her remarks at a press conference of the Congressional Black Caucus (July 19, 2000), Eleanor Holmes Norton, the nonvoting representative from Washington, D.C., in the House of Representatives, chastised the Senate Judiciary Committee for the speed with which it was confirming (or refusing to confirm) minority appointments to the federal bench. According to her statistics, which were researched by The Citizens for Independent Courts' Task Force, during the 105th Congress "minorities and women nominees took significantly longer to gain Senate consideration than White male nominees: 60 days longer for non-Whites than Whites, and 65 days longer for women than men." Given the differential decisions handed down by Black versus White judges (Welch et al. 1988),[2] Norton's remarks are not without consequence.

Other allegations of racial bias in the criminal justice system receive far broader attention, beginning with capital punishment. Even though there is reason to question a race-of-assailant effect, it is quite well established that assailants who murder Whites are significantly more likely to be executed than those who murder Blacks or other minorities (Lewis 1979; Baldus et al. 1983; Radelet and Pierce 1985; Gross and Mauro 1989; Pasternoster 1991; Keil and Vito 1995). The evidence of a race-of-victim effect is equally compelling regarding police-citizen interactions. Relative to crimes involving African-American victims, White victim crimes feature significantly faster police response times (Bachman 1996), significantly higher probabilities of arrest (Smith et al. 1984; Williams and Ferrell 1990) and prosecution (Myers and Hagen 1979), and more "vigilant" investigative strategies (Bynam 1992).

But the literature about police-citizen encounters has also found a substantial degree of bias due to the race of the suspect (Jackson 1989). More specifically, when interacting with African Americans (relative to Whites), police officers have been found to use force more frequently and more severely (Geller 1982; Smith 1986; Jacobs and O'Brien 1998), and to be more often aided by police dogs (Campbell et al. 1998). Further, they are significantly more likely to arrest African-American suspects (Hepburn 1978; Hindleand 1978; Danefer and Schutt 1982; Liska and Chamlin 1984).

Studies by social psychologists show that police officers, like members of the general public, have such a strong association between

[2] In their study of 10 African-American and 130 White judges across more than 3,400 felony cases, Welch et al. (1988) found Black jurists to be more equitable in their decisions to incarcerate Black and White defendants, relative to White jurists who were found to be somewhat less likely to sentence a White defendant to prison.

crime and African Americans that merely thinking about the concept of crime brought Black faces to mind. In addition, merely thinking about Black faces makes it easier for police officers to detect guns and knives when they do not have clear images of these objects (Eberhardt et al. 2004).[3] This and other experimental studies suggest that despite training designed to control discriminatory responses, the police and other justice agents often fall prey to a variety of unconscious biases and associations.

The most high-profile allegations of police bias concern the "driving while Black" cases of racial profiling, in which police officers make decisions about which vehicles to stop according to the race of the driver. Inasmuch as racial profiling is standard policy for police departments in many metropolitan areas, there can be little doubt that African-American motorists face far higher probabilities of being stopped and questioned than do Whites (Georges-Abeyle 1984; Johns 1992; Maclin 1998). A report commissioned by the American Civil Liberties Union (Harris 1999) studied discretionary vehicular stops nationally. Just one example from this study conveys the magnitude of the bias: when spotlighting a section of Interstate 95, the authors documented that even though 75 percent of motorists and traffic violators were White, 73 percent of those searched were African American (33). It is important to note that these racial discrepancies persist even after location, suspect demeanor, and the seriousness of offense are controlled (cf. MacDonald 2001).

One of the reasons why perceptions of bias are so pervasive among many Blacks is that differential (mis)treatment begins very early, even in the sense that Black students are more often victims of corporal punishment relative to White children (Gregory 1995). More significantly,

[3] Other experimental studies using justice agents as subjects also show how implicit racial associations can bias the judgments of decision makers. E.g., after Graham and Lowery (2004) subliminally primed the unconscious racial stereotypes of police officers and juvenile probation officers, they found that officers in the primed condition rated the hypothetical youth offender more negatively (e.g., violent and dishonest), as more culpable for the crime, as more likely to commit similar crimes in the future, and, thus, deserving much harsher punishment. Laboratory simulation studies using undergraduate subjects have also produced race effects. Harsher sentences were meted out for African-American defendants in studies by DeSantis and Kayson 1997 and Mazella and Feingold 1994, and mock jurists were found to be more likely to hand down guilty verdicts for African-American defendants in research by Pfeiffer and Ogloff (1991) and Rector et al. (1993).

once individuals make contact with the juvenile justice system, widespread discrimination appears to be omnipresent (Lieber and Stairs 1999). African-American youths face more punitive "control" at virtually every phase of the juvenile system: they are more likely to be detained by the police (Conley 1994; Bridges et al. 1995; Wordes and Bynum 1995), to be subjects of juvenile court intake (Conley 1994; Frazier and Bishop 1995; Wordes and Bynum 1995; Bridges and Steen 1998), to be held for preliminary detention (Conley 1994; Wordes et al. 1994; Wordes and Bynum 1995), and to be sentenced to a juvenile detention center (Austin 1995; Frazier and Bishop 1995). Wordes and Bynum (1995), moreover, argue that racial bias becomes worse as juveniles are processed deeper into the system: in one department examined, they found African Americans to comprise 35 percent of the city youths, 55 percent of youths in police records, 57 percent of youths referred to court, and 77 percent of those brought to secure detention. Discrimination becomes more pronounced as the stakes become higher (cf. Leonard and Songheimer 1995).

Racial bias in the justice system does not appear to be limited to discriminatory treatment from agents in the system; it can also be argued that discrimination infiltrates the law. The best-known example is the notorious 100-to-1 provision of the Federal Crack Cocaine Law of 1986 (21 U.S.C. 841), which mandates the same five-year prison sentence for one hundred grams of powder cocaine (used primarily by Whites) as for one gram of crack cocaine (used primarily by African Americans), despite the gram-for-gram pharmacological equivalence of the two drugs (Stuntz 1998). But courts have also upheld other laws that affect minorities disproportionately, such as gang loitering laws (*Chicago v. Morales*, 687 NE2d 53 [Ill. 1997]) and public housing authority mass building search laws (*Pratt v. Chicago Housing Authority*, 848 F. Supp. 792 [N.D. Ill. 1994]).

It should by now be clear that examinations of discrimination must be interpreted carefully because the literature is replete with controversy and ambiguity. What constitutes discrimination for one scholar does not do so for another, leading to substantial disagreements between criminological experts. In their review, for example, Lauritsen and Sampson (1998, 75) conclude that "When restricted to index crimes, most individual level studies have shown that a simple direct influence of race on pretrial release, plea bargaining, conviction, sentence length, and the death penalty is small to nonexistent, once legally relevant variables (e.g., prior record) are controlled." In these areas, what were once thought to be obvious race effects proved to be ephemeral once other relevant considerations are taken into account (e.g., Langan 1994; Dixon 1995; cf. Johnson and Jones 1998; Huebner and Bynum 2008).

Walker, Spohn, and DeLone (2004, 359), however, arrive at a different conclusion: "Our analysis of race and crime in the United States suggests that those who conclude that 'the criminal justice system is not racist' are misinformed."[4] Their updated and wide-ranging examination of the statistical evidence concludes that "Persuasive evidence indicates that racial minorities suffer discrimination at the hands of the police ... and within the court system" (358–9). In many of the same areas that Lauritsen and Samson find race effects to be small to nonexistent, Walker et al. conclude that the evidence for discrimination is serious and compelling. What we can say for certain, therefore, is that our justice system is a patchwork, displaying troubling signs of discrimination at some points in the justice process but not in others, in some locations but not others, and by some personnel but not others.

Implications for Perceptions of Fairness

Given the complexity and ambiguity of the available evidence, citizens are forced to formulate their judgments about procedural fairness in an environment of incomplete and highly imperfect information. As a result, they should be quite likely to fill in many of the missing pieces based on their own personal experiences and cultural stereotypes of both the other race and of the agents of the justice system (i.e., police officers and court personnel). We will devote a substantial portion of this book to an analysis of how, exactly, citizens go about filling in these missing pieces.

But the bottom line, as far as we are concerned, is that individuals of both races have perfectly legitimate reasons to perceive bias

[4] To be fair, Walker et al. (2004, 357) reject the extreme position that the criminal justice system is systematically racially biased, or that "discrimination prevails at all stages, places and times." They do, however, interpret the statistical evidence as demonstrating that discrimination is more widespread and serious than Lauritsen and Sampson (1998), in part because they view more complex (e.g., indirect and interactive) influences of race as more important and more robust than do Lauritsen and Sampson.

in their system of justice. We have noted such bias – if not in all places and at all times, at least often enough so that a reasonable person will take note. Even if studies find an absence of direct race effects (in certain phases of justice) "once legally relevant variables ... are controlled," we would argue that many of these controls are heavily race dependent. It may be true, for example, that African Americans receive longer prison terms than Whites, essentially because Blacks have more prior arrests and convictions. In all likelihood, however, many of these "priors" are due to a race effect. Suspect demeanor, which we earlier noted to be a strong determinant of officer arrest decisions, provides another case in point. It is entirely understandable that the police are more likely to detain and arrest suspects who behave belligerently or who attempt to flee from the officer. But when African Americans believe that they are being questioned merely because they are Black (a perfectly understandable assumption in many instances), or attempt to flee because they have been victims of brutality in the past, one must question whether it is really possible to so easily divorce race from the variables that are used as controls in such research.

It is also crucial to evaluate the evidence as a whole, rather than as a series of unrelated parts. For much of what happens in the justice process has a ripple effect that, by necessity, impacts events later in the chain. Not surprisingly, in contexts where levels of discretion are high, such as in the arrest of juveniles and in the targeting of drug crimes, evidence for systematic bias against Blacks is stronger (e.g., Beckett, Nyrop, and Pfingst 2006; Spohn 2009). Given that "prior record" represents such an important explanation for racial disparities at later stages of criminal justice processing, these early interventions appear particularly important in producing the divergent trajectories of Blacks and Whites and likely contribute to a process of cumulative disadvantage (Walker et al. 2004).[5]

[5] In addition, a slew of studies find that certain types of Black offenders are much more likely than their White counterparts to be incarcerated – i.e., males, the young, the unemployed and less educated, those who commit serious drug offenses, and those who victimize Whites (e.g., Albonetti 1997; Spohn 2000, 478). Moreover, there is ample evidence that Black suspects are disadvantaged before sentencing because they are more likely to be incarcerated before trial (Chiricos and Bales 1991; Crew 1991) and because they are more likely to be represented by public defenders instead of private counsel (Holmes et al. 1996).

Most importantly, even if we take the Lauritsen and Sampson conclusion at face value, and even if we are willing to concede that direct race effects are "small to nonexistent" once "legally relevant variables ... are controlled," such findings may be essentially irrelevant, for few individuals are likely to "control" these factors in their minds. Rather, it is perception that matters, and perception is likely to be driven by parsimoniousness. It is patently unrealistic to expect African Americans (or, for that matter, anyone else) to sort through all of the confounding ingredients that lead to the statistics cited in the preceding text – ingredients that even criminologists and social scientists often disagree upon. Instead, as reasonable decision makers, Blacks are likely to base their assessments on the information at hand. Although some of the information may touch upon the demographic and behavioral characteristics of those processed through the criminal justice system, the most prevalent, and the most digestible, information will focus squarely on the gross disproportionalities in outcomes. Thus, despite Tyler's contention that perceptions of process are responsible for the judgments that individuals make of the justice system, we contend (and will do so in more detail in the next chapter) that outcomes are equally important – especially for groups like African Americans who can make obvious inferences based on such outcomes.

What most citizens are likely to notice are the data cited in the preceding text: although African Americans accounted for 12 percent of the American population, they accounted for 28 percent of all arrests and approximately 40 percent of the prison population. They accounted for 41 percent of those sentenced to death between 1976 and 1997 (Bureau of Justice Statistics, 1999). These staggering disproportionalities are not likely to be tempered by an understanding of other characteristics with which race is often correlated. The bottom line, therefore, is that there is plenty of room for African Americans to perceive bias in virtually all nooks and crannies of the criminal justice system, and such perceptions must inevitably contribute in large measure to the racial divide in judgments of fairness.[6] These same

[6] It is quite likely that the perceptions of unfairness held by many African Americans are fueled by another (accurate) set of perceptions – i.e., a reality-based appraisal of an economic system fraught with the type of discrimination that, inevitably, leads to disproportionate levels of criminal behavior among the poor, many of whom are Black.

statistics, however, are likely to be viewed by many Whites (and some Blacks) as evidence of the greater criminality of African Americans rather than a bias of the justice system. Such perceptions are doubtless reinforced by news coverage of crime, which tends to disproportionately portray Blacks as perpetrators of violent crimes (e.g., Gilliam and Iyengar, 2000; Entman and Rojecki 2001).

THE IMPORTANCE OF EXPERIENCE

There are two ways to look at the perception gap in Blacks' and Whites' assessments of fairness: by asking about experiences (Are Blacks more likely than Whites to believe that they, and other Blacks, experience unfair treatment by legal authorities in their communities?) and by asking about more global assessments (Are Blacks more likely than Whites to believe the justice system treats people and groups fairly?).

To be sure, these are not independent beliefs but, rather, beliefs that should be causally related to one another: an individual's experiences with the local justice system should, at least theoretically, influence his or her more global beliefs about the wider system. Blacks who believe that they have been personally mistreated by legal authorities (e.g., police or courts) or who view such mistreatment as being widespread in their communities are, in all probability, likely to perceive the entire system as generically unfair, just as Whites who lack these same experiences are more likely to see the system as being both fair and color blind. Experiences and perceptions at the local level should inform more general beliefs about the fairness of the wider legal system.

We will explore the relationship between citizens' experiences with local authorities and their more global perceptions in the next chapter. Presently, we focus on two types of experiences that diverge considerably across the races: 1) personal experiences with the local police, and 2) vicarious experiences of discrimination by legal authorities in one's community. We are not just interested in cataloguing the huge gap between the races in the way they experience the legal system, however. A far more important theoretical and political question is, to what degree are the two sets of experiences related? To what extent do Blacks (and Whites) generalize from their personal experiences of unfair treatment by the police to more general perceptions of discrimination by the police and the courts in their communities? Ultimately, we hope to be in a position to demonstrate how the radically different experiences of the races go a long way toward explaining their polarized views of the justice system.

In the National Race and Crime Study (NRCS), we asked White respondents if there was "any time in the last five years or so when you felt you were treated unfairly in dealing with police, such as being stopped or followed while driving?" We asked African Americans a more restricted question: "Was there any time in the last five years or so when you felt you were treated unfairly in dealing with police, such as being stopped or followed while driving *because you were African American*?" This distinction is important because it narrows considerably the definition of unfair treatment for Black respondents to only those perceived as being motivated by racial discrimination. Had we asked Blacks the same question used to query Whites, the number of reported incidents of unfair treatment would have undoubtedly been much larger. All respondents who indicated that they had been treated unfairly were then asked to specify if the encounters had happened once, two or three times, or four or more times.

As documented in Table 2.1, Black respondents are much more likely than White respondents to have been subjected to unfair treatment at the hands of the police. To reiterate, the interracial differences in Table 2.1 would, almost surely, be greater if not for the fact that "unfair" treatment for Blacks, but not Whites, is restricted to race-related incidents. Even so, we find that almost one-third of the African-American respondents, an astonishing statistic, believe they were treated unjustly.

Moreover, of the 29.6 percent of African Americans who reported unfair treatment, more than two-thirds (67.5%) complained of mistreatment more than once. This finding from the NRCS converges neatly with the results of a Gallup poll conducted in 1999 (Gallup and Gallup 1999). Those who felt that they "were stopped by the police just because of [their] race or ethnic background" were asked how many times this had happened in the course of their lifetime. Although only a minority (47%) of the Whites who had reported being profiled responded that it had happened three times or more, 70 percent of Blacks reported more than two such instances. Fully 30 percent of African Americans who had been profiled indicated that it had happened at least six times during their lives.

TABLE 2.1. *Reports of unfair treatment by police by race*

Number of Times Treated Unfairly in Last 5 Years	Blacks	Whites
None	70.40%	87.31%
Once	9.63	7.18
Two or Three	13.84	4.01
Four or More	6.13	1.50
N	571	599

Note: Difference across race of respondents is statistically significant (≤ .05).
Source: NRCS data.

Not surprisingly, African Americans were found (Gallup and Gallup 1999) to be almost twice as likely to feel that they "personally" had been "treated unfairly by the police or by a police officer" (43% vs. 24% of Whites). Equally unsurprisingly, although only 16 percent of Whites reported being "afraid that the police will stop and arrest [me] when [I am] completely innocent," 43 percent of Blacks expressed such fear.

VICARIOUS EXPERIENCE

Without question, therefore, relative to the experiences of Whites, the personal contacts between African Americans and police officers are more frequent, more involuntary, and more contentious. But, as noted in the preceding text, an experiential basis on which opinions about the justice system are formed is not necessarily personal in nature. Additionally, many such experiences are acquired vicariously, by hearing, reading, or seeing the experiences of others in one's community.

In Figure 2.1, we present the results of a series of items from the NRCS, all of which are designed to gauge evaluations of the degree to which Blacks are treated unfairly in one's community. The first three items focus on the criminal justice system and are prefaced with the statement: "Now I'm going to read you several statements that some people make about problems with the justice system in their community. As I read each one, please rate how serious it is in your

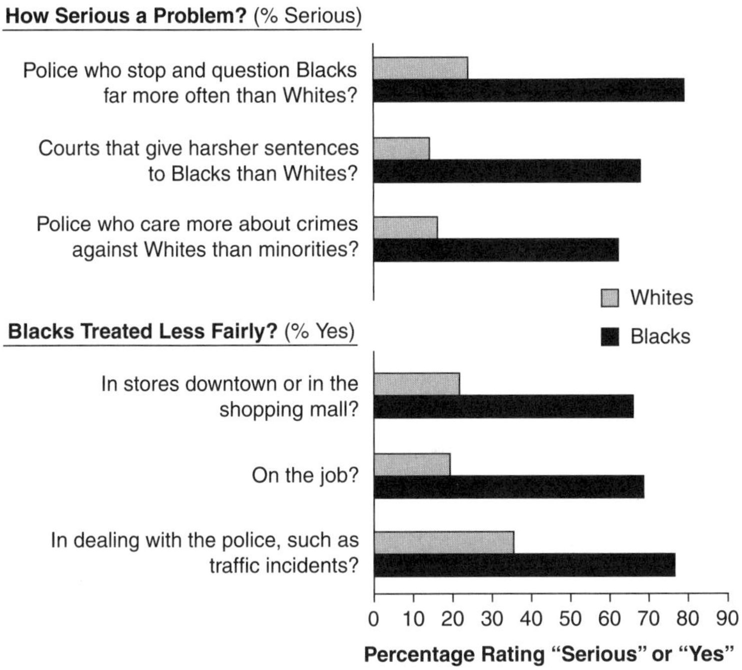

FIGURE 2.1. Perceptions of neighborhood discrimination, by race of respondent. Differences across race of respondent are statistically significant (≤ .05). *Source*: NRCS data.

community on a 7 point scale, where 1 means it is not a problem and 7 means it is a very serious problem." The graph displays the percentage of Whites and Blacks who rate each of the problems as "serious" (i.e., point 5 or higher on the 1–7 scale).

Regardless of the criterion employed, African Americans perceive far more in the way of discrimination in their communities than do Whites and are far more likely than Whites to view such discrimination as "serious." For example, the average percentage of Blacks rating the problems in the first battery as serious is 70 percent versus only 18 percent of Whites. Clearly, there is a large divide in how the races evaluate the gravity of police stopping and questioning Blacks more often, of courts giving harsher sentences to Blacks, and of police caring more about crimes against Whites.

The last three items in the figure reflect the percentage of both Black and White respondents who feel that "African Americans in your community are treated less fairly than Whites" in three conditions: downtown or in malls, on the job, and in dealing with the police. Quite plainly, Blacks are more likely to perceive injustice in numerous contexts but, for our purposes, it is most illustrative that they are more than twice as likely as Whites to believe that they are treated unfairly in dealing with the police (77% vs. 35%, respectively).

JOINT FRUSTRATION

What makes these contentious experiences with law – regardless of whether they are personal or vicarious – particularly unpalatable for many African Americans is their higher level of victimization. The disproportionate victimization rate of Blacks has been well catalogued, perhaps most thoroughly by the National Crime Victimization Survey (NCVS), a project begun in 1973 by the Bureau of the Census for the Bureau of Justice Statistics. More than 150,000 individuals were interviewed from more than 85,000 households in this study, leading to the most exhaustive documentation of crime victimization on record.

Not surprisingly, the NCVS data in 2000 show a higher rate of "household" crimes (e.g., burglary, household larceny, and motor vehicle theft) for African Americans (212.2 per 1,000 households per year) than for Whites (173.3). This disparity was found to be especially true for vehicular theft (13.2 vs. 7.9) and burglary (47.6 vs. 29.4). Racial disparities were found to be even more dramatic for personal victimization – especially crimes of violence (e.g., rape, robbery, and assault). Although 35.3 of 1,000 African Americans were victimized in 2000, the rate for Whites was 27.1.[7] Interracial differences for both household and personal crimes were found to be particularly dramatic in urban and suburban areas for males, and for urban areas for females.

The NCVS documents other notable demographic differences in victimization patterns. For example, although rates per 1,000 individuals are relatively similar for Black and White adolescents (under 16 years of age), as well as for those twenty-five and older, the differences

[7] See Walker et al. 2004, Chapter 2, for a thorough description of the NCVS and the victimization results.

for those in the sixteen- to twenty-four-year-old cohort are profound. Among those between the ages of sixteen and nineteen, for example, approximately seventy-two Whites reported being victimized, while the report rate for African Americans was almost 103 per 1,000.

Additionally, the relationship between victimization and family income exhibits interesting interracial differences. Among Whites, there is a monotonic decrease in victimization as family income increases. Among African Americans, however, although those in the lowest income categories are victims of violent crime most often, and at rates approximately comparable to Whites, those in the highest income brackets are almost twice as likely to fall prey to violent crime relative to Whites. Put differently, Whites earning the least in 2000 were approximately 300 percent more often victimized than Whites earning the most; among African Americans, the poorest were only about 50 percent more often the victims of violent crime. The least prosperous of both races are surrounded by the type of poverty that typically breeds criminal activity. However, although the more affluent Whites are able to insulate themselves from such activity, the more affluent Blacks apparently are not.

Given these demographic patterns of victimization, it is predictable that African Americans are substantially more fearful of crime relative to Whites. As established in the previous chapter, Blacks are considerably more concerned about becoming the victim of numerous acts of violence against them and, consequently, considerably more likely to take various precautions – ranging from carrying guns and mace to installing burglar alarms.[8]

It is therefore unsurprising that the NRCS clearly documents heightened levels of fear among precisely those individuals who are most often the sufferers of violent crime: African Americans.

The interracial differences in concern with crime, as documented in Table 2.2, are profound. Although Blacks are only modestly more likely than Whites to believe that violent crime has increased, they are more than two-and-one-half times as likely to report being "very worried" about falling prey to a violent crime and are nearly twice as likely to rate crime as the most important problem facing the nation.

[8] *Sourcebook of Criminal Justice Statistics Online.* http://www.albany.edu/sourcebook/pdf/t240.pdf (accessed January 2, 2010).

TABLE 2.2. *Fear of crime by race*

Percentage Reporting Fear of Crime	Blacks	Whites
Percentage very worried about self or family member being victim of serious crime (vs. somewhat, only a little, or not worried)	25%*	10%
Percentage rating crime as most important problem facing nation today (vs. no more or less important than other problems)	57*	36
Percentage saying violent crime in our nation increased over last five years (vs. stayed same or decreased)	60	54

* Difference across race of respondents is statistically significant (≤ .05).
Source: NRCS data.

As we will demonstrate, the most regrettable part to this story is that those who are most needy, most fearful, and most often look to the legal system – particularly the police – for protection, instead find that a good many of their encounters are contentious and involuntary, thereby magnifying the discrimination that African Americans perceive when they are stopped in their vehicles, on the streets, or in the malls. In the previous chapter we referred to this as the "joint frustration syndrome" (Meares 1997), or the phenomena whereby African Americans look to the criminal justice system for protection but, instead, experience personal contacts with law enforcement that they believe are inherently unfair.

THE DETERMINANTS OF PERSONAL DISCRIMINATORY EXPERIENCE

How universal are these contacts, and how deeply into the African-American community do such contacts occur? To what degree is racial profiling reserved for "certain types of Blacks" who live in particular types of communities? Are African Americans in the lower end of the socioeconomic spectrum uniquely targeted or, instead, is profiling an experience shared by Blacks at all levels?

To answer these and other questions, it is important to focus not just on the characteristics of *individuals* that affect the likelihood of discriminatory treatment but also on the characteristics of the *social environment* in which individuals live. On the one hand, a variety of individual-level factors should influence the probability of Blacks personally experiencing unfair treatment at the hands of the police. For example, an individual's age, gender, and other demographic characteristics should be associated with frequency of contact and unfair treatment by the police. Younger Black males have often been targeted by police (Walker, Spohn, and DeLone 2004). In addition, various social and political orientations, such as education or ideology, may prompt individuals to interpret negative encounters with police as being motivated by racism. Blacks with a college degree, for example, are much more likely to perceive both societal and personal discrimination than less educated African Americans (Sigelman and Welch 1991; Tate 1993; Dawson 1994), and liberal ideologies are typically associated with a suspicious view of police power (Conover and Feldman 1981).

Apart from the characteristics that define individuals, Blacks who live in particular social environments are more liable to experience incidents of unfair treatment. As suggested by the joint frustration hypothesis, living in a high-crime area doubtless increases the likelihood of negative police encounters for all types of individuals. Additionally, the very definition and presence of racial profiling suggests that police are more likely to target urban communities with higher concentrations of African Americans.

To investigate these and other sources of personal discrimination among Blacks, we regressed the number of reported incidents of unfair treatment (described in Table 2.1) on several demographic factors and political predispositions assessed in the NRCS, along with various characteristics of Black respondents' social surroundings as follows:

Unfair Treatment = Individual Demographic Factors (Gender, Age, Education, Income, South) + Individual Political Predispositions (Ideology, Partisanship) + Social Context (Reported Crime, Percent Black, Large Metropolitan Area)

The predictor variables are described only briefly here and in more detail in Appendix A. The measurement of age, education, and income are straightforward; female is a dummy variable with females designated as 1 and males as 0; and ideology and partisanship are measured on traditional seven-point scales where 1 is "strong liberal" (Democrat) and 7 is "strong conservative" (Republican).

The measurement of the social context variables requires more elaboration. Following prior research,[9] we assessed the racial composition of individuals' communities, percent Black, at the Zip Code level, because Zip Codes are smaller geographic census units that approximate a respondent's immediate neighborhood context much better than, say, county or metropolitan area data. Contextual data at the Zip Code (and the county) level were taken from the 2000 Census (Summary Files 1 and 3). The racial composition of respondents' neighborhoods in our survey, as depicted in Figure 2.2, parallels the extreme residential segregation that exists in most U.S. cities and neighborhoods (e.g., Massey and Denton 1993; Oliver 2010). Whites are heavily concentrated in neighborhoods (Zip Codes) that are almost exclusively White. Approximately one-third of all White respondents live in Zip Codes that are 1 percent Black or less; the next third live in Zip Codes of less than 5.3 percent Black, and the overall mean is only 8 percent. By contrast, the average African-American respondent lives in a Zip Code that is 50 percent Black, and more than a third live in neighborhoods that are more than 60 percent Black.[10]

Reported crime statistics are available only at the county level and are taken from the Uniform Crime Reports (UCR) Program data in 2000. Our measure of the County Crime Index is the number of "index crimes" (i.e., murders, rapes, robberies, aggravated assaults, burglaries, larcenies, and auto thefts) reported in a county per 100,000 inhabitants. As might be expected, the average Black respondent lives in a county with a much higher rate of crime (5,532 reported index crimes) than the average White respondent (3,913).

Finally, we assess whether an individual resides in a county that is located in a metropolitan area with a population of one million or more. Approximately 43 percent of Whites and 60 percent of Blacks in our survey live in such a large metropolitan area.

[9] E.g., in their study of Whites' racial attitudes, Oliver and Mendelberg (2000) make a similar argument in favor of measures of racial composition based on smaller geographic units like Zip Codes. Smaller census units, like the block-group level, used by Gay (2004) in her study of environmental sources of Blacks' racial attitudes, were not available in our survey.

[10] Due to the skewed distribution of the raw percentages of racial composition, we use logged values of percent Black in the analysis in the following text, which has the desirable property of stretching out the distribution of percent Blacks at the lower end and compressing it at the upper end.

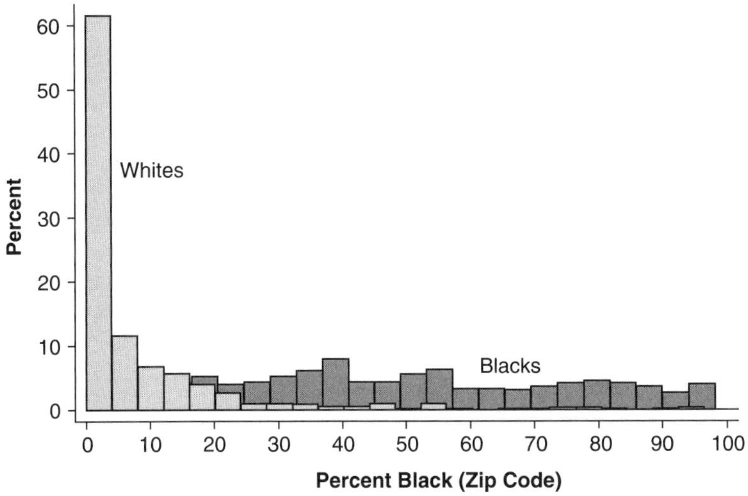

FIGURE 2.2. Percentage of Whites and Blacks living in neighborhoods (Zip Codes) of varying racial concentration.
Source: NRCS data.

Table 2.3 displays the results of the ordered probit regression obtained by estimating the preceding equation.[11] Because the probit coefficients are not directly interpretable, we also present the predicted probability of Black respondents reporting at least one incident of unfair treatment by the police for high and low values of statistically significant predictors (setting all other variables at their means) in Figure 2.3. The results are interesting and revealing. As expected, gender and age are significant predictors of Blacks' unfair treatment by the police (second and third rows of coefficients). Confirming countless observational studies of police profiling (see Harris [2002] for an excellent account), younger Black men are much more likely to experience unfair treatment than Blacks who are older or female. As shown in the figure, after accounting for all the other variables in the equation, Black men are still almost twice as likely as Black women to report at least one racial incident with police (40% vs. 22%, respectively). Similarly, younger Blacks (assessed at 26 years of age) are almost twice as likely (37% vs. 20%) to be treated

[11] Because the dependent variable, unfair treatment, is ordinal, ordinary least-squares (OLS) estimates will be biased. Hence, we use ordered probit to estimate the equation.

TABLE 2.3. *Predicting unfair treatment from social and political factors, Blacks*

	Coefficient	Standard Error
Demographic Factors		
Education	.100*	(.048)
Female	−.529**	(.115)
Age	−.017**	(.004)
Income	−.009	(.043)
South	−.058	(.134)
Political Predispositions		
Party ID	−.020	(.038)
Ideology	−.070*	(.029)
Social Context		
County Crime Index[a]	5.00e-05*	(2.365e-05)
Large Metropolitan Area[b]	1.00	(.141)
Percent Black in Zip Code (logged)	−.07	(.09)
Median Income in Zip Code	−6.15e-06	(5.75e-06)
Cutpoint 1	−.519	(.629)
Cutpoint 2	−.686	(.519)
Cutpoint 3	.077	(.519)
N	563	

*p < .05, **p < .01

[a] Reported county crime rate per 100,000 inhabitants.

Source: Uniform Crime Reporting Program7 Data, 2000.

[b] County in metropolitan areas of 1 million population or more.

Source: 2003 Rural-urban Continuum Codes.

Note: Entries are ordered probit regression coefficients with robust standard errors in parentheses. Higher values on the preceding variables indicate a greater number of reported incidents of unfair treatment, higher formal education, female, years of age, income, living in the Deep South, more Republican, conservative, higher county crime rate, large metropolitan area, and percent Black in Zip Code (logged).

Source: NRCS data.

unfairly by police because of their race than are older Blacks (at age 57). Among Blacks who are younger (18 to 25 years) and male, the probability of at least one incident increases to an astonishing 50 percent (not shown in the figure).

The finding that younger Black men are much more likely to experience unfair treatment than their older or female counterparts should not obscure the important fact that approximately one of every five women

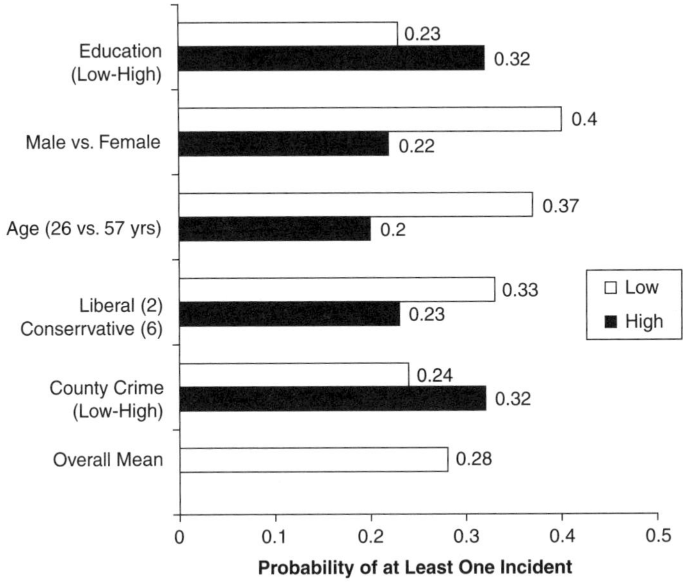

FIGURE 2.3. Predicted probability of at least one incident of unfair treatment, Blacks.

Note: The figure shows how moving from low to high values on the predictor, while holding other predictors at their means, changes the probability that Blacks recall at least one incident of unfair treatment by police. Unless otherwise noted, low and high values correspond to 1 standard deviation below and above the mean (i.e., less than high school vs. a bachelor's degree, male vs. female, 26 vs. 57 years old, not strong liberal vs. not strong conservative, and a county crime rate of 3,340 vs. 7,726 index crimes per 100,000 inhabitants). Probabilities based on the results in Table 2.3.

Source: NRCS data.

and older Blacks report at least one incident of unfair treatment by police, which is a high level by any standard. Generally speaking, in our sample it is hard to find any significant category of African Americans that is sheltered from discriminatory treatment by the police.

The role of education is particularly interesting, for it confirms a paradox of Black opinion often noted in the literature: more educated African Americans are significantly more likely to perceive various types of discrimination relative to less educated African Americans (Tate 1993; Dawson 1994; Welch et al. 2001; Gay 2004). In the present context, the association between education and unfair treatment makes perfect sense, for at least two reasons. In the first place, middle-class Blacks are likely to experience numerous incidents of discriminatory treatment by police. Despite the level of hypersegregation that exists in most U.S. communities, middle-class Blacks are more likely to work (and to a lesser extent, live) in predominantly "White" neighborhoods, which unfortunately means that they become targets of the very kind of racial profiling our question about unfair treatment is designed to tap. (Were you "treated unfairly in dealing with police, such as being stopped or followed while driving because you were African American?") Second, Blacks with more formal education may be more likely to recognize that negative police encounters are not isolated events but are tied to more general discriminatory practices of the justice system.[12]

Turning to the coefficients associated with the two political predispositions, we also see that although partisanship has no effect on the dependent variable, Blacks who consider themselves more liberal report significantly more instances of unfair treatment than their conservative counterparts.[13] It seems likely in this case that the primary influence of ideology is to shape perceptions and interpretations of negative encounters with police rather than to affect the actual frequency of such incidents, because it is difficult to imagine why Black liberals, net of education, demographic factors, and social context, would face more incidents of unfair treatment by law enforcement than conservatives. Given the tendency for liberals to be suspicious of police power the influence of ideology here is not surprising.

Among the indicators of social context, only the reported County Crime Index is significantly tied to the frequency of experiencing unfair treatment at the hands of the police. Moving from counties with a relatively "low" crime rate to counties with a higher one, the predicted percentage of Blacks experiencing police discrimination increases from about one out of every four to one of every three Blacks reporting

[12] After being treated to the ignominy of police harassment, despite their middle-class status, more highly educated Blacks may "perceive more acutely" the kind of racial discrimination from the justice system directed toward Blacks as a group.

[13] In our sample, the mean of the ideology scale among Blacks corresponds roughly to "moderate" (or 4 on the 7-point scale), while "low" corresponds to "not so strong liberal" (at point 2) and "high" is "not so strong conservative" (at point 6). Ideology and partisanship are not highly related among African Americans ($r = .12$).

discriminatory treatment (24% to 32%).[14] Importantly, these findings are consistent with the joint frustration hypothesis: Blacks who are most dependent on the police for protection against higher crime in their communities are at the same time more likely to experience discriminatory treatment from law enforcement. Although our data are limited in being able to pinpoint the exact mechanism by which county crime rates affect the frequency of unfair treatment, the following causal scenario is consistent with our findings and prior research: when police "crack down" on misconduct in high-crime areas, they often target African Americans for "suspicious" behavior, thus subjecting many law-abiding citizens to the daily harassments and ignominy of being stopped and questioned, in part, because they are Black.[15]

THE DETERMINANTS OF VICARIOUS EXPERIENCES

But what influence do such personal experiences have on individuals' more general assessments of legal authorities (e.g., police and courts) and the fairness of the legal system? In Chapter 3 we examine the impact of experiences on more global evaluations of the legal system. Presently, we explore the tendency for perceptions of unfair treatment by the police to shape what we call vicarious experiences – that is, perceptions of racial discrimination by the police and the courts in an individual's community. We know from Figure 2.1 that Blacks and Whites have radically different assessments of the seriousness of such discrimination. But to what extent can these different assessments be traced back to respondents' personal experiences with police, especially among Blacks? Are Blacks who have been treated unfairly by the police more likely to perceive discriminatory treatment against Blacks in their neighborhoods? When Blacks are mistreated by the police, do they generalize from their experience by recognizing that such maltreatment exists on a wider scale?

[14] We obtain basically the same results if we substitute county characteristics (i.e., percent Black, median income) for social context measured at the Zip Code level.

[15] Percent Black does not affect unfair treatment for at least two reasons: 1) most Blacks live in neighborhoods with relatively high concentrations of African Americans, and 2) as suggested by the impact of education, even Blacks who live in predominantly White neighborhoods are subject to racial profiling.

We cannot be certain, or even confident, that individuals will generalize from their personal experiences because, admittedly, a long line of research in political science agrees with Lane's (1962) original conclusion that, for most Americans, the events and experiences of day-to-day life are simply "morselized" instead of seeing them as part of a pattern or larger context with political or social significance. In the economic realm, the failure of citizens to connect their personal experiences to the wider political and economic system is legendary. The unemployed, the poor, and individuals suffering economic setbacks, for example, seldom connect their personal financial misfortunes to more systemic forces, like the national economy or failed economic policies. Rarely do they impugn the fairness of the economic system based on their personal experiences. Rather, the connection between personal experiences and more general perceptions is extremely tenuous and conditional, largely because people seldom attribute responsibility for their personal situation to more systemic forces (e.g., Schlozman and Verba 1979; Lewis-Beck and Stegmaier 2000).

The connection between Blacks' experiences with police discrimination and their perception of similar kinds of discrimination in their community, however, should not be so tenuous. The legal system is responsible for the behavior of its functionaries – for example, cops on the beat or courthouse judges – in a way that the economic system is not. In turn, it is much more easily held accountable when things go badly. Outside of severe economic downturns, jobs are typically assumed to be lost for a variety of reasons, only some of which can easily be traced to more systemic forces. But there are far fewer explanations for police bias. At the end of the day, citizens will inevitably generalize from their encounters with actors of the justice system to the very system. Finally, although various intermediaries (e.g., political parties, politicians, and the media) often fail to help citizens link their personal economic experiences to the public sphere (e.g., Kiewiet 1983; Mutz 1992), a range of agents – including Black leaders, the Black press, the American Civil Liberties Union, and the Justice Department under President Clinton – helped to publicize widespread complaints about racial profiling and "driving while Black" in African-American communities.

In addition, studies in psychology suggest that traumatic personal experiences can lead to more pessimistic estimates of how likely others are to encounter similar experiences. For example, those affected by the 1994 Northridge, California, earthquake were found to be less optimistic about injury in future earthquakes (Helweg-Larsen 1999), patients with unsuccessful organ transplants were found to give lower estimates of population success rates for transplantation (McCauley et al. 1985), and survivors of Hurricane Hugo estimated higher levels of damage from Hurricane Andrew than those who did not experience Hugo personally (Sattler et al. 1995). Quite clearly, a personal experience can have an impact on an individual that is more traumatic and more dramatic than witnessing the event indirectly, through news coverage.

In the legal domain, Tyler's (1990) research is quite clear about the power of negative personal experiences to translate into more general perceptions of an unfair legal system. As Tyler (2001, 431) notes in a recent summary of his research, the "slights and insults that people suffer when dealing with authorities seem to have a big effect on them." For members of minority groups, perceptions of unfair treatment can be especially toxic because such experiences communicate strong signals to group members that their group is neither respected nor valued. Thus, for a variety of reasons, when Blacks are treated unfairly because of their race they are likely to impugn the fairness of the wider system, particularly as it exists in their own community.

Our expectations for Whites are quite different, however. Because Whites were not asked whether they were treated unfairly because of their race, their experiences are, accordingly, less relevant for drawing inferences about racial discrimination in their community.

Measures and Expectations

In the analysis in the following text, we examine whether Blacks' and Whites' ratings of the seriousness of various problems of neighborhood discrimination are a function of negative personal encounters with the law (unfair treatment) as well as various other predictors, such as individuals' political orientations, their stereotypes of Blacks and Whites, various demographic factors, and characteristics of the social environment in which they live. The dependent variable in our analysis, neighborhood discrimination, was created by summing responses to the first two items in Figure 2.1 – that is, police stopping Blacks more often than Whites and courts giving harsher sentences to Blacks (r = .57 for Whites and r = .51 for Blacks), with higher scores indicating that individuals rated justice discrimination as more serious in their community.[16] With scores on the resulting neighborhood discrimination index ranging from 0 (not serious) to 12 (very serious), the average ratings of Whites (3.5) and Blacks (8.7) are remarkably polarized by race. In the following text we present our expectations for key predictors of neighborhood discrimination and describe their measurement.

Political Orientations

Ideological and partisan identifications may shape perceptions of neighborhood discrimination. Conservatives, for example, are reluctant to acknowledge the discrimination that Blacks face in the economic sphere; the same may be true in the legal realm. In addition, as debates about racial profiling and other racial disparities in the justice system move to the political forefront, assessments of discrimination should become politicized, fueled by ideological or partisan leanings. Ideology and party ID are measured as in Table 2.3.

Anti-Black Stereotypes

Individuals' views of racial discrimination are also likely to be influenced by the degree to which they stereotype one race more harshly than the other. Whites who subscribe to negative stereotypes of Blacks, for example, viewing them as lazy or violent, may reject the idea that the justice system discriminates against African Americans in the same way they have been found to deny discrimination in the economic realm (Sigelman and Welch 1991). Individuals who view Whites in a more negative light, rating them as dishonest or prejudiced, may be especially likely to view the justice system (which is dominated by Whites) as discriminating against Blacks. Our measure of anti-Black stereotypes assesses the degree to which individuals view Blacks more negatively than Whites and is created by subtracting ratings of "most Whites" from those of "most Blacks" on a series

[16] We did not include the third item in Figure 2.1, "police care less about crimes against blacks," in the index because responses to this item were not as highly correlated with those from the other two items, and we wanted to avoid loading the index with responses toward the police.

of traits, including "lazy," "prone to violence," "prefer to live on welfare," "hostile," and "dishonest." Maximum scores are diagnostic of respondents who stereotype African Americans more critically than they stereotype Whites, while minimum scores reflect precisely the opposite judgments.

Demographic Factors

As in our analysis of personal discrimination among Blacks, we include several demographic characteristics as predictors: education, female (0 = male, 1 = female), age, income, and living in the South (coded 1 for Deep South, 0 otherwise). Based on research reviewed earlier, we expect to find that more educated African Americans rate discrimination as being more serious in their communities. Controlling for education levels, however, less affluent Blacks, as well as Whites, may view justice discrimination more seriously, insofar as they are more likely to witness or hear about such treatment in their neighborhoods. In light of scanty prior research, our expectations regarding the role of gender, age, and living in the South are understandably less certain.

Social Context

Social context has been found to exert a strong pull on citizens' political and social attitudes quite independently of their individual characteristics (for a review, see Huckfeldt, Johnson, and Sprague 2005), and this is particularly true for racial attitudes, including perceptions of discrimination.[17] A large volume of research, beginning with the seminal work of Key (1949), has investigated the effect of the proportion of Blacks living in a geographic area (e.g., state, county, or neighborhood) on Whites' racial attitudes. More recently, the impact of social context on Black public opinion has received scholarly attention (e.g., Welch et al. 2001; Gay 2004). Although a comprehensive review of this large body of work is beyond our scope (see Oliver 2010 for a recent review), Welch et al. (2001, 8) provide a convenient summary (see also Taylor 1998):

[17] See, e.g., Oliver and Mendelberg (2000) on the influence of social context on Whites' racial attitudes and Gay (2004) on Blacks' racial attitudes. Regarding the influence of social context on Whites' crime attitudes, see Baumer et al. (2003) and Soss et al. (2003).

> Although much inconsistency runs through the findings, a preponderance of evidence suggests that Whites' attitudes towards Blacks (and policies designed to help Blacks) are a curvilinear function of Black population size.

In their own study of racial attitudes in Detroit in the 1990s, the authors found that among both races perceptions of discrimination toward Blacks varied curvilinearly with the percentage of Blacks living in one's neighborhood, with perceived discrimination lower in predominantly White or predominantly Black neighborhoods and reaching its highest levels in racially mixed neighborhoods, where, the authors reasoned, racial tensions are likely to be strongest and Whites have a greater opportunity to observe and hear about discrimination against Blacks. Based on this research, we expect perceptions of vicarious discrimination to vary (curvilinearly) with the percentage of Blacks living in an individual's community (operationalized with logged values at the Zip Code level).[18]

In addition, perceptions of discrimination are expected to vary with the rate of crime reported in one's county of residence. Just as Blacks reported more police discrimination directed against them if they lived in counties with higher crime rates (Table 2.3), so should individuals of both races perceive more discrimination against Blacks as a group in areas where more crime may spark more aggressive policing, racial profiling, and more evidence of discrimination against Blacks by the police and the courts.

Findings

The results of the regression equations, estimated separately for Whites and Blacks, are presented in Table 2.4. The first row of coefficients demonstrates that, as expected, Whites' personal experiences (defined in nonracial terms) with unfair treatment by the police do not form their perceptions of justice discrimination. The coefficients for unfair treatment are small and statistically insignificant. Among African Americans, however, being treated unfairly by the police because one is Black significantly fuels more general perceptions

[18] Using the logged value of percent Black not only reduces skewness but also allows for a slight curvilinear relationship between percent Black and neighborhood discrimination. Logged values outperformed the raw percentages for percent Black for both White and Black respondents.

TABLE 2.4. *Predicting perceived seriousness of neighborhood discrimination*

	Blacks		Whites	
	Coefficient	Standard Error	Coefficient	Standard Error
Unfair Treatment	.63**[a]	(.15)	.17	(.21)
Party ID	−.41**[a]	(.093)	−.013	(.068)
Ideology	.012	(.071)	−.28**	(.074)
Anti-Black Stereotype	−.064**	(.021)	−.057*	(.026)
Local News	.12	(.16)	.22	(.12)
Education	.18[a]	(.12)	−.11	(.091)
Female	.091	(.30)	−.075	(.24)
Age	−.0074	(.0095)	−.0052	(.0077)
Income	−.32**	(.11)	−.15	(.085)
South	−.076	(.33)	−.11	(.29)
Social Context				
County Crime Index	−.000090[a]	(.000065)	.00018*	(.000073)
Large Metropolitan Area	.19[a]	(.34)	.86**	(.26)
Percent Black Zip Code	.36*	(.18)	.16*	(.070)
Constant	1.3**	(1.12)	6.65**	(.83)
N	562	562	595	595
Adj R^2	.082	.082	.103	.103

*$p < .05$, **$p < .01$

[a] Coefficient is statistically different across race of respondents (≤ .05).

Note: Entries are OLS regression coefficients with standard errors in parentheses. Higher values on the preceding variables indicate greater perceived seriousness of neighborhood discrimination, number of reported incidents of unfair treatment, more Republican, conservative, more negative stereotypes of Blacks than Whites, watch more local TV news, higher formal education, female, years of age, income, living in the Deep South, higher county crime rate, large metropolitan area, and percent Black in Zip Code (logged).

Source: NRCS data.

of neighborhood discrimination. The more often Blacks personally experience discrimination by the police, the more likely they are to rate discriminatory treatment in their communities by police and the courts as being serious.[19]

[19] The coefficients for unfair treatment for Whites and Blacks are significantly different at the .05 level.

To gain a sense of the substantive impact of unfair treatment on neighborhood discrimination, as well as other predictors, we display in Figure 2.4 estimates of "first differences," which show the magnitude of change in the dependent variable that results from moving from low to high values on each predictor while holding all other predictors at their means.[20] As is evident in the figure, among Blacks, unfair treatment is one of the more powerful predictors of neighborhood discrimination; moving from low to high values of unfair treatment, while holding all other predictors constant, increases the seriousness of Blacks' assessments of discrimination by more than a full point on the neighborhood discrimination scale. Thus, being stopped and questioned by the police is not viewed as an isolated incident for many Blacks; rather, these encounters are generalized to more fundamental perceptions of the way the police and the courts discriminate against African Americans. Clearly, experience with racial profiling exacts a heavy cost in terms of the perceived legitimacy of the local justice system in their eyes.

We also examined reciprocal effects, because it is conceivable that individuals who perceive a serious problem of discrimination in their community are more likely to interpret encounters with police as unfair or discriminatory treatment, especially among Black respondents. As reported in Appendix B, however, we find no empirical support for such reciprocal influences.

Aside from personal experiences, what other characteristics of individuals influence their perceptions of bias in the legal system? In Figure 2.4, we see that such perceptions are strongly tied to more general political predispositions – namely, partisanship among Blacks and ideological self-placement among Whites. The tendency for Black Democrats to view discrimination as more serious is noteworthy in at least two respects. First, there is much less variation in partisanship among Blacks: 56 percent of the respondents in our sample are strong Democrats (compared with 17% for Whites), and only 9 percent consider themselves Republicans (even if we count those who say they

[20] It should be noted that the low and high values used to calculate the first differences in Figure 2.3, in which "low" and "high" correspond to 1 standard deviation above and below the mean, are different for Whites and Blacks. Although this is the case, they have the attractive property of being based on the densest portion of the distribution of actual observations on each predictor.

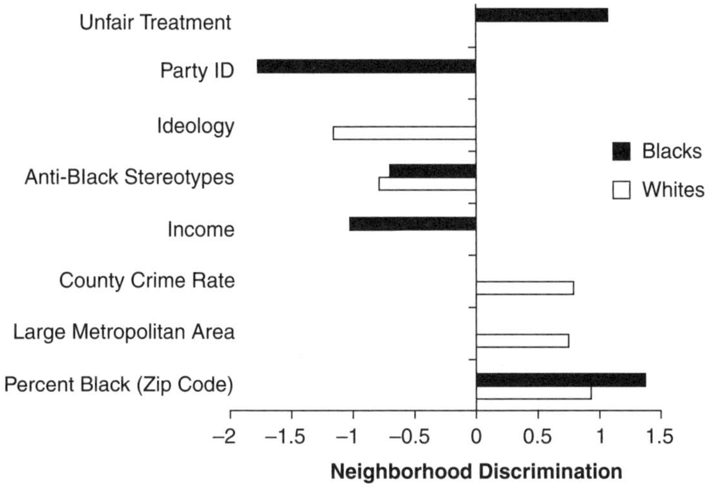

FIGURE 2.4. Substantive impact of select predictors on neighborhood discrimination.

Note: The figure shows "first differences" in neighborhood discrimination – how moving from low to high values on the predictor, while holding other predictors at their means, changes evaluations of neighborhood discrimination. For continuous variables, low and high values correspond to 1 standard deviation below and above the mean for each racial group, with "higher" indicating more incidents of unfair treatment, more Republican, conservative, more negative stereotypes toward Blacks than Whites, higher income, county crime rate, and living in a county in a large metropolitan area. Impact set to 0 if not significant at the .10 level. Based on results in Table 2.4.

Source: NRCS data.

lean toward the party as identifiers). Second, the influence of partisanship likely reflects the more aggressive role that the Democratic Party has traditionally played in targeting racial discrimination, as well as the more specific efforts begun (belatedly in 1999) during the Clinton administration to collect data on racial profiling from traffic stops.[21]

Among Whites, perceptions of discrimination turn more on ideological self-placement than partisanship, though it should be said that

[21] In 2001, President Bush also directed the attorney general to place racial profiling and data collection as a top Justice Department priority. However, when it came time to make the profiling data public, the Bush administration deleted the most critical evidence of racial disparities and demoted the Justice Department official who refused to excise the racial references (Lictblau 2005).

the two predispositions (ideology and partisanship) are highly correlated among Whites (r = .59), though much less so among Blacks (r = .12). White conservatives are much less likely than liberals to view discrimination among the police and courts as serious problems in their communities, a pattern consistent with the tendency for conservatives to perceive less racial discrimination in the economic realm (Kluegel and Smith 1986). An alternative explanation is that ideology biases individuals' attention to, and interpretation of, the available evidence. Among both Whites and Blacks, then, political predispositions appear to serve as perceptual filters rather than as correlates of the degree of "real" discrimination that exists in one's community.

Additional evidence of selective perception can be found in the influence of anti-Black stereotypes in Figure 2.4. For both races, individuals who view Blacks more negatively than Whites are less likely to perceive discrimination by the police and the courts in their community. Compared to the effects of party ID among Blacks or ideology among Whites, however, the effects of anti-Black stereotypes are less powerful predictors of neighborhood discrimination.

Among the demographic factors, aside from race, the only significant effects are associated with income for Black respondents. Less affluent Blacks are more likely than their more wealthy counterparts to perceive discrimination in their communities, presumably because poorer Blacks are more likely to see that Blacks in their neighborhoods are treated more harshly by authorities. In addition, as can be seen by the results at the bottom of Table 2.4 and Figure 2.4, various features of the social environment are selectively important in shaping Whites' and Blacks' perceptions of neighborhood discrimination. All three measures of social context are important for Whites. If they live in counties with higher reported crime rates, large metropolitan areas, or neighborhoods (Zip Codes) with higher concentrations of African Americans, Whites are much more likely to view neighborhood discrimination as a serious problem. Presumably, when Whites have more opportunity to observe or hear about discrimination in their communities, they view it as a more serious problem.[22]

Among Blacks, only one aspect of social context – percent Black – significantly boosts perceptions of justice discrimination. To gain a

[22] It should be noted that although some aspects of Whites' social context – most notably, living in neighborhoods with a greater proportion of Blacks – are associated

better sense of how living in a more racially concentrated neighborhood enhances perceptions of discrimination for Black and White respondents, the predicted values for neighborhood discrimination are plotted against percent Black in Figure 2.5. Two features of the figure stand out. First, African Americans rate justice discrimination as substantially more serious than Whites at all levels of percent Black. Second, especially among Whites, who are clustered at the far left side of the figure in predominantly White neighborhoods, the most rapid increase in perceived discrimination occurs as one moves from 0 to about 15 percent Black, where the number of African Americans becomes a more noticeable presence in one's community.[23]

Admittedly, however, other interpretations of the impact of social context are certainly possible. In particular, self-selection may help to account for an association between context and racial attitudes. As Welch et al. (2001, 91) frame the problem, "perhaps contexts are related to perceptions about race because people choose to place themselves in contexts where their attitudes are most compatible rather than having their attitudes shaped by the contexts in which they find themselves." Thus, instead of predominantly White neighborhoods failing to provide people with opportunities to see racial discrimination, it may be that individuals who are disinclined to perceive discrimination (e.g., conservatives or those who hold negative racial stereotypes) choose to live in all-White neighborhoods.

The case for selection bias is much less persuasive when applied to Blacks, however, because research shows African Americans are much less mobile than Whites – that is, they are "less likely than Whites to move and less likely to improve their housing and neighborhood environments when they do move" (Harding 2003, 683). Even in the case of Whites, we do not find a strong tendency for conservatives or those who stereotype Blacks to live in particular social contexts.[24]

with a greater awareness of racial discrimination in the justice system, such a finding is not inconsistent with the tendency for the same characteristics to engender negative racial attitudes (e.g., Oliver and Mendelberg 2000).

[23] The predicted values track a similar rapid ascent for Blacks, but few Blacks actually live in such predominantly White neighborhoods.

[24] The simple correlations between our measures of neighborhood context (i.e., crime rate, residing in a large metropolitan area, and percent Black), on the one hand, and ideology and anti-Black stereotypes, on the other, tend to be small and statistically insignificant. The sole exception is the correlation between ideology and percent Black which is –.08 and significant at the .05 level.

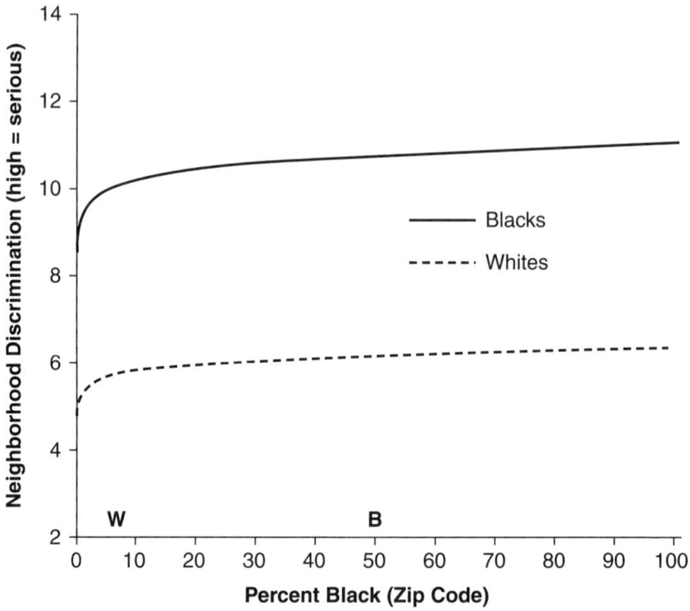

FIGURE 2.5. Predicted values of perceived neighborhood discrimination from percent Black.

Note: The figure shows the tendency for Blacks and Whites living in more racially concentrated neighborhoods (i.e., Zip Codes) to rate racial discrimination in their communities as more serious. Average percent Black among Whites and Blacks indicated by "W" and "B," respectively.

Source: NRCS data.

Nevertheless, because selection effects have occasionally been shown to bias results in complex and unanticipated ways, we remain open to the possibility that some portion of the relationship between social context and perceived discrimination for Whites is due to selection bias, which could exaggerate the estimated influence of social context in Table 2.4 and underestimate the influence of other predictors, such as anti-Black stereotypes.

SUMMARY

In a study of perceptions, it is fitting to begin by assessing the "reality" of racial bias in the justice system. Culling through an exceptionally large body of social science research on the subject, although the evidence is punctuated with a variety of conditions and qualifications, it is impossible to avoid the conclusion that the justice system in America is fraught with discrimination against minorities and, in particular, African Americans. The starting point for an assessment of racial bias is the immense disparity in arrests, incarcerations, and convictions of – and police misconduct toward – Whites versus Blacks in this country. A virtual avalanche of research across the social sciences finds evidence of discrimination in nearly every phase of the justice system and, thus, leads to the conclusion that the contemporary legal system in the United States cannot by any stretch of the imagination be accurately characterized as "color blind."

This chapter's empirical story centers on citizens' experiences with agents of the justice system both personal (i.e., their encounters with police) and virtual (i.e., their perceptions of racial discrimination by police and the courts in their neighborhoods). The dominant theme in our analysis is that the experiences of African Americans are radically different from those of Whites. Our measure of personal experiences reveals that one of every three Blacks reports being treated unfairly by police because of their race, whereas the number of Whites reporting unfair treatment – in which *unfair* is defined in a completely open-ended fashion – is closer to one in ten. Our measures of virtual experiences, assessed by asking respondents about the seriousness of discrimination by the police and the courts in their communities, expose a huge rift in the way Whites and Blacks experience discrimination in the neighborhoods where they reside. Upward of 75 percent of Blacks view racial discrimination by police as "serious" in their community, whereas only 25 percent of Whites do. These disparities in experience reprise a basic finding from studies of perceptions of economic discrimination, in which Sigelman and Welch (1991, 65) conclude: "It is hardly an overstatement to say that Blacks and Whites inhabit two different perceptual worlds. Whites do not acknowledge the persisting prejudice and discrimination that are so obvious to Blacks."

Tracing the antecedents and consequences of these experiences speaks volumes about how Whites and Blacks begin from fundamentally different reference points when thinking about or reacting to the justice system, its agents, and its policies. Personal experiences of discriminatory treatment by the police (e.g., racial profiling), for example, are all too common in the African-American community. Although such contacts are much higher among younger African-American men and those living in areas with higher rates of crime, we do not find that Blacks in the lower end of the socioeconomic spectrum are uniquely targeted. Rather, more educated Blacks are more likely to report discriminatory treatment by the police than the less educated, presumably because middle-class Blacks are more likely to work (and to a lesser extent, live) in predominantly "White" neighborhoods, where they become targets of racial profiling by the police.

Our study shows that these personal experiences with discrimination shared by so many Blacks create a powerful lesson: when Blacks are mistreated by the police, they generalize from their experience by recognizing that such maltreatment exists on a wider scale in their communities. Among Blacks, unfair treatment by the police is the most potent predictor of perceiving discriminatory treatment by the police and the courts in their neighborhoods, even after controlling for a variety of other potential antecedents (as well as reciprocal linkages). Interestingly, because Whites were not asked about being personally mistreated by the police because of their race, their personal experiences were not at all significantly connected to perceptions of neighborhood discrimination. What matters for Whites, but less so for Blacks, is their neighborhood context: because so few Whites live in integrated neighborhoods, most Whites have neither the opportunity nor the inclination to view racial discrimination by the police and the courts as a serious affair. Among the small percentage of Whites who live in neighborhoods with a nontrivial presence of African Americans, however, or who live in high-crime areas where the police are active, there is a greater recognition of the seriousness of racial discrimination.

To place these findings in perspective, it is important to remember the proportion of Blacks and Whites who either report unfair personal treatment or perceive discrimination in their neighborhoods: the percentage of Blacks is staggering, while the percentage of Whites is minuscule. In our analysis of the antecedents of these experiences, although individual predictors often moderated the size of the interracial divide, they did not come close to eliminating it. No matter what the level (high or low) or the type (individual or environmental characteristics) of the predictor variable considered, there is still a huge interracial gap in personal and virtual experiences with the justice system. Even if, in a purely hypothetical world, we were to assume that Whites shared many of the same characteristics as Blacks (or vice versa) – for example, living in predominantly Black neighborhoods or occupying similar socioeconomic status – the interracial gap in experiences would still be stark.

In the following chapter we turn our attention from experiences to more global evaluations of the criminal justice system. There we find that experiences are critical in shaping the races' beliefs about whether the justice system in America is fair, and whether it dispenses justice equitably to African Americans.

3

The Role of Fairness

In the previous chapter, we examined the dramatically different experiences of Whites and African Americans in the criminal justice system. After discussing the historical and criminological documentation for such interracial differences, we focused on the experiences of the National Race and Crime Survey (NRCS) respondents – experiences that are felt personally and vicariously. Unsurprisingly, we found that African Americans are substantially more likely to report being treated unfairly by the police relative to Whites, particularly Blacks who are younger males, liberal, better educated, and living in high-crime communities.

We also explored vicarious experiences – or perceptions that Blacks are treated discriminatorily in their communities by the police and the courts. Although we were not surprised to find that Blacks see discrimination differently from Whites, we were not prepared for the enormity of the divide between how Blacks and Whites evaluate the severity of the problem. Overwhelming majorities of African Americans, but only trivial percentages of Whites, perceive problems of racial discrimination as being "serious," regardless of whether the problem is defined in terms of courts giving harsher sentences to Blacks, police stopping and questioning Blacks disproportionately, or police caring more about crimes committed against Whites than against Blacks.

Most importantly, contrary to the conventional wisdom that personal experiences rarely translate into more general perceptions, we found a strong association among African Americans between personal discriminatory treatment during encounters with police officers and their perceptions of discrimination in the community. But what difference does it make if African Americans perceive injustice – either directly or vicariously in their communities? Inevitably, the answers to this question bring us to the fundamental issue of fairness, for it is almost inconceivable that individuals who have experienced discrimination from the justice system will perceive that system to be anything but unfair.

Fairness, to be sure, is an interdisciplinary concept, prevalent in literatures as diverse as those found in political science, sociology, economics, psychology, criminology, law, linguistics, and even zoology. It is so important to these varied disciplines because it has been found to explain so much else, ranging from attitudes toward welfare payments (e.g., Gilens 1999) to foreign policy (e.g., Liberman 2006).

We begin this chapter with a detailed conceptual discussion of fairness, tracing its interdisciplinary lineage and, more specifically, beliefs with which it is associated. We then turn to the important question of why it is such an instrumental explanatory concept. After detailing our approach to the measurement of fairness, we turn to an empirical analysis of the antecedents of fairness judgments, paying particular attention to interracial differences in fairness beliefs.

THE MEANING OF FAIRNESS

As noted, fairness (or justice, as we will label it as applied to the criminal justice domain) has been studied in many different forms and for many different purposes. Despite these varied approaches, scholars from a variety of disciplines agree that the desire for justice is a powerful motivator for individuals – almost a basic human need. It has been tied to an organic physiological response (Vermunt and Steensma 2003), and Hibbing and Alford (2004) argue persuasively that the need to be treated fairly (or not taken as a "sucker") is even rooted in Darwinian biology in the sense that such needs are now "'hardwired' into our nature" (64).

Part of the reason why justice, as a concept, is so pervasive in these literatures is related to its multidimensionality. When individuals consider the question of fairness, they do not use one evaluative criterion.

To the contrary, at least in the justice arena, no fewer than three principles can be taken into consideration: is the legal process fair (procedural justice); is punishment an appropriate response to those who violate the rules (retributive justice); and is the outcome evenly distributed (distributive justice)?

Although all three dimensions of justice are of potential relevance to our study, the focus in much of the extant literature has been squarely on procedural justice, which, it has been argued, is likely to be of paramount importance in understanding the different ways that citizens approach criminal justice issues. Procedural justice in the justice domain is concerned not with outcomes (e.g., a speeding ticket or a jail sentence) but, rather, with the process by which policy decisions are made and implemented. According to Tyler (1988, 103), procedural justice is based on "(1) the degree to which those authorities were motivated to be fair; (2) judgments of their honesty; (3) the degree to which the authorities followed ethical principles of conduct; (4) the extent to which opportunities for representation were provided; (5) the quality of the decisions made; (6) the opportunities for error correction; and (7) whether the authorities behaved in a biased fashion." In short, procedural justice is concerned with making and implementing decisions according to fair processes that ensure "fair treatment."

On its face, retributive justice is also relevant to any discussion of crime,[1] for almost all crime policies in any legal system have, as an important purpose, the punishment of law violators. Even some of the most ardent proponents of the death penalty concede that it does little to deter crime but, nonetheless, support it because of its punitive function.[2] Some have argued, quite simply, that we want rule breakers to suffer; a desire to punish may be so important that we prefer to discipline violators even at a personal cost to ourselves (Tyler et al. 1997; Fehr and Gachter 2002).

Retributive justice is not terribly important for our purposes, however, essentially because at the abstract level Blacks and Whites tend to agree on the role of punishment, and when the races do part

[1] This is in stark contrast to studies of the economic system in which retributive fairness is conceptually irrelevant.

[2] Jones, Jeffrey M. June 3, 2003. "Understanding Americans' Support for the Death Penalty." Available at http://www.gallup.com/poll/8557/Understanding-Americans-Support-Death-Penalty.aspx (accessed January 3, 2010).

company at the policy level they diverge most sharply when they disagree on whether policies violate principles of procedural justice. In the abstract, Whites and Blacks essentially agree about the appropriateness of punishment. The NRCS includes a two-item punitiveness inventory, designed to assess the degree to which respondents advocate harsh punishment for disobedience in the abstract.[3] On a scale ranging from 0 to 6, with higher values indicating greater punitiveness, the average placement of Blacks (mean = 2.1) on the scale is nearly identical to that of Whites (2.3). In short, there is no compelling evidence that African Americans and Whites differ fundamentally in their support for the principle of retributive justice, at least when viewed in isolation from the principle of procedural justice.

In contrast to retributive justice, which focuses on punishment as a suitable response to law breaking, distributive justice raises questions regarding the evenness with which law enforcement and sanction is applied – whether justice *outcomes* are distributed fairly. Distributive justice is a multidimensional construct, inasmuch as liberals and conservatives seem to interpret and evaluate it quite differently (Rasinsky 1987; Skitka and Tetlock 1992). Specifically, liberals tend to focus on the equality principle, or the degree to which outcomes (either financial or, in this case, punishment) are distributed uniformly across different groups in society. Conservatives are more likely to employ an equity criterion, evaluating punitive measures based on whether they are appropriate to the degree of culpability and criminal intent. Regardless of the ideologically based interpretation, distributive justice, by any definition, focuses on outcomes.

As we have noted previously, however, a veritable avalanche of research by Tyler and associates (e.g., Tyler and Folger 1980) has found that individuals are much more willing to accept adverse outcomes when they judge the process used to derive such an outcome to be inherently fair.[4] It is tempting to draw the conclusion, consequently,

[3] The punitiveness scale sums responses to the following Likert statements: "One good way to teach certain people right from wrong is to give them a good stiff punishment when they get out of line" and "Parents need to stop using physical punishment as a way of getting their children to behave properly" (reversed).

[4] The importance of procedure to litigants' judgments of fairness was first emphasized by Thibaut and Walker (1975) and has subsequently been replicated by numerous studies (e.g., Lind 1982; Walker and Lind 1984).

that at least in the criminal justice domain, questions of procedural justice take precedence over questions of distributive justice, particularly given the well-established finding that evaluations of procedures buffer the vicissitudes of outcomes. Certainly, an emerging literature in the political domain focuses precisely on this expectation – that is, process plays a much more important role in citizens' evaluations than does outcome.

For example, in their provocative book, *Stealth Democracy: Americans' Beliefs about How Government Should Work*, Hibbing and Theiss-Morse (2002) make the forceful argument that, in contrast to the conventional wisdom that citizens care most about outcomes and policies, evaluations of the processes of government (e.g., the way decisions are made) can have a far greater impact on political evaluations and behavior. Using survey and focus group data, the authors conclude that dissatisfaction with governmental procedures causes citizens to disapprove of their government, support reform initiatives and protest candidates, and even believe that they need not comply with the laws passed by government. Process concerns are most relevant for explaining the public's disdain for the U.S. Congress, a body for which policy outputs matter little in generating disapproval but for which perceptions of its procedures are of paramount importance. There is more than a kernel of truth to the cliché that legislation is one of two things we should never observe being made (the other being sausage), for the legislative process is on display in Congress, and the public does not like it. Not only is the Congress viewed as being inefficient in deriving decisions, but also it is seen as unduly influenced by special-interest groups and unfair in the way that it allocates benefits. In short, we loathe Congress because we believe it to be procedurally unfair.

Individuals employ much the same calculus when evaluating the fairness of the economic system. Based on her in-depth interviews with twenty-eight respondents, Hochschild (1981) concludes that people partition the world into social, political, and economic domains and, more importantly, treat the economic domain differently in one important respect: although they expect egalitarian outcomes in the social and political worlds, they want and expect differentiation in the economic world. Put differently, provided that individuals receive reasonable reassurance of equality of economic opportunity (i.e., procedural fairness),[5] they are not disturbed by vast inequalities in the distribution of economic rewards (distributive unfairness).

This finding is remarkably consistent with a great many other studies in political science and sociology – studies examining Americans' judgments of economic fairness. A persistent conclusion, for instance, is that individuals dislike policies designed to generate equal economic outcomes (e.g., across-the-board minimum incomes), although they are relatively supportive of policies that enhance economic opportunities such as job-training programs (Kluegel and Smith 1986). By the same logic, Lipset and Schneider (1978) argue that Whites are strongly oppositional to affirmative action programs that mandate hiring and admissions decisions through explicit quotas, largely because such policies are seen to go beyond the limits of equal opportunity and into the realm of equal outcomes. According to Bobo and Kluegel (1993), this is particularly true when policies are targeted to Blacks (as opposed to the poor).

Justice in the Criminal Justice Arena

As a consequence of the pioneering work of Tyler in the criminal justice domain, and of numerous scholars focusing on other domains, one is led quite naturally to the expectation that citizens' fairness judgments in the criminal justice domain should be determined almost exclusively by perceptions of procedural fairness. We propose, however, that this expectation, and the evidence on which it is based, is somewhat facile in nature and that it masks important differences in how Whites and Blacks evaluate the justice system. Although we certainly do not discount the importance of citizen judgments of process, we do believe that it is problematic to ignore the important role that distributive justice judgments play as individuals formulate evaluations of the system.

To be sure, Tyler and his associates have made extraordinary contributions to our understanding of citizen evaluations. We do not take issue with his empirical finding, referenced in the preceding text, that

[5] The acceptance of the doctrine of equality of economic opportunity is also a significant predictor of a variety of policy attitudes (including welfare spending, social services, education spending, and minority aid) and even candidate evaluations (Feldman 1988).

motorists' levels of satisfaction with legal authorities hinge more on whether they believe they are treated fairly (i.e., the process) than whether they like the outcome (i.e., the distribution). We do wonder, however, whether this methodology – examining citizens' personal encounters with police officers – is the best way to understand how individuals really do evaluate the criminal justice domain.

We prefer to adopt an integrative approach to fairness evaluations, as utilized by fairness heuristic theory (e.g., Van den Bos et al. 1997), which explicitly attempts to describe the conditions under which individuals rely on outcome (distributive) rather than process (procedural) information. According to the authors,

> when persons do not have information about the outcomes of others they will use the information that is available. This suggests that in such situations people may turn to the fairness of the procedure to judge the fairness of their outcome and how satisfied they are with their outcome.... However, we also propose that when a person does have information about the outcome of another person, he or she will use this social comparison information to assess how fair his or her outcome is and how satisfied he or she is with the outcome. *In other words, we argue that when people do have information about the outcomes of other people, procedure information is not easier to interpret than outcome information.* (1036, emphasis added)

Along with Van den Bos et al., we believe that whether people base their views of the fairness of the justice system on procedures or outcomes depends on what type of information is available to them when formulating their judgments. Although personal experiences with police officers may lead individuals to emphasize procedural criteria, as in the Tyler protocol, beyond the occasional traffic citation, only a relative minority of citizens have firsthand contact with the justice system, especially in the White community. Even in the African-American community, where approximately one-third of the males have entered the penal system in one way or the other, majorities of Blacks lack direct confrontations with the law. To be sure, individuals of both races witness, and evaluate, acts of police officers that may be taken as evidence of procedural unfairness. At the same time, we do not believe that the "data" used by citizens must come exclusively, or even primarily, from such a source.

Like most evaluations, especially those pertaining to matters of importance, fairness judgments of the justice system are manifestly complex and, consequently, exceedingly unlikely to emanate from a single source. We have demonstrated (Chapter 2) that personal experiences with the justice system count for a great deal when individuals formulate their broader judgments. But for those without such experiences (or, for that matter, even those with such experiences), there are numerous other cues in the environment – cues provided by friends, family members, educators, the media, opinion leaders, political elites, chiefs of police, and many others, all of whom serve to inform an individual in his or her evaluative process.

Much of the information supplied by such sources is tied to outcomes in the justice system – information that is often more accessible and less ambiguous than procedural information. By contrast, process can be confusing to citizens, especially to the degree that it is hidden from view. It can involve negotiations that take place in a judge's chamber or even arcane statistical analyses designed to address questions such as whether a given group is being treated unfairly simply because it is punished disproportionately. We strongly suspect, therefore, that individuals often gravitate toward available information that bears on outcome – that is, information pertaining to the distribution of arrests, convictions, and punishments across various groups. They may be fully aware of facts pertaining to disproportionate numbers of African Americans in penitentiaries – numbers that are far in excess of their place in the general population. They may be less certain of whether such disproportionalities are a consequence of procedural bias or, instead, higher levels of Black criminal behavior. By the same token, many citizens are doubtless aware of the fact that African Americans are more likely to be stopped and questioned in traffic, while they may be unaware of facts pertaining to whether police officers had probable cause to question Blacks more frequently than Whites.

Our point is not that procedural justice is irrelevant, or even unimportant, to citizens as they evaluate the justice system. To the contrary, process matters in at least two ways. For one, people are often motivated to go beyond "raw" outcome data to make inferences about whether disparities in outcomes can be traced back to unfair procedures or process. Second, as argued by Tyler, citizens tend to tolerate unfavorable outcomes when they evaluate the process as fair.

Rather, our point is that as citizens are exposed to increasing amounts of outcome-based justice information – which is true for many African Americans who have ample access to a great deal of evidence regarding rates of interrogation, apprehension, arrest, and incarceration of Blacks – they are increasingly likely to incorporate distributive justice evaluations into their overall beliefs of the criminal justice system. Thus, to minimize the importance of outcomes is to mischaracterize the way that individuals reason and the types of information to which they turn.

We also suspect that Whites and African Americans may translate outcome-focused information into procedural justice judgments in different ways. To anticipate the findings of the next chapter, Whites may look at disproportionate incarceration rates and see no evidence of procedural injustice, explaining the outcome instead as a function of Blacks being more likely to get into trouble, more violent, and less respectful of authority. African Americans may take that same information, put it in the context of either personal or vicarious information that they have regarding inappropriate police behavior, and conclude that the justice system is procedurally unfair. We will return to this discussion in the following text.

THE IMPORTANCE OF JUSTICE PERCEPTIONS

Whether defined distributively or procedurally, individuals' general belief systems about the fairness of the justice system are of substantial importance. In his seminal 1964 chapter, Philip Converse wrote about two properties of belief systems: range and centrality. Belief systems with wide ranges and with high levels of centrality, he argues, "can be presumed to have some relevance to political behavior" (209). To be sure, general fairness beliefs assume both of these properties.

Range refers to the number and importance of issues that are subsumed under the umbrella of the abstraction. Beliefs with a narrow range encompass only a modest number of ideas (Converse provides the example of the effects of changes of weather on health) and, consequently, are relatively useless outside of the venue that is covered by the abstraction. Belief systems with a wider range, such as ideologies, values, or general beliefs and perceptions, are far more useful to the individual simply because they are applicable to a far wider array of topics. Liberals, for instance, support governmental intervention across a number of policy domains.

By the same token, perceptions of (in)justice also have extraordinary range. We use them to evaluate not only how criminals are treated but also to evaluate economic outcomes and processes. Additionally, we use them to evaluate political actors, crime policies (e.g., Hurwitz and Peffley 2005), and even the political system (Hibbing and Theiss-Morse 2002).

The *centrality* of ideas refers to "the role that they play in the belief system as a whole" (Converse, 208). Any belief system consists of a number of interconnected ideas, some of which, inevitably, will change. For the elements within the system to remain internally consistent, other ideas must also change. A strong proponent of legalized abortion, for instance, may enthusiastically endorse a candidate who also supports abortion rights. But if the candidate changes his or her views on the policy, the citizen must either reassess his or her views on abortion or views toward the candidate – at least for purposes of consistency. According to Converse, "the element more likely to change is defined as less central to the belief system than the element that, so to speak, has its stability ensured by the change in the first element" (208). By any account, beliefs and perceptions about justice constitute a central idea element. As such, they assume two properties that any highly central idea element assumes: they are stable and influence the formulation of other, more specific, beliefs and perceptions.

Central beliefs are stable because, by definition, they are unlikely to change in response to changes in other beliefs within the system. More important for our purposes is the role that such general beliefs and perceptions play in shaping more specific idea elements – particularly policy attitudes and perceptions of agents of the justice system. Certainly the consistency between general beliefs, perceptions, and values, on the one hand, and policy attitudes, on the other hand, is incontrovertible (e.g., Peffley and Hurwitz 1985; Feldman 1988; Zaller 1992); additionally, such general beliefs are highly correlated with perceptions of out-groups (e.g., Kinder and Sanders 1996) and even forms of political behavior (Borg 1995).

We cannot completely rule out the possibility that general beliefs are endogenous to the belief-policy attitude relationship, such that more specific policy attitudes influence broader judgments rather than vice versa (see, e.g., Seligman and Katz 1996). Nonetheless, evidence (e.g., Peffley and Hurwitz 1992, 1993; McCann 1997) strongly supports the likelihood that general orientations – whether in the form of beliefs, values, or perceptions – are, for the most part, causally antecedent to more specific forms of attitudes.

We are uncertain, and even relatively unconcerned, about the precise microlevel mechanism by which general beliefs translate into more specific policy attitudes and evaluations of particular actors. Nevertheless, the process is fully consistent with findings from the voluminous literature on political information processing (e.g., Sniderman, Brody, and Tetlock 1993) which, collectively, contends that because citizens are cognitive misers they use abstract, general beliefs to structure the type of information that is attended to, retained by, and recalled from memory. When citizens encounter new or novel information – whether about specific policies, candidates, or agents of the criminal justice system, they are highly likely to interpret it such that it is consistent with their more general beliefs and the expectations with which such beliefs are associated. It is wholly unsurprising, therefore, that beliefs about human nature (e.g., laziness vs. hard working) structure attitudes toward welfare policy (Gilens 1999), or that in the international sphere, general beliefs about the use of military force, nationalism, and images of our allies and enemies guide attitudes toward policies ranging from defense spending to international trade (Hurwitz and Peffley 1987). Neither is it surprising that the general beliefs we form regarding the groups around us (i.e., stereotypes) largely determine how we respond to any specific representative from that group. To a great extent, for example, our judgments and perceptions of specific candidates are influenced by our partisan (e.g., Rahn 1993) or gender (Huddy and Terkildsen 1993; Koch 2000) stereotypes. Our point is that most of the specific beliefs, attitudes, and perceptions that we hold are derived from more abstract idea elements – in this case, whether the justice system is perceived to be generically fair.

It is easy to envision individuals (particularly African Americans) who have strong doubts about the fairness of the justice system. As such, they may be hypersensitive to information in the community that points to discriminatory treatment at the hands of the police. Additionally, they may be more likely to understand that crime rates among certain groups are at least partly a function of poor educational and occupational opportunities and, as such, may also be more likely to support policies designed to redress these disadvantages. As well, they may also oppose more punitive policies, believing them to be unfairly strong and even applied in a discriminatory fashion. As will be shown in the following text, they often develop substantially lower levels of trust in the U.S. criminal justice system. It is easy to envision, consequently, such individuals responding much more favorably to the O. J. Simpson acquittal and much more negatively to the acquittals of police officers who brutalize Whites, relative to others. To take this one step further, it is easy to envision that such cynicism toward the justice system may well lead to various forms of noncompliance with the law (e.g., Tyler 1990), civil disobedience as exemplified in the Los Angeles riots of 1965 and 1992 (e.g., Sears and McConahay 1982; Bobo et al. 1994, respectively), jury nullification (Dilworth 1996), and to perceptions of the entire U.S. political system as unfair (Lind and Tyler 1988).

But fairness judgments do not affect only those who are disillusioned with the equity of the justice system. To the contrary, individuals have a very powerful tendency, almost a need, to perceive the world as a fair place – to subscribe to the "just world" phenomena (e.g., Lerner 1980; Lerner and Lerner 1981). Individuals appear to prefer a world that is orderly, predictable, and fair, a world where people get what they deserve. Upon encountering evidence that the world is unjust, our response is to attempt to restore justice – either by helping the victim or by persuading ourselves that no injustice has occurred, which typically results in blaming or derogating him or her (Haynes and Olson 2006). Such a phenomenon, often called "blaming the victim," has been employed countless times to explain, for example, jury acquittals of alleged rapists whose victim is a provocatively dressed woman – who, according to theory, "got what she deserved."

We know that conservatives and those with the most negative attitudes toward underprivileged groups are most likely to believe in the just world (Rubin and Peplau 1975). We have also shown that conservatives are more likely to perceive the justice system to be fair and, by extension, to believe that individuals get what they deserve in the justice system. It is precisely the individuals who are most likely to perceive the system as fair (who are disproportionately conservative in nature) who are also most likely to believe that those charged with crimes deserve to be dealt with punitively – *not* because they necessarily are guilty (in fact), but because they *must* be guilty given their belief that the system is fair. In this ironic sense, the belief in a just world may become a substitute for legitimate justice – particularly among those who are most convinced that the system is just in the first place.

JUSTICE AS AN INHERENTLY RACIAL CONCEPT

At least in the United States, it is essentially impossible to think about the concept of justice without also thinking about race, and, contrariwise, it is essentially impossible to think about race without also thinking about justice. Quite simply, justice is a construct that is inherently comparative in nature, and in this country the dominant sociodemographic comparison has been between Whites and African Americans for most of its history.

It has become increasingly clear to economists that satisfaction with gains is relative – that is, relative to the gains of others and not absolute (Frank 1999).[6] Thus, regardless of the size of the distribution, individuals will be more satisfied with small awards when they are equal and be less satisfied with larger awards when they are unequal.

Admittedly, this line of research focuses on satisfaction at the individual level not at the aggregate level. It is not, however, a large inferential leap to conclude that members of a group who perceive members of another group to be receiving a disproportionate share of the pot will feel aggrieved and, in our vernacular, a sense of injustice. To be sure, this is precisely what Hochschild (1995) uncovered in the course of her lengthy conversations with Americans of both races. Although both Blacks and Whites accept unequal economic outcomes as a result of the American Dream (and its emphasis on the fruits of hard labor), many African Americans now regard the dream as an artifice, largely because they see equality of opportunity as a myth. Although they are willing to accept greater rewards for those who earn them, they are less sanguine about greater rewards that are distributed to individuals merely on the basis of their majority group status. Not surprisingly,

[6] In a two-player game, e.g., player 1 will be far more satisfied with a gain of \$A when the total pot of money is \$A × 2 (indicating an equitable distribution of the pot) than when the pot of money is \$A × 2 + B (indicating that player 2 receives more money than player 1).

these doubts about the American Dream are most intense among the Black middle class, quite possibly because they have taken the steps necessary to reap large economic rewards (e.g., by attending college) but have not experienced rewards commensurate to those accrued by Whites. Inevitably, under these circumstances African Americans will conclude that the system is inherently unjust.

There are many factors that lead to the perception of injustice, most especially in the criminal justice arena. In his seminal work, Leventhal (1980) identified six conditions, the absence of any of which may lead to pervasive beliefs that the system is unjust: consistency, the ability to suppress bias, decision quality or accuracy, correctability, representation, and ethicality.[7] Barrett-Howard and Tyler (1986) further break consistency into, first, consistency across time and, second, consistency across individuals. Of all the evaluative criteria, research has repeatedly shown that consistency is the most important of the six conditions and, within this category, consistency across individuals and groups matters the most (e.g., Barret-Howard and Tyler 1986; Greenberg 1986).

We recognize that evaluations of fairness and justice are manifestly complex and multidimensional. Yet we also recognize that, minimally, individuals expect laws, and the application and enforcement of such laws, to be applied fairly across individuals and groups in society and, by extension, across groups within society. When expectations of procedural justice are violated, citizens are much more likely to conclude that the justice system is, almost by definition, flawed and unfair.

Naturally, the most powerful evidence of an unfair justice system for an individual is the perception that authorities, such as the police and the courts, have treated the individual unfairly. But perceived injustice is even more pernicious for those in minority groups, who tend to think about justice as generalized to their group, unlike those in the majority, who typically think about justice as applied to the individual (Azzi 1992). We referred earlier (Chapter 2) to a group values model (Tyler 2001), which underscores the importance of fair process, largely because perceptions of *un*fairness will convey to group members (especially minority group members) the message

[7] Other lines of research emphasize different criteria by which individuals evaluate the fairness of a justice system. Thibaut and Walker (1975), e.g., recognize the importance of control – control that individuals feel they have over the opportunity to present evidence and control over the final decision.

that neither the individual nor the group is respected or valued. In light of the indisputable fact that Black citizens are far more likely to be treated unfairly by legal authorities than Whites, they should also be far more likely to view the justice system as patently unfair – to themselves and to their group.

MEASURING FAIRNESS JUDGMENTS

Having established the conceptual importance of fairness beliefs, we now turn to an empirical analysis of the determinants of such judgments. Specifically, what are the individual-level and contextual determinants of beliefs that the criminal justice system is (un)fair, and how, if at all, do such determinants differ interracially? But how are we to measure beliefs about fairness in the justice system? Unfortunately, the concept does not surrender to easy or facile instruments. Different people have different things in mind when they think about the property of fairness and, consequently, different measurement strategies must be considered.

In the previous chapter, we examined perceptions of justice discrimination at a very specific and concrete level: do individuals believe the police and the courts discriminate against Blacks in their own neighborhoods? Thus, we asked respondents to indicate the severity of explicit alleged problems: "Courts that give harsher sentences to African Americans than to Whites"; "Police who stop and question Blacks more often than they stop Whites"; and "Police who care more about crimes against White people than crimes against minorities." To a large extent, our focus was narrow (and we consequently adopted this specific measurement strategy) because of our interest in the relationship between personal experiences with the justice system and perceptions of neighborhood discrimination.

Presently, however, it is essential to broaden our thinking of fairness, examining beliefs about the wider criminal justice system. Although more concrete perceptions should shape an individual's broader beliefs about the fairness of the justice system, once formed, it is these more general beliefs that should guide individuals' responses toward a wide range of specific events and issues in the justice domain – a pattern that is consistent with research on attitude constraint and information processing.

Important clues about how to conceptualize and measure such beliefs are provided by scholars studying fairness appraisals in other (mostly economic) domains. For example, an emerging interdisciplinary literature on the psychology of legitimacy[8] argues that fairness appraisals can occur at several levels: 1) the system level, where individuals assess the fairness of the system that produces outcomes, whether economic, social, or criminal justice outcomes; 2) the group level, where individuals assess whether the allocation of outcomes to one group relative to others is fair or just; and 3) the individual level, where people assess whether their own outcomes are fair or unfair (Major and Schmader 2001, 180). We have earlier addressed individual fairness appraisals (Chapter 2); our interest at this point is in fairness beliefs pitched at the system and group levels.

System-Level Beliefs

It is easy to find examples of fairness beliefs at the system and group levels in the economic realm. The belief in equality of opportunity, for instance, is essentially an assessment of the (procedural) fairness of the economic system. Not only do such beliefs guide an individual's responses to a variety of specific issues and political evaluations, they provide ready-made explanations for economic inequality. For as long as one believes that the economic system affords people an equal opportunity to get ahead, inequities in wealth and income can be attributed to a failure to take advantage of the opportunities believed to be available to everyone. Embracing a belief that the criminal justice system is fair should provide a similar function in that once an individual believes the system to be fair, all sorts of disparities in outcome can be attributed to the failure of individuals to follow the rules and obey the laws of an imminently fair system.

In contrast to the economic domain, however, where an overwhelming majority believes equal opportunities exist (Feldman 1988), there is likely to be less consensus about whether the justice system can be described as fair. There is no "hidden hand" distribution of outputs by impersonal market forces; rather, all-too human agents – the police, the courts, and other officials – administer justice with doubtless more

[8] See, e.g., Jost and Major (2001).

discretion, bias, and fallibility than many people perceive to be the case for the wider economic system. Although agents of the justice system are, in theory, bound by impartial rules and laws, people are more likely to believe that laws are more subject to the human frailties of the legislative process, which many people believe is flawed, and even corrupt (Hibbing and Theiss-Morse 2002). In addition, because the justice system is likely to be viewed in terms of the agents (e.g., police) and offices (e.g., courts) that make up the system, beliefs in this domain are likely to be used to generate expectations about the behavior of such agents in specific situations. Although beliefs about economic fairness tell us little about the expected behavior of the local plant manager, justice beliefs tell us a great deal about the level of fairness to expect from the cop on the beat or judges in criminal court. Thus, not only is there likely to be more skepticism about the fairness of the justice system compared to the economic system, but also, more so than in the economic realm, system fairness beliefs are likely to generate evaluations of actors and events within the justice system.

Unlike individual- or neighborhood-level fairness judgments, which are often assessed in terms of specific activities, and unlike group fairness (to be discussed in the following text), which is often assessed in terms of specific targets, views of system fairness should be pitched at a more general level, devoid of the kinds of references to such activities (e.g., the police stopping and questioning Blacks more than Whites) or groups (e.g., Blacks). System fairness is about procedural justice and the extent to which the system renders judgments impartially and fairly.

Our index of perceived system fairness, therefore, is guided by the importance of eliminating specific references – to specific actors (e.g., the police or a given race) and specific forms of activity. It consists of two Likert items: "The justice system in this country treats people fairly and equally"; and "The courts can usually be trusted to give everyone a fair trial" (r = .59).

Group-Level Beliefs

In thinking about fairness appraisals at the group level, we also find a number of parallels in the economic domain, where individuals routinely make a variety of assessments about whether their group is receiving a fair distribution of outcomes vis-á-vis other groups.[9] A good deal of research that cuts across several disciplines finds that people possess an assortment of naïve theories or explanations of why groups receive unequal economic outcomes – that is, why the poor are poor, why Blacks are worse off than Whites, or why males are generally paid more than females. For the most part, such beliefs take the form of causal attributions, locating the locus of the cause of good or poor outcomes to either internal forces (e.g., individual effort, ability, and other dispositions) or external ones (e.g., an unfair system or bad luck). Such attributional beliefs are also found to be subject to various biases. In Western societies, for example, the tendency to attribute most outcomes or behaviors to individuals rather than situations or systems is so pervasive it has been called the "fundamental attribution error" (Nisbet and Ross 1980).[10] This bias also can be found at the group level, where entire groups are blamed for their collective fates, a bias called the "ultimate attribution error" (Pettigrew 1979).

An analogous set of causal attributions should be every bit as important in the justice domain. Explanations of criminal behavior are also found to be heavily dispositional, or biased toward internal explanations for crime versus systemic ones (Iyengar 1989). More pertinent for our study, however, is the question of how Whites and Blacks explain one of the more troubling racial disparities of our time: why do Blacks receive far greater punitive treatment at the hands of the justice system than Whites?

It might strike many liberals as unthinkable that any individual could consider a system fair if it treats given groups more harshly. Such treatment of groups would constitute *prima facie* evidence to any fair-minded person that the justice system is inherently unjust. But just as the existence of poverty does not automatically impugn the fairness of

9 E.g., Conover (1988, 57) argues that the primary consideration dominating people's views of groups, which in turn should influence their views on political issues, is a desire to know what the group is getting and whether it has been treated fairly – that is, whether the outcome is deserved. Moreover, Mutz and Mondak (1997) found such judgments of group fairness (operationalized as whether people thought the rich were better off than Blacks or the poor) to exert a greater impact on voting decisions in the 1984 presidential election than assessments of national and personal economic outcomes.

10 More specifically, individuals tend to attribute the outcomes/behaviors of others to internal dispositions but attribute their own outcomes/behaviors to external forces.

the economic system for many conservative individuals, so may harsher treatment of some groups say little directly about the basic fairness of the justice system, if, for example, unequal outcomes (poverty or punishment) are deemed appropriate and deserved. If the system is assumed to be fair, unequal outcomes may be viewed by some (primarily conservative) individuals as highly desirable, for they represent an incentive (deterrence) to individuals to apply more effort, in the case of the economic inequality, or to avoid unlawful behavior, in the case of a disparity in punishment directed toward individuals and groups.

Causal beliefs often play a central role in shaping public support for governmental policies directed toward particular groups precisely because such attributions imply an evaluation of blameworthiness and whether the group deserves to be treated by government in this fashion (Brickman 1982; Iyengar 1989). In the economic world, there is ample evidence that we are far more likely to support government assistance for the poor if we believe poverty to be a function of environmental factors (e.g., poor schooling or widespread unemployment) rather than of internal or dispositional factors such as laziness (see, e.g., Iyengar 1989; Gilens 1999; Applebaum 2001). In short, we are more likely to support government assistance when we perceive the targets as deserving, and we see them as deserving when we believe that poverty is environmentally, rather than dispositionally, determined.

When the target is not a welfare recipient but, instead, an alleged criminal, the concept of blameworthiness takes on a fundamentally different meaning – that is, does the target deserve a given penalty and its presumed severity? The answer to this question, we argue, depends largely on the extent to which we perceive the criminal as singly responsible for committing the crime, and there is substantial evidence (e.g., Young 1991; Grasmick et al. 1993; Cochran et al. 2003) that those who attribute crime to dispositional considerations are more likely to approve punitive sanctions than those who attribute it to environmental (or other mitigating) factors.

Numerous reasons exist as to why we may attribute the greater levels of involvement of Blacks in the criminal justice system to environmental rather than internal factors. We may decide, for example, that some individuals are almost forced into criminal activity given the lack of jobs, quality education, or health care available in many African-American communities. More to the point, however, is the conclusion reached by many that Blacks are disproportionately likely to be arrested, convicted, and incarcerated because the justice system is inherently biased against them. If so, African Americans are often treated unfairly, with excessive punitiveness.

For this reason, we rely heavily in this study on a measure of attributions of Black treatment, designed to assess respondent explanations of racial disproportionalities in arrest and incarceration rates. Specifically, we inform them that

Statistics show that African Americans are more often arrested and sent to prison than are Whites. The people we talk to have different ideas about why this occurs. I'm going to read you several reasons, two at a time, and ask you to choose which is the more *important reason* why, in your view, Blacks are more often arrested and sent to prison than Whites.

- First, is it because the police and justice system are biased against Blacks, *or* because Blacks are just more likely to commit crimes?[11]
- Next, is it because the police and justice system are biased against Blacks, *or* because many younger Blacks don't respect authority?[12]

[11] It could be argued that the pairings require a false choice, because some people might rate "both" or "neither" internal or external reasons as important, if they were allowed to rate their importance one at a time. We firmly believe, however, that the advantages of forcing people to choose in an ipsative format outweigh the benefits of using more conventional rating scales. The former strategy requires people to think about their choices, whereas the latter often leads to "satisficing" responses, in which people mindlessly rate all objects as equally important (Krosnick 1999). In addition, although respondents were not read "both" or "neither" response options during the interview, such answers were recorded if the respondent volunteered them (about 10 to 15% of the sample did so). We coded these responses to the midpoint of the two scales used to construct the Black treatment index, with each scale coded 0 (external reason), 1 (both/neither), or 2 (internal reason). The validity of this coding scheme is demonstrated by the fact that the predictive power of the Black treatment index is just as high when "both" and "neither" responses are included in the measure as when they are excluded.

[12] It could also be argued that some respondents may not view "younger Blacks do not respect authority" as a dispositional factor if the police are seen as (unfairly) retaliating against younger Blacks whom they view as disrespectful. This interpretation of the second item, however, seems unlikely for two reasons. First, in the course of our cognitive interview pretest, a number of participants mentioned "don't respect authority" as an explanation for Black crime. Second, because the "younger blacks" item follows the first, which clearly poses a trade-off between an external and an internal attribution, we believe it is quite likely that the first question serves to frame the second in the mind of the respondent, thus ensuring that both items will be interpreted similarly.

The responses to these items are summed to create an attributions of Black treatment scale (r = .42 for Whites, r = .35 for Blacks) in which external explanations of African-American crime (police bias) are coded 0, while internal explanations (more likely to commit crime, don't respect authority) are coded 4. By using this scale, we simultaneously require respondents to focus particularly on Black crime and explain their judgments about the degree to which African Americans deserve punishment.

Antecedents of Fairness Beliefs

How do our two measures of fairness – that is, system fairness and attributions of Black treatment – differ from one another, empirically, and how do they contribute to the racial polarization of attitudes in the justice system? One way to address this question is to examine the consequences of such beliefs, a topic we explore in Chapters 4 and 5; another way is to investigate the different sources of these two sets of beliefs, which we explore presently.

We begin by examining the huge gulf between Whites' and Blacks' beliefs about system fairness and attributions of Black treatment. Figure 3.1 shows the percentage of Whites and Blacks who characterize the justice system as either "unfair" (in the case of the two system-fairness items [top]) or "biased against Blacks" (the two attributions items [bottom]) in response to the individual questions. The race gap averages about 30 percentage points. Clearly, even when fairness appraisals are pitched at a more general level, the cleavage is staggering. We gain even more perspective on racial polarization by comparing responses, not to individual items but to the full additive scales, system fairness and attributions of Black treatment. For example, on the system fairness scale, which ranges from 0 (very unfair) to 6 (very fair), the average Black respondent falls close to the "very unfair" end of the scale (1.2), while the average White falls much closer to the opposite "very fair" end of the system fairness scale (3.4). The modal response of Blacks is 0, while that of Whites is 4.

Responses to the attributions scale are just as polarized, if not more so. On a scale ranging from 0 (attributions to racial bias) to 4 (Blacks are entirely to blame), the average African American again scores toward one end of the scale (system blame, 1.47) and the average

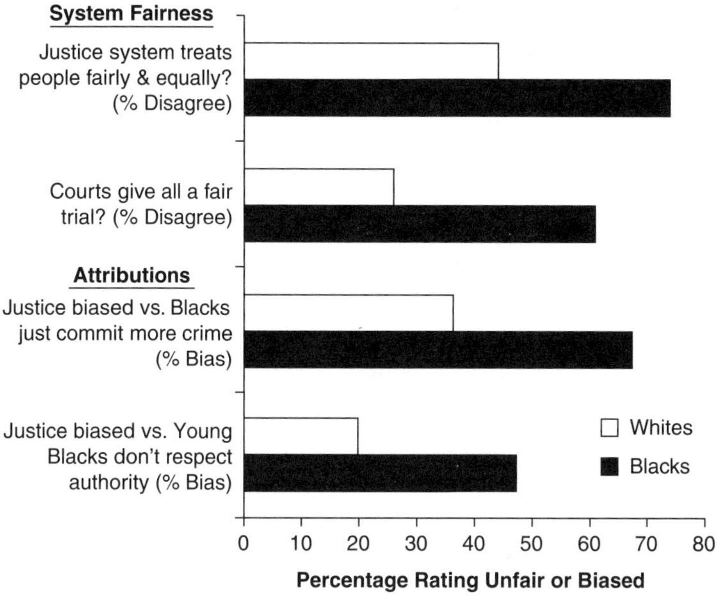

FIGURE 3.1. Racial differences in beliefs about system fairness and attributions of Black treatment.

Note: The figure shows the percentage of Whites and Blacks who characterize the justice system as either "unfair" (system fairness) or "biased" (attributions). Differences across race of respondent are statistically significant (≤ .05).

Source: NRCS data.

White falls closer to the opposite end (2.5, blame Blacks). On this measure, the modal responses of Blacks and Whites are the extreme end points of the scale: 0 among Blacks and 4 among Whites. It is, therefore, no exaggeration to conclude the races are polarized in their assessments of fundamental questions about the fairness of the justice system at the system and group levels.

We also expect the two measures of fairness to be correlated because individuals who are convinced the justice system treats people fairly should be more likely to attribute the harsher treatment of Blacks to the dispositions of Blacks rather than to a racially biased justice system. Understandably, the association is greater for African Americans (r = .26) than for Whites (r = .19), given the tendency for a group to assess fairness in terms of how that group is treated by authorities (Tyler 2001). Another way of characterizing the correlations is that, for most Whites, who view the justice system as fair and color blind, the only reasonable explanation as to why Blacks are more likely to be arrested and imprisoned is that they deserve it, given the belief that justice is dispensed equitably. Among the majority of African Americans who view the system as extremely unfair, however, the unequal treatment of Blacks can be readily attributed to an unfair and racially biased justice system.

Although the correlations between the two fairness measures make perfect sense, it is worth noting that the strength of the associations is fairly modest. Not only are the two sets of beliefs largely independent of one another, but they can be expected to have different sources (examined in the following text) and consequences (examined in Chapters 4 and 5). The evidence in this chapter and the next, therefore, supports our contention that system fairness and attributions of Black treatment tap two conceptually distinct constructs.

Sources of System Fairness

In terms of citizens' appraisals of system fairness, our most critical concern is whether Whites and Blacks generalize their personal and vicarious experiences with legal authorities (i.e., the police and the courts) to the wider justice system. Are general assessments of the justice system (i.e., system fairness) based on unfair treatment with police and perceptions of neighborhood discrimination that we explored in Chapter 2? If so, the racial polarization that exists in assessments of fairness at the system level may be traced, in large measure, to the radically different treatment by agents of the system that Blacks and Whites experience in their everyday lives.

With respect to personal experiences, prior research reviewed in Chapter 2 yields conflicting expectations about how negative encounters with police are likely to influence the formation of more global system beliefs. In the economic realm, for example, personal economic discontents generally play only an anemic role in shaping general beliefs about the fairness of the economic system. But as we argued earlier, it is doubtless easier to link unfair treatment by the police to an unfair justice system than it is to infer that a decline in one's income is due to an unfair economic system.

Among Black citizens, negative experiences with the justice system are likely to have a ripple effect on system beliefs. As we saw in

Chapter 2, Blacks' negative encounters with the police also feed into their perceptions of justice discrimination in their neighborhoods. Individuals who see serious problems of neighborhood discrimination should see the overall system as less fair. Thus, among Blacks, our personal experiences measure, unfair treatment, is likely to exert a direct and an indirect effect on system fairness, mediated through perceptions of neighborhood discrimination.[13] Among Whites, for whom unfair treatment was found to be entirely independent of neighborhood discrimination in Chapter 2, there is no mediating role to speak of.

Naturally, beliefs about system fairness should also be shaped by a variety of other attitudinal (e.g., partisan and ideological identifications) and demographic characteristics of individuals, and these factors are included in the analysis in the following text as "control variables." Several studies, some cited in the preceding text, for example, suggest that ideological conservatives, and by extension, Republicans, are likely to differ in their assessments of system fairness from their liberal and Democratic Party counterparts. Among the demographic factors, Blacks with more formal education are not only more likely to perceive discrimination, as we found in Chapter 2, but they are also more likely to question the fairness of the economic and social stratification systems (Tate 1993) than less educated Blacks and Whites. Finally, we expect females to be more critical in their evaluations of the justice system than males. As noted by Hutchings and his colleagues (forthcoming), "a variety of cross-national studies have found that women are more likely than men to endorse social group equality, express concern for the disadvantaged, self-identify as political liberals, and support structural explanations for racial inequality" in addition to supporting more racially egalitarian political appeals (Hutchings et al. 2004).

Table 3.1 presents the results obtained from regressing system fairness beliefs on unfair treatment, neighborhood discrimination, and various control variables among Blacks (column 1) and Whites

[13] Recall that unfair treatment ranges from 0 (none) to 3 (4 or more) reported incidents of being treated unfairly by police, where Blacks (but not Whites) were asked about being treated unfairly because of one's race (see Table 2.1). Neighborhood discrimination ranges from 0 to 12, with 0 indicating that respondents rated racial discrimination in one's community by both the police and the courts as "not a problem," and 12 indicating that both forms of racial discrimination were rated as "very serious." We did not include the item "police care less about crimes against blacks" in order to avoid loading the index with items about the police.

TABLE 3.1. *Predicting system fairness beliefs across race of respondent*

	Blacks	Blacks, Curv.	Whites	Whites, Curv.
Unfair Treatment	−.21**[a] (.08)	−.20** (.08)	−.48** (.11)	−.47** (.11)
Neighborhood Discrimination	−.11** (.02)	.18[a] (.11)	−.14** (.02)	−.02 (.09)
Neighborhood Discrimination^2		−.02** (.01)		−.01 (.01)
Anti-Black Stereotype	.03 (.01)	.01 (.01)	−.01 (.01)	−.01 (.01)
Fear Crime	.05 (.07)	.06 (.07)	.15 (.08)	.15* (.08)
Party ID	.09 (.05)	.08 (.05)	.01 (.04)	.02 (.04)
Ideology	−.01 (.05)	−.001 (.04)	.07 (.04)	.06 (.04)
Education	−.10 (.06)	−.12* (.06)	−.02 (.05)	−.02 (.05)
Female	−.12[a] (.15)	−.08 (.15)	−.66** (.14)	−.66** (.14)
Age	−.01 (.01)	−.01 (.01)	.003 (.004)	.003 (.004)
Income	−.03 (.06)	−.03 (.05)	.10* (.05)	.10* (.05)
South	.09 (.17)	.10 (.17)	.17 (.17)	.16 (.17)
Social Context				
County Crime Index	7.1e-06 (3.e-05)	1.-e5 (3.e-05)	2.e-05 (4.e-05)	1.e-05 (4.e-05)
Large Metropolitan Area	.27 (.18)	.28 (.17)	.23 (.14)	.23 (.14)
Percent Black Zip Code	.19 (.10)	.17 (.10)	−.08 (.05)	−.09 (.05)
Constant	3.04** (.66)	1.91* (.78)	3.86** (.50)	3.55** (.54)
N	528	528	531	531
Adj R^2	.10	.11	.19	.19

*p < . 05, **p < .01

[a] Coefficient is statistically different across race of respondents (≤ .05).

Note: Entries are OLS regression coefficients with standard errors in parentheses. Higher values on the preceding variables indicate greater system fairness, more serious neighborhood discrimination, higher incidents of unfair treatment, more Republican, conservative, more negative stereotypes of Blacks than Whites, higher formal education, female, years of age, income, living in a state of the Deep South, higher county crime rate, large metropolitan area, and percent Black in Zip Code (logged).

Source: NRCS data.

(column 3). In the first row of coefficients, we see that among individuals of both races, being treated unfairly by the police is associated with sharp decreases in appraisals of system fairness. The size of the coefficients suggests that the effect is larger for Whites than it is for Blacks, something we did not expect to find. There are two possible explanations for this seemingly anomalous finding. One reason why the coefficient for unfair treatment is smaller among Blacks is that some of the influence of unfair treatment on system fairness is indirect and is being mediated by neighborhood discrimination. This is true only for Blacks, however, not for Whites – for whom we found unfair treatment and neighborhood discrimination to be unrelated (Table 2.4). Consistent with this interpretation, if we eliminate neighborhood discrimination from the system fairness equation for Blacks, the coefficient for unfair treatment increases significantly (from –.20 to –.29), though it still lags behind that for Whites (b = –.49).

Another explanation is that the races likely differ in the impact that any single piece of information is likely to have on their general beliefs about system fairness. Many Blacks doubtless encounter a wide range of information and experiences that lead them to conclude that the justice system is unfair, including secondhand information of negative encounters with the police and other agents from family members and friends, Black opinion leaders, and others. Thus, each individual piece of negative information, including being treated unfairly by the police, should have less of an effect on their overall beliefs. Most Whites likely begin with a comparatively naïve view of the justice system as fair and color blind, so Whites who are treated unfairly by the police are more strongly affected by such experiences.[14]

A similar story unfolds when we turn our attention to the association between neighborhood discrimination and system fairness in the second row of Table 3.1, where we see that the more serious discrimination in one's community is perceived to be, the less fair one is likely to view the criminal justice system. The coefficients for neighborhood discrimination are roughly the same size among Blacks and Whites. Once again, we are confronted with a seeming anomaly, because Blacks' views of the justice system should, if anything, be more likely to be filtered through the lens of race than Whites' views. How can we account for this? The answer to this question lies in the next row of coefficients in Table 3.1, where we estimate a curvilinear relationship

[14] Still another explanation for the discrepancy is that Whites were asked about incidents of unfair treatment by the police, while Blacks were asked about a special class of unfair treatment – i.e., because of their race. The more general phrasing of Whites' experiences may provide a better match with the more general assessment respondents were asked to make about the fairness of the justice system.

between neighborhood discrimination and system fairness for Blacks, based on the supposition that, especially among Blacks, "positive" information about system fairness should carry less weight than negative information.[15]

Figure 3.2 compares the predicted (curvilinear) relationship for Blacks to the (linear) one estimated for Whites, based on the results in Table 3.1. The first thing to notice in the figure is the more positive evaluation of the justice system among Whites compared to Blacks at all levels of neighborhood discrimination. But the most dramatic difference occurs among Whites and Blacks who see little discrimination in their communities, on the left side of the figure. The vast majority of Whites, who see little evidence of injustice in their neighborhoods (67% fall between .5 and 6.5 on the discrimination scale), are likely to evaluate the justice system quite favorably (i.e., very fair). By contrast, Blacks who also see little discrimination in their own neighborhoods are much less likely to generalize their rosy perceptions to the system as a whole. Compared to Whites, they remain fairly cynical in their views of system fairness, as if waiting for further evidence to convince them that the system, overall, is just. Neighborhood discrimination carries more weight for Blacks only when discrimination is viewed as quite serious. When the majority of Blacks rate neighborhood discrimination as very serious (67% fall between 5.5 and 12 on the scale), they are more apt to generalize these perceptions to the system as a whole than are Whites, adopting a nearly universally cynical and negative posture that the system is unjust.

Overall, then, both races base their evaluations of the justice system, in part, on their personal and vicarious experiences with the criminal justice system. In addition, because many Blacks are doubtless bombarded with information questioning the fairness of the

[15] In light of the highly skewed distribution of perceptions of discrimination revealed in Figure 2.1, in preliminary analyses we included the square of neighborhood discrimination, along with the first-order term, in order to detect evidence of a curvilinear (quadratic) relationship between neighborhood discrimination and system fairness, which we found to be significant for Blacks but not for Whites. Hence, we included the quadratic specification in Table 3.1. The second and third rows of coefficients in Table 3.1 show that among Blacks, the relationship between neighborhood discrimination is curvilinear because the coefficient for the squared discrimination term is statistically significant.

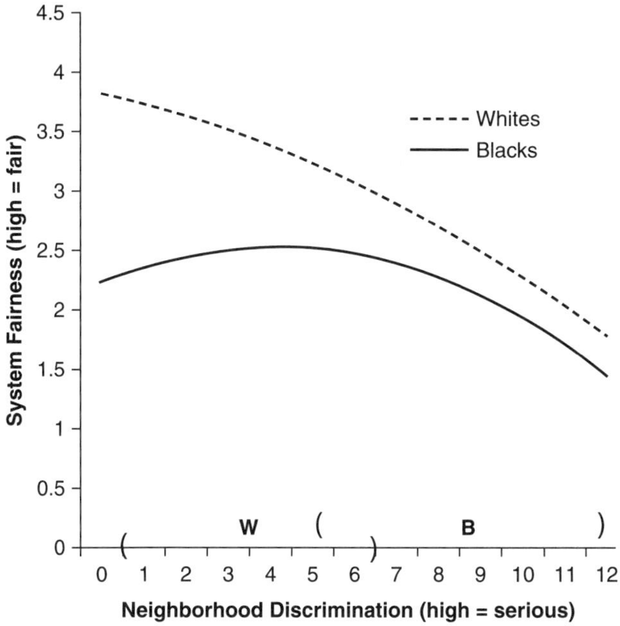

FIGURE 3.2. Predicting system fairness from neighborhood discrimination.
Note: The figure plots predicted values of system fairness (Table 3.1) to show the curvilinear effect of neighborhood discrimination on system fairness among Blacks but not Whites. "W" and "B" indicate groups means, with parentheses indicating 1 standard deviation below and above the mean.
Source: NRCS data.

criminal justice system, a "ceiling" effect exists that limits the degree to which an absence of negative experiences can buoy more positive evaluations of the system. The bottom line, however, is that the evidence is consistent with the conclusion that personal experiences (i.e., unfair treatment and neighborhood discrimination) are generalized to more fundamental views of system fairness.

Looking at the coefficients associated with the control variables in Table 3.1 (column 2), we see more concrete evidence that Blacks' views of an unfair justice system stem from a variety of sources – in this case, formal education. Independent of their experiences with the justice system, more educated Blacks are significantly more likely to believe the system is unfair – consistent with the tendency for middle-class Blacks to perceive injustice most starkly (e.g., Gay 2004).

With a larger complement of significant predictors for Whites, it is useful to compare the magnitude of their substantive impact in Figure 3.3, which displays estimates of "first differences," or the amount of change in system fairness that results from moving from low to high values on each predictor while holding other predictors at their means. Although the results in Table 3.1 indicate that males and the more affluent are more likely to believe that the justice system is fair than do females and those with less income, the figure clearly shows that gender trumps income in the size of its impact. Consistent with other studies finding women to be more supportive of egalitarianism than men (e.g., Hutchings et al., forthcoming), women are much more skeptical of the claim that the justice system treats people fairly and equally. Although the impact of gender is on par with that of unfair treatment, it is approximately half that of neighborhood discrimination.

The findings in Table 3.1 and Figure 3.3 also reveal that neither political orientations (partisanship and ideology) nor social context

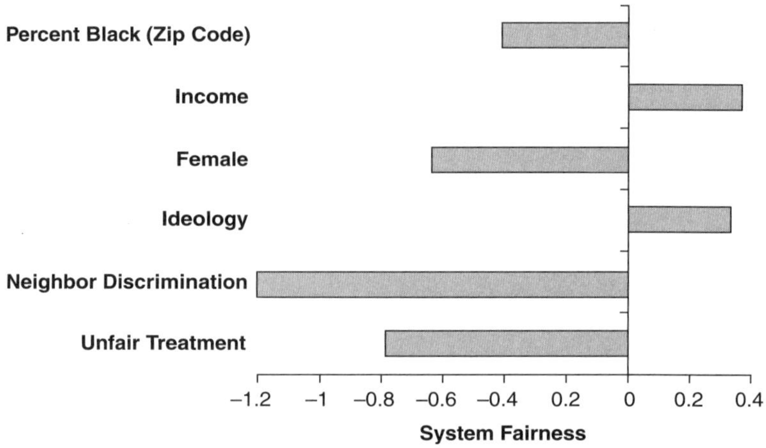

FIGURE 3.3. Substantive impact of select predictors on system fairness for Whites.

Note: The figure displays "first differences" – that is, the degree of change in system fairness that results from increasing a given predictor from a low to a high value, holding all other predictors at their means. For continuous variables, low and high values correspond to 1 standard deviation below and above the group mean, with higher values indicating greater percent Black, income, female, conservative, more serious neighborhood discrimination, and more incidents of unfair treatment. Based on the results in Table 3.1.

Source: NRCS data.

(e.g., percent Black) appear to play a significant role in shaping system fairness, a pattern to be repeated in the following text, when examining sources of our other measure of fairness, attributions of Black treatment. One reason why social context fails to influence general fairness assessments directly is that its impact is mediated primarily through personal and vicarious experiences (i.e., unfair treatment and neighborhood discrimination), both of which were found to be associated with contextual variables in Chapter 2.

Exactly why political orientations fail to shape fairness assessments requires more explanation, especially because, in the economic sphere, conservatives are much more likely than liberals to judge the economic system as being fair (e.g., Kluegel and Smith 1986; Bartels 2008). Elites very seldom offer "dissenting" positions on crime, fearful of the label "soft on crime." Consequently, citizens typically do not perceive differences between parties or, most likely, between liberals and conservatives. Without clear elite cues, ideology may only structure fairness views among more sophisticated individuals who follow politics more closely and think about such issues in ideological terms (Zaller 1992). As is often the case in American politics, ideology may be more important for more educated or politically aware individuals. This explanation fits well for Whites but not for Blacks. In Figure 3.4, we display the predicted values of system fairness for extreme liberals and conservatives at different levels of education for both Whites and Blacks. Among Whites, liberals and conservatives become more polarized at higher levels of education, with highly educated conservatives showing a strong tendency to view the justice system as fair and with educated liberals rating the system as much less fair. Among Blacks, however, ideological differences are nonexistent (and nonsignificant) across education levels. Instead, greater formal education is associated with rating the justice system as increasingly unfair. But even Blacks at fairly low education levels rate the justice system as less fair than liberal Whites at much higher levels of education. The analysis suggests that Blacks do not depend on liberal elites for guidance on criminal justice issues the way Whites do.[16]

[16] Equations including interaction terms are not shown. Of note, we found a very similar interactive pattern among Whites (but not for Blacks) when substituting

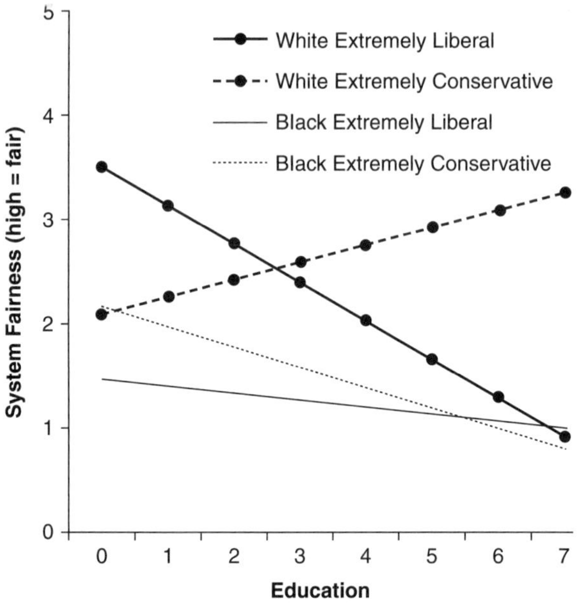

FIGURE 3.4. Impact of ideology on system fairness across education.
Note: The figure shows how the impact of ideology on system fairness increases among Whites with higher education. The impact of ideology on system fairness is statistically significant among the 47% of Whites with a bachelor's degree or higher. Predicted values based on Table 3.1.
Source: NRCS data.

Narrowing the Race Gap?

The robust impact of our two experiential measures – unfair treatment and neighborhood discrimination – on beliefs about system fairness raises an interesting question: if the experiences of Whites were more like those of Blacks, to what extent would the racial gap in fairness beliefs be narrowed? The expressions "where you stand depends on where you sit" and "walk a mile in my shoes" convey in different ways

attributions of Black treatment for system fairness. We can only speculate about the finding that ideology is interactively significant (with education) for Whites but not for Blacks. Most likely, the unfair nature of the justice system is just more "obvious" to African Americans and, therefore, less dependent on any ideological cues that may otherwise be helpful to structure such perceptions. Also worthy of comment, we have not found partisanship to be statistically significant in these equations, most likely because party elites do not tend to differ substantially in the public positions they take on crime and justice.

the power of individuals' life experiences to mold their views. In order to gain more insight into the forces that separate the races in their appraisals of the justice system, we explore how Whites' views of fairness would change if their experiences were identical to those of Blacks. If we assume, quite hypothetically, that Whites, on average, have the same experiences of unfair treatment and neighborhood discrimination as Blacks, to what degree would Whites abandon their more rosy views of the justice system in favor of the more cynical views of Blacks?

In an attempt to answer this question, we compare Whites' and Blacks' average view of system fairness under three conditions in Figure 3.5. In the "baseline" condition, depicted on the left-hand side of the figure, we estimate the race gap in its "natural state" – that is, when all fourteen predictors of system fairness in Table 3.1 are set to their respective

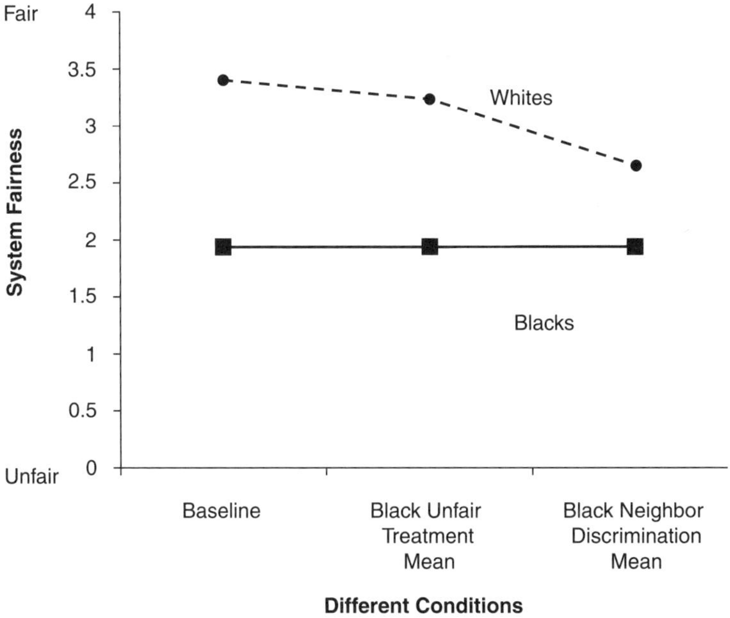

FIGURE 3.5. Reducing racial polarization in system fairness under hypothetical (simulated) conditions.

Note: The figure shows how racial polarization in system fairness beliefs decreases from the baseline condition to simulated conditions when Whites take on the same average value on unfair treatment or neighborhood discrimination as Blacks. The simulations are based on the regression estimates in Table 3.1.

Source: NRCS data.

(and usually quite different) means for the races. In the middle of the figure, however, we predict system fairness views for Blacks and Whites presuming that Whites have the same level of personal experience with unfair treatment as Blacks. In practical terms, we set the mean of unfair treatment for Whites to the average for Blacks. On the right-hand side of the figure, we assume that Whites rate neighborhood discrimination identically to Blacks.[17]

In the baseline condition, the race gap in system fairness judgments is a substantial 1.5 points along a seven-point scale. By assuming Whites have the same experience of unfair treatment as the average Black respondent, the race gap is narrowed only slightly, by about 12 percent. But when Whites are assumed to rate neighborhood discrimination the same as Blacks, the gap in system fairness beliefs narrows considerably, closing by more than half (51%). Notably, in this scenario, Whites traverse from the "fair" end of the system fairness scale (above point 3) to the "unfair" end of the scale (below point 3). In our hypothetical world, then, Whites' global views of fairness become more like Blacks' when they are assumed to share similar experiences. In reality, it is important to point out that only a small percentage of Whites actually score at or above the average Black response on unfair treatment (13%) and neighborhood discrimination (7%), so the likelihood of Whites actually having such experiences is extremely remote. The overall lesson from this exercise is clear: experiences matter – they play a large role in determining the race gap in global views of the fairness of the justice system.

Sources of Attributions of Black Treatment

Our purpose in examining the sources of our second measure of fairness, attributions of Black treatment, is slightly different from our analysis of system fairness. Here we are mostly interested in determining

[17] See Kinder and Winter (2001) for a more complete description of this method in a more elaborate application. As indicated, these simulations are hypothetical and not completely realistic. E.g., Blacks and Whites are asked different questions in order to assess unfair treatment. Nevertheless, this exercise provides an indication of how much the race gap in system fairness beliefs would, potentially, be narrowed if African Americans and Whites had comparable experiences with the justice system.

the degree to which attributions of Black treatment should be interpreted as constituting a more subtle form of prejudice or, at minimum, racially insensitive beliefs about African Americans. As noted (Figure 3.1), most Whites attribute Blacks' harsh treatment to the failings of Blacks, with no real weight given to the biases of the justice system. In the economic sphere, Whites' denial of racial discrimination has been termed "laissez-faire racism" (Bobo, Kluegel, and Smith 1997) because, it is argued, the maintenance of racial hierarchies no longer requires widespread endorsement of the idea that Blacks are genetically inferior. Rather, it presumes that all major obstacles facing Blacks as a group have been removed, making government-sponsored efforts to reduce racial inequality unnecessary. By the same token, by denying the discrimination that Blacks face in the justice system, Whites are free to "blame the victim" or turn a blind eye to the many injustices that Blacks suffer at the hands of the police and the courts.

Accordingly, an important goal in the analysis in the following text is to assess whether attributions of Black treatment among Whites are associated with anti-Black stereotypes, or the tendency to stereotype Blacks more negatively than Whites. Such an association would be consistent with the view that attributions of Black treatment are not simply dispassionate causal explanations of the degree to which Blacks are responsible for their fate in the justice system but also, to some degree, reflect racial animus.

The equation estimating Black treatment is identical to that of system fairness with one important exception. In the analysis in the following text, we include not only the usual control variables[18] but also individuals' explanations of crime, in general, because attributions of why Blacks receive harsher treatment in the justice domain are likely to depend, in part, on explanations of crime in general. For example, some people (e.g., conservatives) may feel that structural forces are wholly unimportant in explaining crime and arrest rates among all groups, not just Blacks. Therefore, we include a measure of general

[18] The controls are especially important in this case in order to eliminate spurious effects from the common dependence of racial stereotypes and Black attributions on various attitudinal (e.g., conservatism or fear of crime) and demographic factors (e.g., lower education, age, gender, and living in the Deep South). Recall, also, that our measure of anti-Black stereotypes includes a built-in control for any tendency to rate all groups harshly, because it is constructed by subtracting ratings of "most Whites" from those of "most Blacks" on a series of traits (e.g., lazy or violent).

attributions of crime that parallels our measure of attributions of Black treatment in that respondents were asked to choose between pairs of dispositional and structural causes, but instead of asking about Blacks, we asked whether generic causes of crime – for example, poverty versus being too lazy to get an honest job – were more important reasons for crime in America these days. General attributions of crime range from 0 (structural attributions) to 4 (dispositional attributions).

The regression results are displayed in Table 3.2. As a general pattern, aside from the significant impact of neighborhood discrimination (row 2), where rating discrimination less seriously is associated with blaming Blacks for their harsher treatment in the justice system, we see a different set of predictors impinging on Black treatment than was the case for system fairness. Notably, personal experiences with unfair treatment, which were critical in shaping system fairness, are wholly unimportant for Black treatment (row 1). To be sure, one difference is due to model specification: general attributions of crime is only included in the Black treatment equation, where we find, unsurprisingly, that individuals of both races who attribute crime to dispositional forces are also more likely to blame Blacks for their harsher treatment in the justice system (row 3).[19]

The most important difference is the significant coefficient for anti-Black stereotypes (row 4) in Table 3.2. Stereotyping Blacks more negatively than Whites is strongly associated with blaming Blacks for their harsher treatment in the justice system, particularly among White respondents (b = .043 for Whites, b = .031 for Blacks). Further, among White respondents we also see that older individuals and Southerners are much more likely than younger, non-Southerners to blame Blacks for their harsher treatment (rows 10 and 12). This regional difference should not be surprising. A number of studies have documented that although more open expressions of racial animus have declined markedly among southern Whites over the years, large regional differences reappear when unobtrusive instruments are used to measure racial prejudice (e.g., Kuklinski, Cobb, and Gilens 1997). Using their list experiments,[20] for example, Kuklinski and his colleagues found that

[19] Even so, if we include general attributions in the system fairness equation, we find that it plays no significant role in shaping fairness for either race.

[20] The list experiment enables the researcher to ask respondents about matters of racial prejudice in such a way that individuals do not realize they are being queried. They are, consequently, unaware that they may have revealed prejudicial responses.

TABLE 3.2. *Predicting attributions of Black treatment*

	Whites	Blacks
Unfair Treatment	−.075 (.100)	−.066 (.064)
Neighborhood Discrimination	−.091 (.019)**	−.047 (.017)**
General Attributions of Crime	.184 (.040)**	.176 (.040)**
Anti-Black Stereotype	.043 (.013)**	.031 (.008)**
Fear Crime	−.086 (.066)	−.091 (.054)
Party ID	.058 (.033)	.019 (.039)
Ideology	.029 (.036)	.064 (.029)*
Education	−.069 (.045)	−.131 (.050)**
Female	−.312 (.118)**	−.339 (.123)**
Age	.010[a] (.004)**	.000 (.004)
Income	.001[a] (.041)	−.127 (.044)**
South	.511[a] (.147)**	.029 (.136)
Social Context		
County Crime Index	7.1e-06 (3.e-05)	4.-e5 (3.e-05)
Large Metropolitan Area	.071 (.124)	.020 (.141)
Percent Black Zip Code	−.006 (.041)	.084 (.076)
Constant	2.277 (.437)**	2.299 (.518)**
N	526	537
Adj R^2	.20	.21

*p < . 05, **p < .01

[a] Coefficient is statistically different across race of respondents (≤ .05).

Note: Entries are OLS regression coefficients with standard errors in parentheses. Higher values on the preceding variables indicate attribute Black treatment to Blacks, general attributions more dispositional, more incidents of unfair treatment, more serious neighborhood discrimination, more negative stereotypes of Blacks than Whites, greater fear of crime, more Republican, conservative, higher formal education, female, years of age, income, living in a state of the confederate South, higher county crime rate, large metropolitan area, and percent Black in Zip Code (logged).

Source: NRCS data.

the gap between Southerners and non-Southerners in their expressions of anger at the idea of a single "Black family moving next door" or "Black teens dating White teens" ranged from 20 to 30 percent.

It is worth repeating that the impact of anti-Black stereotypes and living in the South are independent of an array of controls, most notably conservative ideology, beliefs about the general causes of crime, and perceptions of discrimination. It is not the case that Southerners or negative stereotypers attribute more blame to Blacks because they happen to be more conservative or because they attribute crime to dispositional forces regardless of race. Rather, the results show that it is *Black* crime, in particular, that receives a more dispositional attribution from Whites who live in the South and stereotype Blacks more negatively than Whites.

Having shown that attributions of Black treatment are based on anti-Black stereotypes, is it fair to conclude that our attribution scale is simply another measure of racial prejudice? The problem with such an interpretation is that the attributions of not only Whites but also Blacks are based on a variety of other antecedents that are only weakly tied to racial prejudice, if at all. This can be seen most clearly in Figure 3.6, which displays the amount of change (i.e., "first differences") in Black treatment that results from moving from low to high values on each significant predictor, for both White and Black respondents.

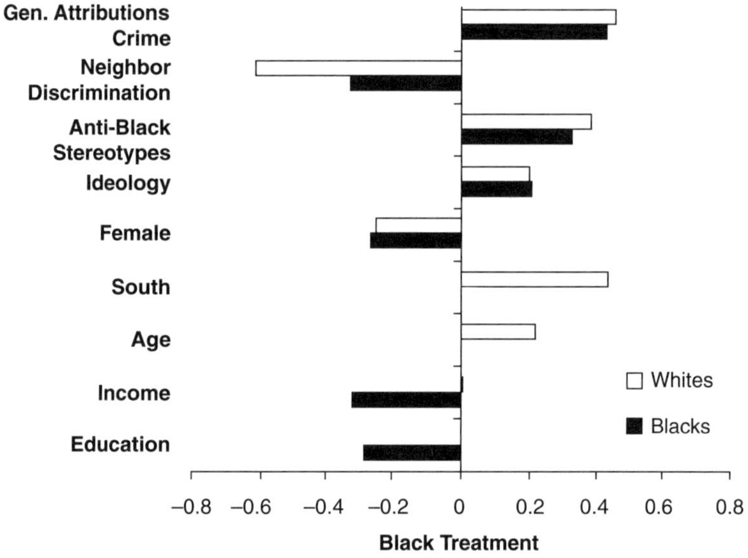

FIGURE 3.6. Substantive effects of select predictors on Black treatment.
Note: The figure shows the degree of change in Black treatment associated with moving from low to high values on select predictors, when holding other predictors at their means (i.e., first differences). For continuous variables, low and high values correspond to 1 standard deviation below and above the mean for each racial group, with "higher" values indicating more dispositional attributions for Black treatment and general attributions of crime, more serious evaluations of neighborhood discrimination, more negative stereotypes of Blacks than Whites, more conservative, female, living in the Deep South, older, higher income, and education. Nonsignificant effects are set to 0. Based on the results in Table 3.2.
Source: NRCS data.

Among Whites, the substantive impact of anti-Black stereotypes and living in the Deep South is not trivial, but then neither is the impact of other predictors, such as general attributions of crime and perceptions of neighborhood discrimination.[21] Although the substantive impact of ideology appears small for both races in Figure 3.6, when we focus on more educated Whites, as we did for system fairness, conservatives are far more likely than liberals to attribute Black treatment to Blacks (analysis not shown).[22]

Admittedly, cross-sectional survey data are not ideal for sorting out causal influences of racial prejudice versus other variables. In addition, others might interpret these findings quite differently. Measures of "New Racism," for example, implicitly assume that the denial of racial discrimination is a key component of prejudice (e.g., Kinder and Sanders 1996; Henry and Sears 2002). We are inclined to agree with Huddy and Feldman (2009), however, in arguing that while attributions of discrimination are useful predictors of policy attitudes, when they are employed as measures of racial prejudice they tend to be plagued by ambiguity. According to the authors:

> If discrimination is difficult for experts to conclusively demonstrate, can we flatly state that the denial of racial discrimination among ordinary people reflects racial prejudice? Isn't it possible that the denial of discrimination is due to the inherent difficulty in attributing unequal racial outcomes specifically to differential treatment, especially for individuals unschooled in scientific research methods? Some whites may feel they have never witnessed or seen direct evidence of such categorical discrimination. The denial of discrimination could also arise from ideological considerations that make it more difficult for political conservatives to accept the existence of discrimination as a determinant of an individual's economic and educational outcomes. In the same way, the willingness to blame black poverty on discrimination could arise from an ideological belief in the pervasiveness of

[21] To some extent, neighborhood discrimination (as well as general attributions of crime) is shaped by anti-Black stereotypes, along with other predictors. Nevertheless, one interpretation of the impact of neighborhood discrimination in this case is that the social context in which many Whites live encourages them to downplay discrimination as an explanation of the harsher treatment of Blacks.

[22] Compared to the full sample of Whites, in which moving from low (liberal) to high (conservative) values on the ideology scale produces rather small differences in attributions of Black treatment (first difference = .25), the impact of ideology doubles among Whites who at least completed some college (first difference = .5) and becomes quite strong among Whites with a college degree (first difference = 1.5).

structural inequities in American society....[and] [s]everal recent studies suggest that common psychological processes may in fact limit people's willingness and ability to attribute unequal outcomes to discrimination. (432)

To summarize, attributional beliefs about Black treatment clearly differ from beliefs about system fairness in the degree to which the former are based on anti-Black stereotypes, especially among Whites. But further examination also suggests that even though such attributions are surely influenced, in many instances, by prejudice, they are also the product of other beliefs and orientations, such as ideology (at least among more educated Whites), general attributions of crime, and evaluations of neighborhood discrimination.[23] Among African-American respondents, higher education and income are associated with a greater appreciation of the discriminatory context that Blacks face in the justice system. These findings suggest that our measure of Black treatment is not merely a proxy for prejudice. Rather, individuals, especially Whites, who place the blame for the harsher treatment of African Americans entirely on the dispositions of Blacks, are, at best, either naïve about or insensitive to the realities of discriminatory treatment in the justice system. At worst, many are doubtless motivated by some degree of racial animus. In either case, they fail to appreciate the substantial environmental obstacles faced by many Blacks on a chronic basis. It is important to remember that regardless of the motivation for denying discrimination, the consequences of such beliefs are likely to be the same (e.g., Huddy and Feldman 2009).

CONCLUSIONS

In this chapter, we have underscored the multidimensionality of fairness. When applied to the criminal justice domain, justice (a term that we have used interchangeably with fairness) can be understood as retributive, distributive, or procedural in nature. Our essential argument has been that, even if procedural concerns feed most directly into appraisals of the justice system, citizens will base a great deal of

[23] Consistent with research on support for social equality, among both races women are more likely than men to attribute the harsher treatment of Blacks to the biases of the justice system than to Blacks.

their knowledge of procedural justice on outcomes – or distributive justice criteria.

Fairness is also multidimensional in another important sense – that is, it can be assessed with regard to the beneficiary of equality. The psychology of legitimacy literature referenced in the preceding text is quite explicit in this respect: observers evaluate a system (whether economic or justice) according to how it impacts an individual, how it impacts a particular group, and how it impacts the society at large. In Chapter 2 we focused on judgments at the individual level, examining Blacks' and Whites' responses to questions about their personal confrontations with the justice system, as well as the confrontations with which they became familiar vicariously. In Chapter 3, we have established that individuals of both races who believe their encounters with law enforcement have been tainted by discrimination also tend to be substantially more likely to see discrimination at the systemic (or societal) level as well (though not at the group level).

In this chapter, we turned our attention to evaluations at the societal and group levels. To assess societal fairness, we administered a two-item system fairness battery asking whether the justice system and the courts treat "people" or "everyone" fairly and equally. As noted, these items are void of any reference to race (or, for that matter, any group), activity, or policy. To measure group fairness (attributions of Black treatment), we asked respondents to tell us why African Americans are more often "arrested and sent to prison than Whites," asking twice to select between dispositional (Blacks more likely to commit crimes, or Blacks don't respect authority) and societal (the police and justice system are biased against Blacks) causes.

Although there is modest overlap between them (i.e., individuals who believe that the justice system is unfair at the broadest [societal] level also tend to believe it is unfair to African Americans), our examination of their antecedents suggests that they are quite different for the most part. Beliefs about system fairness are based primarily on personal and vicarious experiences with the justice system (i.e., unfair treatment and neighborhood discrimination, respectively), and the radically different experiences of the races largely accounts for the substantial gap in their assessments of the fairness of wider systems, with Whites being far more likely than Blacks to view the justice system as fair. By contrast, attributions of Black treatment are based on beliefs about African Americans (i.e., anti-Black stereotypes) as well as more general beliefs about the causes of crime and ideological identifications. Only vicarious experiences about discrimination toward Blacks (i.e., neighborhood discrimination) matter for such attributions, not personal experiences. These empirical findings, along with our theoretical expectations, bolster our assumption that the two fairness measures will have very different consequences in the chapters ahead.

We have argued that people use general fairness beliefs (at the societal and group levels) to guide their responses to inherently ambiguous events and objects in the justice domain. Specifically, we will show in subsequent chapters that the different views that Whites and Blacks hold about fairness in the justice system go a long way toward explaining racially polarized responses to events (Chapter 4) and policies (Chapter 5). In Chapter 4, for example, we examine responses to various vignettes designed to capture incendiary incidents of police brutality and racial profiling. We investigate support for a variety of punitive policies that divide the races, such as capital punishment, in Chapter 5.

However, we do not expect societal and group judgments to play the same role in each of the forthcoming chapters. System (societal) fairness beliefs refer to generic assessments about the degree to which authorities in the system can be expected to adhere to fair procedures – that is, whether the process by which specific decisions are made are likely to be fair or biased. As such they are likely to be especially useful for making judgments about the conduct of particular authorities.

In Chapter 4, we rely on a series of scenarios that pit civilians against police officers and essentially ask respondents if they are more sympathetic to the former or to the latter. More specifically, we ask whether the police are likely to launch a fair investigation in a police brutality case and whether the police acted fairly in searching two men in a racial profiling case. In these and similar incidents, individuals are expected to rely on their prior beliefs about the general fairness of the justice system to assess the fairness of authorities in concrete situations.

Causal attributions, which serve as our measures of group fairness, should play a central role in shaping support for punitive justice policies because such attributions imply an evaluation of blameworthiness and whether the governmental policy is deserved and appropriate (Brickman 1982; Iyengar 1989). In particular, because many punitive crime policies are widely believed to be applied in a racially biased fashion, individuals' attributions of Black treatment, as well as their more general attributions of crime, should assume center stage in accounting for individuals' support for a range of crime programs and policies.

In the end, we will show that the expected division of labor in the explanatory roles played by the two sets of fairness beliefs is supported by the empirical evidence: system fairness beliefs account for responses to events that question the fairness of authorities, while attributional beliefs account for policy support.[24] We hasten to mention that one limitation of our analysis in this chapter is that we were unable to determine whether the direction of causality runs from experiences to fairness beliefs, as our models assume, or whether fairness beliefs shape reports of experiences. A jaundiced view of system fairness, for example, could lead to more negative evaluations of individuals' personal and vicarious experiences, as well as the reverse.[25]

Fortunately, Tyler's (1988, 1990) research on this question provides some reassurance, for he finds that although prior expectations of fairness often shape evaluations of encounters with police and other authorities, this should not be taken to mean that people's experiences with authorities are mere figments of their imagination. On the one hand, Tyler's research clearly shows that individuals' (e.g., citizens or convicted felons) expectations about fairness can influence their evaluations of encounters with authorities (e.g., police or attorneys). Those who expected fair treatment were more likely to see fair treatment than those who expected unfair treatment. On the other hand, these same studies found that prior views did not overwhelm the nature of the experience. The reality of individuals' encounters with

[24] Although we do not report the results, we also examined the influence of both sets of beliefs (system fairness and group attributions) in explaining responses to events (Chapter 4) and policies (Chapter 5) and found no significant departures from the expected division of labor. To simplify the analyses, therefore, and to avoid obscuring the effects we do find, we rely on system fairness beliefs to do the heavy lifting in Chapter 4 and causal beliefs to do likewise in Chapter 5.

[25] Correcting for this endogeneity problem is much more difficult in the present context than it was in Chapter 2 (Appendix) because we were unable to create strong (Two-Stage Least Squares) instruments for the endogenous explanatory variables.

authorities (i.e., how they were actually treated) had a greater impact on their evaluations of the encounter than their perceptual biases. By the same token, the tendency for large portions of Blacks from every walk of life in our study to report experiences of racial discrimination across a range of measures should be viewed as evidence that their experiences are real, not merely the product of imaginary slights and biases. Thus, although we must acknowledge that our analysis of the association between people's experiences (i.e., unfair treatment and neighborhood discrimination) and fairness beliefs in Tables 3.1 and 3.2 may overstate any causal influences, there are good reasons to believe that the bias in our estimates is small.

4

The Consequences of Fairness

Polarized Reactions to Police Brutality and Racial Profiling

In the previous chapter, we made two important claims: first, that fairness beliefs should be central elements in mass belief systems in the justice domain, and second, that such beliefs are essential to understanding the different ways that Whites and Blacks evaluate criminal justice issues. Accordingly, we proffered two measures of fairness, one asking respondents in the National Race and Crime Survey (NRCS) to evaluate the fairness of the wider system (i.e., system fairness) and another asking them to explain the harsher treatment of African Americans by the justice system (attributions of Black treatment). Unsurprisingly, we found a huge race gap in responses to both measures, with most Blacks rating the system as patently unfair and attributing Blacks' harsher treatment to biases in the system, and most Whites taking the opposite view, believing the system is fair and that Blacks deserve their harsher treatment. Our analysis of the sources of our two fairness beliefs led us to conclude that, as expected, even though the two measures overlap, they are substantially independent of one another. Specifically, judgments about the general fairness of the justice system are, to a great degree, experientially determined; quite commonly individuals will think about their own experiences, and those of their neighbors, as they evaluate the system as a whole. In contrast, at least for Whites, stereotypes of African Americans figure prominently into assessments of whether the justice system treats Blacks fairly.

Having investigated the content and the sources of fairness beliefs, we turn in this chapter and the next to the more important question: what are the political consequences of these beliefs? More to the point, to what degree can racial polarization on specific events and policies in the justice domain be traced to the interracial chasm underscored so dramatically on our two measures of fairness documented in Chapter 3? As described in Chapter 2, fairness heuristic theory (Van den Bos et al. 1997, 1035) argues that people form general fairness beliefs based on various types of information (e.g., about outcomes as well as processes), and that "once a person has established a fairness judgment, perceived fairness serves as a heuristic that guides the interpretation of subsequent events."

Our analysis follows the division of labor justified in Chapter 3, in which we argued that attributional beliefs should play a central role in explaining policy attitudes while system fairness beliefs are much more relevant for interpreting events involving legal authorities. Accordingly, in Chapter 5, we examine the role of attributions of Black treatment in accounting for Blacks' and Whites' support for anticrime policies. We turn our attention here to the role played by system fairness beliefs in shaping reactions to events in the justice domain.[1] The question we take up is an important one: why do Whites and Blacks diverge so sharply in their reactions to potentially incendiary events in the justice system, such as police brutality and racial profiling? As we point out in the following text, public reactions to incidents of police misconduct, from highly publicized cases like the Rodney King beating to more commonplace occurrences of racial profiling, constitute "flashpoints" in the racial divide. To understand how two groups of people, each viewing the same phenomena, can come to such radically different interpretations, we focus on interracial differences in system fairness beliefs as major culprits in generating the different perceptual realities of Whites and Blacks.

Our study departs in several important respects from prior investigations. We are certainly not the first to examine polarized public reactions to incidents of police brutality and racial profiling. For decades, a slew of commercial polls (and a handful of academic studies reviewed in the following text) has clearly documented the huge

[1] As we point out in the following text, we also estimated equations in the current chapter that included attributions of Black treatment (and other variables) as well as system fairness, but because the results did not change and the effects of Black treatment rarely achieved statistical significance, we do not report the more fully specified equations.

chasm that exists. What has not been clear is how these interpretative disagreements are fueled by more fundamental divisions in the way the races perceive the fairness of the justice system. We will demonstrate that these dissimilar judgments of system fairness strongly affect how both races interpret the same incidents so differently.

Another point of departure for our study is that we rely on a series of survey experiments describing police-civilian interactions in instances of racial profiling and police brutality – experiments where we randomly vary the race of the civilian. With such leverage, we can examine not only whether an individual's overall judgment of the fairness of the system influences his or her interpretation of such events but also the circumstances under which system fairness beliefs influence the interpretation of potentially racially charged events. Although, alternatively, we might have asked respondents to reveal their sympathies in "real life" events such as the Amadou Diallo case, the limitation of such methods is that they would not enable us to experimentally and randomly manipulate the race of the civilian, thus making it impossible to determine whether the race, or some other characteristic of the civilian, affects the responses.

As will become clear from the analysis in the following text, not only do the races diverge sharply in the content of their beliefs about system fairness (as demonstrated in Chapter 3), but also these beliefs influence the interpretation of police misconduct quite differently for Blacks and Whites, suggesting that "fairness" often takes on a radically different meaning for the races. Among Blacks, system fairness beliefs clearly carry strong racial connotations; fairness beliefs are much more predictive of their reactions to the scenarios when the civilian is Black. Among Whites, however, we find an extraordinary level of naiveté; their tendency to view the system as fair and essentially color blind prompts them to ignore important differences between Black and White civilians during their encounters with the police.

INCIDENTS OF POLICE BRUTALITY AND RACIAL PROFILING

We began this book with a brief litany of highly publicized incidents of police brutality against Blacks that serve as striking examples of the different realities that Blacks and Whites face, as well as the highly polarized reactions that such incidents elicit. A brief review of the chronology of some of the most publicized cases deserves mention here, for survey studies show that they often leave a lasting mark on public opinion. It is the public's polarized responses to such high-profile occurrences that provided the genesis for this book, as, time after time, we are left wondering why Whites respond one way, and Blacks respond another, to real-world situations.

Undoubtedly, the most publicized incident of police beating an African American occurred in 1991, when a bystander videotaped Rodney King being beaten by four White police officers of the Los Angeles Police Department, who used a stun gun and repeatedly kicked and beat King with batons. As noted by Sigelman et al. (1997, 777–8, emphasis added),

> For weeks afterward, the beating received saturation coverage in the news media; according to the *Vanderbilt Television News Index and Abstracts* (1992), from March 5 (the evening the story broke) through the end of March, the tape was shown twenty-seven times on the three network evening news programs alone. Expressions of outrage echoed across the nation.... Approximately fourteen months later, the trial of the four officers ended in verdicts of not guilty, with a hung [mainly White] jury on one count. Los Angeles exploded in violence that produced approximately sixty deaths and an estimated billion dollars in property damage.... *Blacks and Whites drew diametrically different lessons from the verdict.* Asked whether it "shows that Blacks cannot get justice in this country," 66 percent of White respondents said no, but 78 percent of Black respondents said yes.

Six months after the verdict in the King case, Malice Green, a Black resident of Detroit, was repeatedly kicked, punched, and bludgeoned by several members of the Detroit Police Department, and died as a result of what was officially ruled homicide by "blunt force trauma to the head." Abner Louima, a Haitian immigrant, was arrested outside a Brooklyn nightclub in 1997. On the way to the police station, he was severely beaten by officers in the patrol car and sodomized with the handle of a toilet plunger in the station house while the officers shouted racial slurs. Amadou Diallo, while being questioned about a rape in his New York City neighborhood, died after being shot forty-one times while reaching for his wallet (which police mistakenly took for a gun) in 1999. Nathaniel Jones died in 2003 after being clubbed repeatedly by Cincinnati officers – an incident occurring less than three years after the Ohio city was racked by race riots over alleged incidents of police brutality against African Americans. There have been countless other examples of police brutality around the country, which seem to occur on a periodic basis.[2] In November 2006, for example, five police officers in New York City were put on paid administrative leave after firing fifty rounds into the car of Sean Bell, a Black resident of the city, outside a Queens nightclub, killing Bell, a bridegroom, and seriously wounding two of his companions.

As intimated in Chapter 1, such incidents have a ripple effect emanating from the cities where they occur to the country as a whole. Most dramatically, police brutality and patterns of police misconduct against African Americans have even been linked to the outbreak of racial disturbances and riots in some American cities. Ironically, the 1991 Christopher Commission report, published in the aftermath of the King beating and nine months before the Los Angeles disturbances, warned that

> Within minority communities of Los Angeles, there is a widely-held view that police misconduct [against minorities] is commonplace. The King beating refocused public attention to long-standing complaints by African-Americans, Latinos and Asians that Los Angeles Police Department (LAPD) officers frequently treat minorities differently from Whites, more often using disrespectful and abusive language ... and engaging in use of excessive force when dealing with minorities.[3]

Remarkably similar conclusions were reached in the 1968 Kerner Commission Report almost forty years ago in which the number one complaint among Blacks in the twenty-one cities where race riots had occurred was police harassment "and a 'double standard' of justice and protection – one for Negroes and one for Whites."[4] Clearly, then, incidents of police misconduct against Blacks, particularly those involving the use of deadly force, have historically provided a combustible mixture in major American cities.[5]

[2] For a long litany of police brutality incidents, see Human Rights Watch (1998), *Shielded from Justice: Police Brutality and Accountability in the United States.*

[3] Christopher, Warren, ed. "Report of the Independent Commission on the Los Angeles Police Department" (The Christopher Commission), 1991, 32.

[4] U.S. National Advisory Commission on Civil Disorders. "Report of the National Advisory Commission on Civil Disorders" (The Kerner Commission), 1968, 206.

[5] To be sure, recent legal reforms and the response by some city officials have significantly reduced the number of people killed by police officers (from 559 in 1975 to

But the impact of highly publicized police brutality incidents extends far beyond the cities where they occurred. In their study of various trends in attitudes toward the police from 1977 to 1997, for example, Tuch and Weitzer (1997) concluded that events like the Rodney King beating were followed by an erosion of support for the police at the local and the national levels. Although Blacks' and Whites' views of the police became more negative, Blacks' attitudes were much more likely to sour after such events, and the effects were more long-lasting than they were for Whites.

The authors could not (and did not) claim that their results demonstrate a cause-and-effect relationship, because their study did not control for a variety of confounding events and factors (e.g., police responses after the incidents, contamination from other incidents, and news coverage). However, Sigelman et al. (1997) were able to construct a more controlled, quasi-experimental design by taking advantage of the 1991 General Social Survey (GSS), which (purely fortuitously) interviewed some respondents before and some after the Rodney King incident. The authors' findings were roughly similar to those of Tuch and Weitzer. Blacks interviewed after the King beating were more likely to take a more pessimistic view of racial discrimination in the United States than Whites, but both races became less approving of the conditions under which a police officer is justified in striking a citizen after the incident, and the effects were found to persist for several weeks. In summary, the available evidence suggests that police brutality fuels interracial tensions, eroding faith in, and reinforcing polarized perceptions of, the criminal justice system.

But brutality is not the only phenomena to which citizens pay attention. It does not go without notice, for instance, that African Americans are far more often the subjects of police stop-and-search procedures – that is, racial profiling. As documented in Chapter 2 (Table 2.2), Blacks are far more likely than Whites (51% vs. 5%) to believe it is a serious problem in their community that "police ... stop and question Blacks far more often than Whites." Moreover, they are more than twice as likely as Whites (77% to 35%) to believe that African Americans are treated less fairly in their communities "in

300 in 1987), with a corresponding drop in the ratio of Black to White suspects killed falling from 7 to 1 to 3 to 1 during this period (Beckett and Sasson 2004, 149).

dealing with the police, such as traffic incidents." These data from the NRCS are borne out by a 1999 Gallup survey, reporting that Blacks (70%) are far more likely than Whites (47%) to report being "stopped by the police just because of [their] race or ethnic background" on at least three occasions.[6] Not at all surprisingly, according to Weitzer and Tuch (2002, 2004), such incidents of racial profiling and police misconduct have a corrosive impact on attitudes toward the police.

ANALYSIS: THE IMPACT OF SYSTEM FAIRNESS ON PERCEPTIONS OF THE POLICE

Our intention in this chapter is to explore the impact of system fairness judgments (i.e., the degree to which individuals believe the justice system to be generically fair) on evaluations of the police in situations of alleged brutality and profiling. Using a series of survey experiments, we place police officers in a conflictual situation with either a Black or White civilian and assess whether the sympathies of the respondent lie more with the officer or with the civilian. Although every method has its own particular mix of strengths and weaknesses, survey experiments (using vignettes) provide a needed combination of external and internal validity for our purposes. By randomly assigning respondents to different question-wording conditions, experiments embedded in national surveys combine the generalizability and representativeness of opinion surveys with the control and internal validity gained from experiments (e.g., Sniderman and Grob 1996).[7]

The advantages of our design compare favorably with other methods used to investigate the connection between race and crime in public opinion. In the studies reviewed earlier, for example, analysts focused on public reactions to "real-life" events involving highly publicized incidents of police brutality, such as the Rodney King beating. The problem with such studies, from our perspective, is that every real-life event and brutality victim is unique in a variety of ways,

[6] See http://www.gallup.com/poll/3421/Racial-Profiling-Seen-Widespread-Particularly-Among-Young-Black-Men.aspx (accessed January 3, 2010).

[7] As detailed by Sniderman and Grobb (1996), Rossi and Anderson (1982) spearheaded the development of one of the precursors of modern, computer-assisted survey experiments with the vignette method, in which descriptions of crimes were randomly varied to determine how such descriptions affected the public's recommended punishment for various crimes.

making it impossible to "control" for extraneous factors and pinpoint what feature of the incident is responsible for shaping responses to it. A given individual may, for instance, be unsympathetic toward King because he is African American. Any number of other attributes (e.g., some behavior seen in the infamous videotape of his beating, his manner of speech, and his dress) may quite easily account for such feelings. By instead describing a brutality vignette that is exactly the same in every respect except for the race of the victim, however, we can determine whether and how the target's race (vs. some other characteristic) affects people's responses.

Another benefit of manipulating the race of the civilian is that it helps to reduce social desirability bias when assessing the impact of race on public opinion (e.g., Peffley, Hurwitz, and Sniderman 1997). We could have asked every respondent about scenarios involving both Black and White civilians, but such a procedure would surely pressure individuals to react similarly to the two vignettes. Because each respondent is only asked about *either* a Black *or* a White brutality victim, the purpose of the experiment is presumably "hidden" to respondents; neither the respondent nor the interviewer is aware of the randomized manipulation.

Finally, our methods hold some advantages over laboratory experiments used by social psychologists to study the effects of manipulating the race of target individuals on a variety of phenomena, such as jury decisions (e.g., Bodenhausen 1988) and stereotyping (Hamilton and Sherman 1994). Although laboratory experiments can provide subjects with more realistic stimuli (e.g., videotapes) than can survey questions, their primary limitation, for our purposes, is that the subject pool is rarely representative of the general population of either Black or White citizens. College sophomores or other willing and accessible subjects can sometimes be poor substitutes for members of the general population, particularly when it comes to studies of race and crime (e.g., Sears 1986).

Expectations: Testing Two Theories

Our goal in this chapter is more ambitious than merely documenting that Black and White respondents will differ in their relative sympathies toward the officer and the civilian. Additionally, through the use of our survey experiments, we investigate the power of two very different explanations of Whites' and Blacks' reactions to incidents of police brutality and racial profiling, the first of which focuses on the sentiments toward one's own racial group, with the second focusing on different views of the races about the fairness of the justice system. According to the in-group favoritism model, Blacks and Whites may react chiefly to the race of the civilian in confrontations with the police by employing a simple in-group favoritism bias (e.g., Brewer and Brown 1998), with Blacks being more sympathetic toward Black civilians (while disparaging White targets), and Whites being more sympathetic to White than to Black civilians. Importantly, the in-group favoritism model maintains that individuals of *both* races will respond in a similar way to show greater sympathy for the in-group (i.e., their own race) than the out-group.

The tendency toward in-group favoritism often appears as a ubiquitous facet of social life in social psychology research and has been used to account for the biases of a wide range of social and political groups in addition to racial and ethnic groups. A large volume of research, for example, finds not only that individuals hold favorable attitudes toward practically any group they are associated with but also often discriminate against and derogate out-groups (e.g., Huddy 2004). One of the attractive features of the in-group favoritism hypothesis – that is, its general applicability to a range of groups, biases, and circumstances – can also be one of its greatest deficiencies. For without identifying more specific mechanisms and conditions under which group biases arise, explanations of in-group favoritism can become tautological – that is, groups are biased because that is their nature (e.g., Hewstone et al. 2002; Jost et al. 2004).

Thus, as an extension to the in-group favoritism model, we also expect individuals to be more likely to disparage a member of the out-group when they hold more negative stereotypes of that group. Several studies have found that Whites with more negative stereotypes of African Americans – viewing them as lazy or violent – evaluate Black criminal suspects or welfare recipients more negatively than White targets (e.g., Hurwitz and Peffley 1997; Peffley, Hurwitz, and Sniderman 1997; Gilens 1999). Although there has been less attention to the impact of racial stereotypes on Blacks' judgments, it is likely that African Americans who view Whites more negatively are more prone to sympathize with Black civilians in their confrontations with police. In short, in-group favoritism, or the degree to which one's sympathies toward the civilian are affected by the civilian's race, should be affected by one's stereotypes of the out-group.

In contrast to the in-group favoritism model, the perceived fairness model turns on beliefs about the fairness of the justice system held by individuals. One set of expectations should apply universally to Blacks and Whites and is rather straightforward: we expect those who believe the justice system is grossly unfair to be more suspicious of the behavior of agents of the system (e.g., police) under a variety of circumstances, including charges of racial profiling or police brutality. Beliefs about fairness, doubtless, serve the same cognitive function as any other type of general beliefs – that is, they guide the interpretation of novel or ambiguous stimuli. In the same way that beliefs about the political parties shape perceptions of Democratic Party and Republican candidates (e.g., Rahn 1993), or that beliefs about the "American Dream" shape judgments of who is responsible for economic misfortunes (e.g., Schlozman and Verba 1979; Hochschild 1995), beliefs about system fairness should guide inferences about particular agents of the system in specific situations.

The impact of fairness beliefs is likely to vary across the races, however, in light of the markedly different content and experiential basis of such beliefs among Blacks and Whites documented in earlier chapters. Not only do the races diverge in the content of their beliefs about system fairness, but also such beliefs are likely to be used in very different ways when interpreting justice events. Quite simply, fairness and equality in the justice system are likely to mean different things to Blacks and Whites. Whites, who tend to think the system is fair and color blind, are likely to think about system fairness in a race-neutral manner. Even Whites who think the system is unfair may believe that injustice (e.g., crooked cops or judges) is color blind as well; they may, for example, naively assume that both races suffer equally from the malfeasance in the system.

By contrast, given the experiences of Blacks, their notions of fairness and equality should take on important racial connotations. It stands to reason that many African Americans will base their beliefs about the fairness of the justice system on how it is seen to treat Blacks, for a system that is believed to be heavily tilted against one's own group is unlikely to be viewed as fair and impartial overall. Thus, when Blacks are asked about fairness in general, they are likely to think about whether the system is fair to Blacks as a group.

It is also likely that confrontations with police will be racially charged for African Americans when the target is Black. If we know anything about the differential experiences of Blacks in the criminal justice system, it is that, given the history of racial bias in the system, Blacks should be especially vigilant to signs of discrimination during encounters between police and Black civilians. Brutality and profiling are so familiar to many Blacks, that they constitute chronically accessible "scripts" that are frequently primed and likely to guide interpretations of ambiguous events. Thus, Blacks as a group are likely to view confrontations between the police and Black civilians as yet another instance of police discrimination. An accumulating body of research in social psychology strongly supports such a prediction. Because of their more frequent encounters with prejudice in their everyday lives, minority group members (e.g., Blacks or women) are naturally more vigilant to any signs of prejudice and discrimination in their social environment than majority group members (see Feldman-Barrett and Swim 1998), in part because prejudice tends to be more central and accessible for members of such groups than it is for other individuals (Inman and Baron 1996).[8]

As such, although Blacks may perceive confrontations between the police and White civilians in a relatively neutral fashion, confrontations between the police and Black civilians should heighten suspicions among Black respondents, who should be simultaneously more sympathetic to the Black civilian and concerned about his or her unfair treatment at the hands of the police. We expect that fairness judgments should *interact* with the race of the target, such that Blacks who see the justice system as generally unfair should be especially suspicious of the police in confrontations with Black civilians. Yet because "fairness" has fewer racial connotations for Whites, who naively believe the system to be essentially color blind, the race of the civilian should be essentially irrelevant.

[8] Vigilance to discrimination is activated in a particular context. We do not mean to imply that Blacks are hypersensitive to discrimination and prejudice, or that Blacks as a rule evaluate all events and issues through a racial lens (e.g., White 2007). We return to this matter in the conclusions.

Thus, in contrast to the in-group favoritism model, the interactive version of the perceived fairness model predicts that the race of the target matters more to Blacks than to Whites, and for quite different reasons. Simply stated, rather than underscoring the natural and inevitable tendency of people to favor individuals of their own group, the perceived fairness model instead highlights the concerns of African Americans (but not Whites) with the likelihood of discriminatory treatment at the hands of the justice system. This model holds that Black respondents will be more sympathetic toward Black targets, therefore, not simply because the target is a member of the in-group, but instead because he or she serves to remind the respondent of the worst aspects of the discriminatory character of the justice system.

As noted, testing these models requires an experimental design that manipulates the race of the civilian in confrontations with police. In the analysis to follow, we present respondents with scenarios involving police-civilian interactions; in one instance, an officer is accused of brutalizing a man described as either White or Black, and in the other the police search men (again, either White or Black) for drugs. Although the details of the two experiments differ, in both respondents are essentially asked whether they are more sympathetic to the police or the civilian side of the confrontation – confrontations designed to reflect salient and incendiary "real-world" events.

Police Brutality Experiment

In our first experiment, we ask respondents about "a recent incident in Chicago in which a police officer was accused of brutally beating a [White/Black] motorist who had been stopped for questioning. The police department promised to investigate the incident." By randomly varying the race of the motorist in the scenario, we are able to determine whether and how the race of the target influences respondents' answers to two subsequent survey questions:

A) How likely do you think it is that the police department will conduct a fair and thorough investigation of the policeman's behavior? (1 = very likely, 4 = very unlikely);

B) If he is found guilty of beating the motorist, how should the policeman be punished – should he be suspended (1), fired (2), sentenced to one year in prison (3), or sentenced to two or more years in prison (4)?

For each of the two judgments, the following equation was estimated separately for Black and White respondents using ordered probit procedures:

Judgment = Race of Motorist + System Fairness + Race of Motorist*Fairness + Anti-Black Stereotype + Race of Motorist*Stereotype

The variables in the equation are measured in the following manner. The first dependent variable, Fair-Investigation-Unlikely, is a four-point scale ranging from "very likely" (point 1 on the scale) to "very unlikely" (point 4) that the police department will conduct a fair investigation. The second dependent variable, Punish-Guilty-Officer, ranges from the minimum punishment of suspending the officer (at point 1) to the maximum punishment of two or more years in prison (point 4).

Race of motorist is a dummy variable coded 0 when the motorist is Black and 1 when the motorist is White. System fairness is measured as before (Chapter 3),[9] with one important difference: to ease the interpretation of the race of motorist variable, system fairness was rescaled so that the midpoint of the scale is 0 and the extremes run from −3 (very unfair) to +3 (very fair). The *first* interaction term is the product of race of motorist and system fairness. Following the perceived fairness model, which presumes that African Americans' beliefs about fairness are more likely to be activated when the brutality victim is Black, we expect this interaction term to be significant for Black respondents but not for Whites. Anti-Black stereotypes are also measured as before, with higher scores reflecting more negative stereotypes of African Americans versus Whites. Because the impact of racial stereotypes should vary depending on whether the target is Black or White, an interaction term, Race of Motorist*Stereotypes, was added to the equation.[10]

[9] Respondents were asked the degree to which they agree with the statements: "The justice system in this country treats people fairly and equally," and "The courts can be trusted to give everyone a fair trial."

[10] We also estimated equations that included attributions of Black treatment, unfair treatment, political orientations (party ID, ideology), demographic factors (e.g., education, gender, and income), and contextual variables (e.g., racial composition or county crime) as control variables; but because the results did not change and the effects of the control variables rarely achieved statistical significance, we do not report the more fully specified equations here.

In the first four columns of Table 4.1.A we display the ordered probit results for the fair investigation question. Given the coding of the variables, the coefficients for system fairness and stereotypes indicate the effect of these variables for the Black motorist only, while race is assessed at the midpoints of the fairness and stereotypes scales.[11] At first blush, the results appear to provide provisional, though inconsistent, support for the in-group favoritism model. On the one hand, judging from the race of motorist coefficients (first row), we find that Black respondents are more sympathetic to Black brutality victims in that they are much more dubious about the police conducting a fair investigation into the incident when the victim is Black than when he is White ($b = -.49$, first row, column 1). On the other hand, we do not find Whites, on average, to be significantly more sympathetic to White brutality victims ($b = .15$, $p > .05$), which is inconsistent with the in-group favoritism model.

This is not to say that race makes no difference to Whites, however. It clearly does when we turn to the influence of anti-Black stereotypes (rows 3 and 5), where we find that Whites who view Blacks more negatively are suddenly more optimistic that the police investigation will proceed fairly ($b = -.03$), but only when a Black motorist is brutalized ($b = .04$). Anti-Black stereotypes have no discernible effect for Black respondents. Once again, therefore, support for the in-group favoritism model is mixed.

On balance, we find much stronger support for the perceived fairness model. In the first place, judging from the coefficients associated with system fairness (row 2), we see that for both races, consistent with the literature on procedural justice, fairness beliefs matter ($b = -.16$ and $b = -.26$ for Black and White respondents, respectively). People who do not think the justice system treats people fairly are quite pessimistic about the police conducting a fair investigation of

[11] The coefficients for the substantive variables (race, fairness, and stereotypes) are conditional effects indicating the impact of the predictor when the variable(s) with which it interacts equal(s) 0 (Jaccard, Turrisi, and Wan 1990). Thus, the coefficient for race of motorist indicates the impact of race when system fairness and stereotypes equal 0, the midpoint of the system fairness scale and the approximate mean of the stereotypes scale. The coefficients for fairness and stereotypes give the effect of these variables for the Black motorist only (the 0 point on the race of motorist scale). However, coefficients at other values of the interacting variables can be easily computed.

TABLE 4.1. *Predicting responses to the police misconduct experiments*

4.1.A. Police Brutality Experiment

Independent Variables	Fair Investigation Unlikely? Blacks	Fair Investigation Unlikely? Whites	Punish Guilty Officer? Blacks	Punish Guilty Officer? Whites
Race of Motorist (0 = Black)	−.49** (.11)	−.15 (.09)	−.10 (.11)	−.32** (.09)
System Fairness	−.16** (.04)	−.26** (.04)	−.16** (.04)	−.05 (.04)
Anti-Black Stereotypes	−.004 (.01)	−.03* (.01)	−.01 (.01)	−.03* (.01)
Race X Fairness	.12* (.05)	−.03 (.06)	.14* (.06)	−.03 (.10)
Race X Stereotype	.01 (.01)	.04* (.02)	−.01 (.02)	.04* (.02)
Cutpoint 1	−1.06 (.09)	−1.00 (.08)	−1.39 (.10)	−1.50 (.09)
Cutpoint 2	−.22 (.08)	−.24 (.07)	−.40 (.09)	−.46 (.08)
Cutpoint 3	−.45 (.08)	.95 (.08)	−.10 (.08)	−.01 (.07)
N	559	570	554	565

4.1.B. Stop-and-Search Experiment

Independent Variables	Not Reasonable Search? Blacks	Not Reasonable Search? Whites	Believe Police or Men? Blacks	Believe Police or Men? Whites
Race of Men (0 = Black)	−.11 (.11)	−.17 (.10)	−.53** (.16)	−.20 (.24)
System Fairness	−.16** (.04)	−.08* (.04)	−.08* (.04)	−.14** (.04)
Anti-Black Stereotypes	.002 (.01)	.01 (.01)	−.01 (.01)	−.01 (.02)
Race X Fairness	.10* (.05)	.003 (.05)	.08 (.06)	−.018 (.07)
Race X Stereotype	−.01 (.01)	−.03 (.02)	.02 (.02)	.02 (.02)
Cutpoint 1	−.79 (.09)	−1.02 (.15)	−1.09 (.10)	−.25 (.07)
Cutpoint 2	−.13 (.08)	.21 (.07)	−.01 (.09)	1.10 (.09)
Cutpoint 3	.81 (.09)	.90 (.08)	.96 (.10)	1.82 (.13)
N	551	576	444	505

*p < .05, **p < .01

Note: Entries are ordered probit regression coefficients with standard errors in parentheses. Higher values on the preceding dependent variables indicate: fair investigation unlikely, more severe punishment of guilty officer, judging the police search as unreasonable, and believing the men vs. the police. Higher values on independent variables indicate: White motorist/victim of police brutality, White men, believing the justice system is fair, and more negative stereotypes of Blacks than Whites.

the brutality incident. They use their general beliefs about the fairness of the justice system to guide their reactions to the vignettes.

What merits our most careful attention, however, is the significant support for the interactive model among Black respondents. As expected, fairness matters a good deal more when the brutalized motorist is Black. And, as expected, this interaction is only important for Black respondents ($b = .12$), not Whites ($b = -.03$, $p > .05$).

To better understand the nature of the interaction, Figure 4.1 displays a graph of the predicted probability that respondents think a fair investigation is likely (combining "very" and "somewhat likely"), broken down by race-of-motorist and race-of-respondent, and arrayed across the system fairness index.[12] The judgments for Black respondents are depicted by solid lines, with dotted lines used for Whites. One is struck, first, by the higher level of cynicism among Black respondents, who quite clearly believe, relative to Whites, that a fair trial is unlikely. Additionally, the figure documents the large impact of the race of the motorist among African-American respondents who think the justice system is unfair (i.e., the left-hand side of the fairness scale). Blacks who think the system is very unfair (at −3 of the fairness scale) are more than twice as likely to think the police investigation will be fair when the motorist is White (55%) than when he is Black (24%). Clearly, Blacks who are cynical about the justice system are extremely pessimistic about a Black victim of brutality receiving justice at the hands of the police, compared to a White victim. Blacks who believe the system is very fair (on the right-hand side of the scale) think a fair investigation into the officer's conduct is about as likely for a Black motorist (60%) as for a White motorist (65%).

The figure also neatly documents that general fairness beliefs do not play the same role for Blacks as they do for Whites. Perhaps the greatest single difference in the way the races respond to the scenario is that, among African-American respondents, general fairness beliefs are much more important in shaping their evaluation of the incident when the brutality victim is Black than when he is White. Among

[12] Predicted probabilities were generated based on the ordered probit results in Table 1.A using the Spost program (Long and Freese 2006) for Stata 9.0. Predicted probabilities are generated for a likely (very + somewhat likely) response, varying race of motorist, system fairness, and their interaction, while holding other variables at their mean.

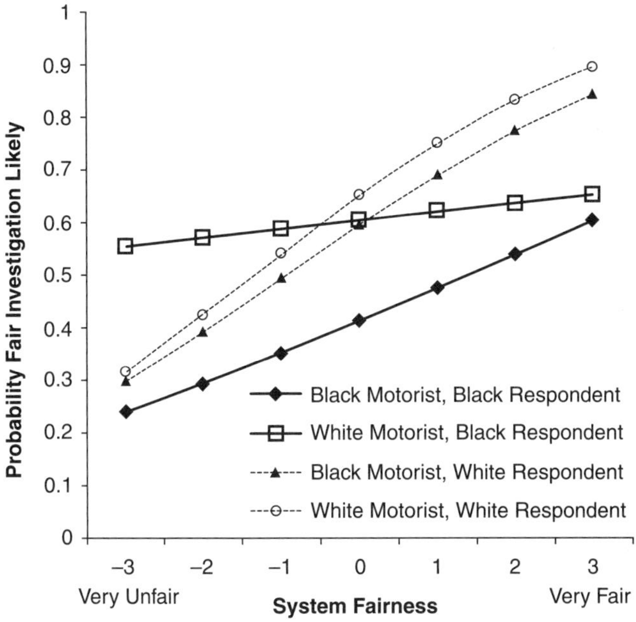

FIGURE 4.1. Probability of judging a fair police investigation, police brutality experiment.

Note: The figure displays predicted probabilities of thinking a fair investigation is likely (very + somewhat likely) across system fairness, race of motorist, and race of respondent, based on Table 4.1.A. System fairness recoded to −3 to +3.

Source: NRCS data.

White respondents, however, the probability estimates are nearly identical, regardless of the race of the victim. Whites (who tend to assume that the system is color blind) apply their fairness beliefs as if the race of the victim has no bearing on whether the police would conduct a fair investigation.

Put differently, Blacks are quite suspicious about the police primarily when an African American is an alleged victim of police brutality – particularly Blacks who think the system is unfair. Thus, if African Americans are "biased" toward Black victims, it is because they believe the justice system is extremely unfair to begin with.[13] We

[13] To place these judgments in context, we note that about two-thirds of the Black sample falls at the three most "unfair" points along the system fairness scale (with only about 7% at the two most fair points of the scale), while about two-thirds of Whites fall at the most "fair" points along the scale.

do not, therefore, find a consistent tendency for African Americans to habitually support members of their own group. Rather, any apparent "bias" toward Black victims is evidenced only among those who see the justice system as fundamentally unfair.

In many respects, the results for African Americans are more consistent with the perceived fairness model. At the same time, however, the impact of stereotypes among Whites clearly conforms to the in-group favoritism model. Although Whites apply their general beliefs about fairness as though oblivious to the race of the victim, those who hold negative stereotypes of African Americans tend to have greater confidence in the police when the victim is Black.

The second question in the police brutality experiment, which asks respondents how the officer should be punished if he is found guilty of attacking the motorist, yields a different pattern (particularly for White respondents), as reflected in the coefficients in the right-hand panel of Table 4.1.A (the punish guilty officer model). Whites' judgments in this case turn less on their general fairness beliefs[14] than on the race of the motorist ($r = -.32$), the coefficient for which is larger for White than for Black respondents. Although most Whites appear to assume that the justice system is color blind, when they are confronted with a clear case of an officer brutalizing a Black motorist (inasmuch as the question specifically informs them of the officer's guilt), they, even more so than Black respondents, recommend a stiffer punishment for the officer who beats the African-American motorist. These results run counter to the in-group favoritism model, which predicts a race of motorist coefficient of the opposite sign for Whites.

However, close inspection of the stereotype and Race*Stereotype interaction indicates that, as before, Whites' judgments are also more strongly colored by anti-Black stereotypes (row 3), but only when the motorist is Black (row 5). Whites with more negative stereotypes of African Americans recommend a lighter punishment for the officer found guilty of beating the Black motorist, despite the officer's clear-cut guilt ($b = -.03$, $p < .05$; $b = .01$, $p > .05$ for the White motorist). Overall, among Whites, we see mixed support for the in-group

[14] Among Whites, the impact of the race of the motorist on punishing the guilty officer is almost twice that of system fairness, judging from predicted probabilities computed across low and high values of the two variables, holding other predictors at their means.

favoritism model. Although Whites on average are sensitive to the race of the motorist being brutalized when the officer is unambiguously guilty, Whites who negatively stereotype Blacks are also significantly more sympathetic to the guilty officer who brutalizes Black, but not White, civilians.

Once again, the interaction between race of motorist and system fairness is significant, but only for Black respondents – again consistent with the perceived fairness model. To better understand the nature of these effects, we return to Figure 4.2 in which the predicted probability of recommending the maximum punishment for the offending officer (point 4 of the officer punishment scale, the modal category for both races) is plotted by the race of the respondent and the race

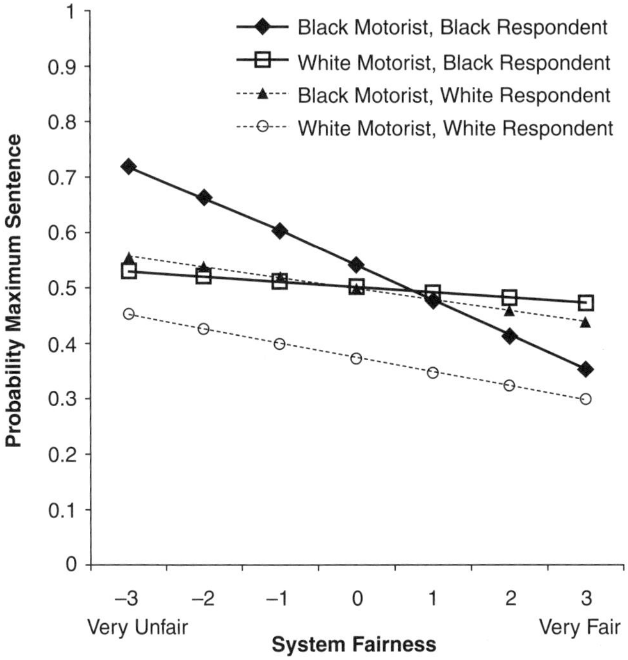

FIGURE 4.2. Probability of maximum sentence for guilty officer, police brutality experiment.

Note: The figure displays predicted probabilities for recommending the maximum sentence for the guilty officer across system fairness, race of motorist, and race of respondent, based on Table 4.1.A.

Source: NRCS data.

of the motorist across the fairness scale. As before, the effect of race is much stronger for African-American respondents who think the justice system is very unfair, where the percentage of Blacks recommending a stiff prison sentence for the guilty officer is much greater when the victim is Black (72%) rather than White (53%). By contrast, the effect of race is much smaller (and even reversed) among the small number of Blacks who rate the system as very fair (on the right-hand side of the figure). Thus, once again, the tendency for Black respondents to express more sympathy for the African-American target is particularly strong among Blacks who feel the system is unfair, and race plays little if any role among African Americans who see the justice system as fair.

In sum, we find impressive similarities across the two questions in the police brutality experiment. In both instances, we find that the race of the motorist does not matter to White respondents in predicting a fair investigation and, further, that Whites are actually more punitive against the officer who brutalizes a Black civilian than an officer who brutalizes a White civilian. In both instances, the results are contrary to the simple in-group favoritism model. Race among Whites, however, does play a role, as closer inspection suggests that Whites who negatively stereotype African Americans are more likely to exhibit an in-group bias across both questions. Although Blacks initially seem to exhibit an in-group bias, it soon becomes clear that the responses of African Americans are most consistent with the perceived fairness model: the greater suspiciousness of the police is found primarily among African Americans who are most cynical of the justice system.

Stop-and-Search Experiment

Although perhaps not as incendiary as police brutality, racial profiling can provoke intense emotions – even to the degree that profiled individuals base their evaluations of the justice system on these encounters with the law. Therefore, we now turn to the stop-and-search experiment to determine if the same factors responsible for activating beliefs about the brutality incident also activate beliefs about profiling.

The stop-and-search experiment is similar to the brutality experiment in that respondents are presented with scenarios that involve potentially explosive police-civilian interactions. The scenarios differ, however, in two important respects. First, because the search experiment makes no reference to physical force used by the officer, it allows us to examine responses to an issue that is somewhat less incendiary than police brutality. More important, however, the stop-and-search experiment places the civilian in a more compromising position. As noted in the following text, the civilians are seen walking "near a house where the police know drugs are being sold," suggesting a potentially dangerous neighborhood. Such a context may be interpreted by some to imply the guilt of the civilians, while for others it may suggest the familiar scenario of racial profiling.

The question posed was: "In another incident, the police see two young [African-American/White] men about 20 years old. They are walking very near a house where the police know drugs are being sold. The police search the two men and arrest them for carrying drugs."

A) Do you think this is definitely a reasonable search (coded 1), probably a reasonable search (2), probably not a reasonable search (3), or definitely not a reasonable search (4)?

B) Who are you more likely to believe in this case – the police, who claim the two men were carrying drugs (1= very likely to believe the police, 2 = somewhat likely to believe the police), or the two men, who claim the police planted the drugs on them (3 = somewhat likely to believe the men, 4 = very likely to believe the men)?

By varying the race of the suspect, we can determine the degree to which respondents' judgments of the search (was it reasonable?) and the judged credibility of the police versus the men (did the police plant the evidence?) are affected by fairness beliefs and racial stereotypes, as well as by the suspects' race.

Table 4.1.B displays the ordered probit results obtained from estimating equations very similar to those in the police brutality experiment, in which the dependent variables in this case refer to the degree to which respondents are critical of the search (unreasonable search?) and the police (believe men?). For both questions, as indicated in the second rows, when the men are Black, evaluations of the search by both African-American and White respondents are significantly shaped by general fairness beliefs, consistent with the perceived fairness model: those rating the justice system as unfair are both more likely to see the search as unreasonable and to believe the Black civilians rather than the officer. Another notable similarity across questions is that racial stereotypes play virtually no role in the judgments of respondents of either race.

The most important difference across questions is that, although the Race*Fairness coefficient is never even remotely significant (or close in magnitude to that for Black respondents) for White respondents, it is statistically significant in the first (but not the second) equation for African-American respondents. African Americans who are initially cynical about the justice system become particularly critical of the police in the case of Black drug suspects.

The interaction for the reasonable search question, as revealed in a predicted probability plot in Figure 4.3, demonstrates a familiar

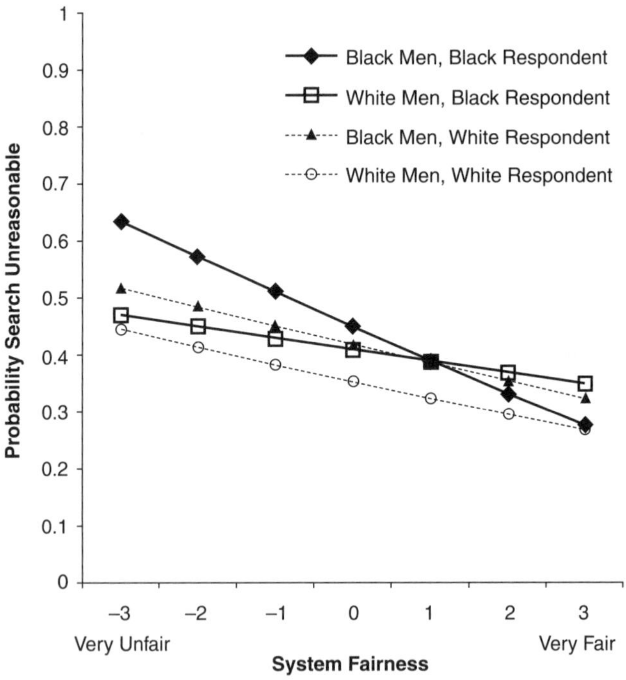

FIGURE 4.3. Probability of judging search unreasonable, stop-and-search experiment.

Note: The figure displays predicted probabilities for judging the police search of the men unreasonable (somewhat + very unreasonable) across system fairness, race of men, and race of respondent, based on Table 4.1.B.

Source: NRCS data.

pattern: Black respondents are not indiscriminately biased toward Black targets. Rather, those who think the system is very unfair are much more critical of the search when it is directed against the African-American men (63% think it is unreasonable) than against White men (47%). But for Black respondents who perceive the justice system as fair, the only bias (though modest) is in favor of White civilians.

Although the interaction is not quite significant (column 3, row 4, Table 4.1.B, b = .08), the same pattern is at work for the second question and displayed in Figure 4.4, which depicts the predicted probabilities for believing the men ("very" and "somewhat") versus the police. Blacks at every point along the fairness scale are much

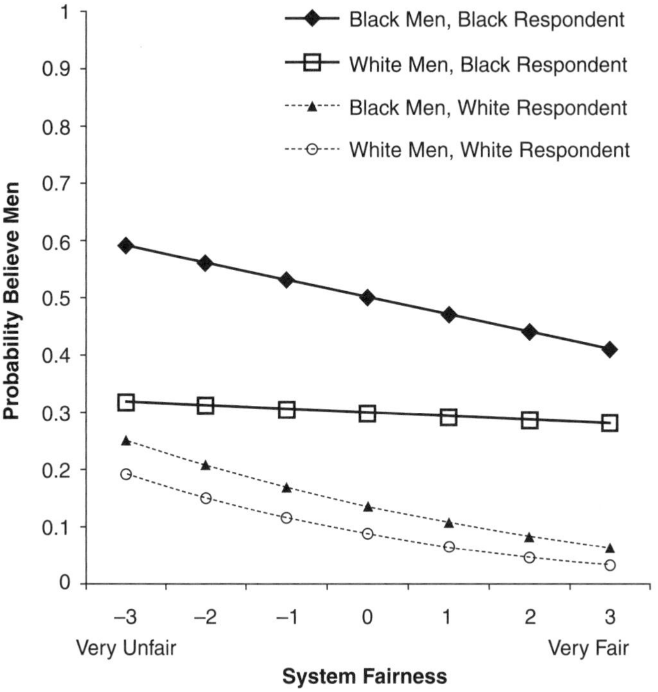

FIGURE 4.4. Probability of believing men vs. police, stop-and-search experiment.

Note: The figure displays predicted probabilities for believing the men (very + somewhat likely) vs. the police across system fairness, race of men, and race of respondent, based on Table 4.1.B.

Source: NRCS data.

more likely to side with the civilians over the police than are Whites (whose predicted probability of believing the men approaches 0!), and this is particularly true if the suspects are African American and the respondent holds cynical views of the justice system. It is also notable that Black respondents are even more suspicious of the police relative to White respondents when the civilian is White – particularly if the respondent perceives the justice system to be unfair. Presumably, many African Americans have become so skeptical of police officers that they are often skeptical of any behavior.

All told, the results from the stop-and-search experiment are most consistent with the perceived fairness model, as opposed to the in-group favoritism model. White respondents do not appear to be more sympathetic toward the police (with either question) when the suspect is of the other race (even when they negatively stereotype Blacks); and African-American respondents exhibit an overall tendency to distrust the police, particularly when they generally distrust the criminal justice system.

SUMMARY AND CONCLUSIONS

Procedural fairness judgments, as measured by system fairness, exert a dramatic impact on individuals' interpretations of potentially incendiary events unfolding within the justice system, such that those with more cynical beliefs are far less likely to believe that the police department can fairly investigate a charge of police brutality, are more punitive toward the officer if he is found guilty, are less likely to see the search of the two men as reasonable, and are less likely to believe the police vis-à-vis the civilians.

More important is the question of whether Black and White respondents translate these beliefs in different ways when interpreting the police-civilian interactions. We initially offered two competing theories of how individuals interpret these interactions. The in-group favoritism model, which is supported by voluminous research in social psychology, holds that Blacks and Whites are both more sympathetic to targets of their own race, particularly when they hold pejorative stereotypes of the out-group. The perceived fairness model assumes that many African Americans, being far more sensitized to the discriminatory character of the justice system, should base their interpretations on the race of the civilian (especially to the degree that Blacks see the justice system as inherently unfair), relative to Whites, who are far less attentive to the biases of the system. Exploring the verisimilitude of these two models requires an experimental design enabling us to manipulate randomly the race of the target.

Overall, although we uncovered evidence for both theories, our results are more consistent with the perceived fairness model. Although it is initially tempting to conclude that the in-group favoritism model is characteristic of African-American respondents, closer inspection of our results tells a different story. Blacks do not habitually gravitate toward civilians of their own race; rather, they tend to be more sympathetic toward Black civilians only if they believe the criminal justice system to be chronically unfair – the response predicted by the interactive version of the perceived fairness model.

We found important, though limited, support for the in-group favoritism model. In the police brutality experiment (but not the stop-and-search experiment), when the brutalized motorist was Black, Whites who negatively stereotype African Americans were more likely to side with the police. Such a result is consistent with a variety of other studies that find that Whites' judgments of Black targets are often biased by their views of Blacks as violent and lazy (Hurwitz and Peffley 1997; Gilens 1999; Gilliam and Iyengar 2000). To put these findings in perspective, however, even in the brutality experiment, Whites' stereotypes were not the dominant force driving responses to the scenario.[15] One reason, we conjecture, that stereotypes are not as important here as elsewhere (e.g., Peffley, Hurwitz, and Sniderman 1997) is that the questions focus more on judgments about authorities (i.e., police) than civilians (e.g., brutality victim or search suspects). Although the justice system may represent racism to many (especially African-American) respondents, the race of the

[15] If we compare estimated changes in predicted probabilities obtained by fixing all variables at their means and then shifting the value of a single predictor from one standard deviation below its mean to one standard deviation above its mean (i.e., "low" and "high" values), we find that the change obtained for anti-Black stereotypes (for the Black civilian condition) for the two questions of the brutality experiment for Whites (Table 4.1.A and 4.1.B) is about one-third as large as that for fairness beliefs for the police investigation question (.10 vs. .31) and about two-thirds the size of the race-of-target for the officer punishment question (.10 vs. .15).

officer is never specified in our questions, thereby muting whatever impact stereotypes may play.

On balance, support for the in-group favoritism model pales in comparison with what we have termed the perceived fairness model. Race manipulation matters primarily among the majority of African-American respondents who perceive unfairness in the justice system, as they judge the police more harshly when the targets are Black. This pattern makes perfect sense inasmuch as an overall judgment of unfairness should influence evaluations in specific situations only, or at least primarily, when the system is believed to be at its weakest – that is, when it "processes" African Americans. It does not appear, therefore, that Blacks are unconditionally supportive of in-group members merely because of their in-group status. Rather, in-group status is important only insofar as it reinforces (or serves as a reminder of) one's extant cynicism toward the justice system. Although not vast in numbers, Blacks who are relatively trusting of the justice system demonstrate no particular bias toward own-race civilians.

Nor do the responses of Whites conform to a simple rendition of the in-group favoritism model. Instead of finding a uniform tendency for Whites to favor members of their group, we find that the race of the civilian activates anti-Black stereotypes among some Whites under some conditions. But in only one instance does the race of the civilian affect Whites' judgments overall, and the direction of the bias in this case is contrary to expectation – namely, White respondents are substantially more likely to punish the officer severely for brutalizing the Black man than for brutalizing the White man.

Why does the race of the brutality victim matter more to Whites in this case? We believe that this exception provides an interesting contrast in the perceptual differences between White and African-American respondents. Under "normal" circumstances, Whites appear oblivious to the possibility of police discrimination against African Americans and, therefore, apply their beliefs about justice system fairness similarly to Black and White targets. But when interpreting responses to this item, it is essential to recall that individuals were asked about the appropriate punishment for an officer who is explicitly identified as guilty of brutality. It becomes, therefore, impossible to ignore the likely discriminatory behavior of the officer. When they are "hit between the eyes" with a case of likely racial discrimination by a police officer, Whites react against the offending officer. But in no other case do they appear to perceive discrimination.

African-American respondents, however, need no such prompting to remind them of Blacks as targets of police discrimination, particularly if they are already predisposed to believe the justice system to be unfair. What seems obvious to many African Americans, namely that they face profound unfairness from the justice system, apparently does not register with most Whites who, unless confronted with overwhelming evidence, regard the playing field as level. This finding is reminiscent of the conclusion reached by Sigelman and Welch (1991, 65) in their study of perceptions of racial economic inequality: "It is hardly an overstatement to say that Blacks and Whites inhabit two different perceptual worlds. Whites do not acknowledge the persisting prejudice and discrimination that are so obvious to Blacks."

As further evidence of diverging racial perceptions, fairness beliefs are much less important in affecting African-Americans' responses to scenarios featuring White targets. In each of the graphs in Figure 4.1, fairness beliefs clearly matter when Blacks are asked about Black civilians, as the line slopes steeply upward; but when the focus shifts to White targets, the lines flatten. Thus, when African Americans are asked about their general assessments of the fairness of the justice system, even though no mention is made of race, they are much more likely to interpret such questions as an evaluation of whether the system is fair and equal to African Americans. Consequently, such beliefs are more likely to be activated when Black respondents are asked about African-American targets. White respondents, however, naively process the fairness items in a racial vacuum, as if it is possible to evaluate the fairness of the justice system without reference to race. Thus, not only do Blacks and Whites come to the scenarios with very different prior beliefs, but also their responses to the scenarios diverge, in part, because the actual meaning of fairness beliefs varies across the races.[16]

[16] Nelson, Sanbonmatsu, and McClerking (2007, 420–1) unearth similar results in their experimental study, in which they find that the racial gap in Blacks' and Whites' judgments of an incident of police misconduct disappears when they take into account respondents' general beliefs about the fairness of the justice system, as well as other beliefs.

An important implication of our findings is that both races appear susceptible to biases in their interpretations of potentially incendiary incidents in the justice system. Many Whites, for example, despite an undeniable history of actual racial discrimination in the justice system, seem to adhere steadfastly to a color-blind perspective in their reactions to the scenarios, unless the racial dimensions of the incident are, as in the question of the officer's punishment, made plain. At the same time, many African Americans may seem quick to assume the worst motives on the part of police involved in confrontations with Blacks. Although Whites may naively discount evidence that the system does not provide the level playing field symbolized by the balanced scales of justice, many African Americans may begin with the belief that the system is biased against them, and when they see an example of potential racial bias, they see this belief confirmed. These reactions doubtless contribute to misperceptions and interracial tensions, as Blacks see Whites as insensitive racists and Whites see Blacks as responding to a simple in-group favoritism bias.

We are struck by the extraordinary naivety of many Whites – a naivety that, in our view, is diagnostic of the type of racial insensitivity labeled as "laissez faire racism" (e.g., Bobo et al. 1997). This phenomenon is marked less by overt racial animosity than by a blind eye toward the prevalent discrimination faced by African Americans. For only when information is blatant and unmistakable, as when respondents were asked whether to punish the guilty officer in the police brutality experiment, do Whites distinguish between Black and White targets. Under other circumstances, when the information is of the ambivalent sort found in the "real world," many White respondents fail to appreciate what is painfully obvious to African Americans – that is, that the races are treated differently in the halls of justice.

For better and (mainly) for worse, generalized judgments of fairness are consequential because of their role in the downward spiral of cynicism typical of many African Americans in the United States Although we are limited in our conclusions because of the correlational nature of our data, the following scenario seems entirely plausible to us. African Americans, far more often than Whites, are the subject of unfair and discriminatory treatment from law enforcement officers. Because so much of one's general sense of whether the justice system is fair is experientially determined, these encounters (whether experienced personally or vicariously) contribute heavily to creating in much of the African-American community a profound understanding that the justice system is inherently biased against them. We know that this understanding – far more prevalent among Blacks – encourages an interpretation of specific police-civilian encounters that casts heightened suspicion and sympathy on the police and civilian, respectively. Finally, though spirals are never fully closed, these interpretations "loop back" to reinforce and intensify one's initial generalized judgment that the justice system is inherently unfair.[17] In this way, fairness beliefs operate much like stereotypes (or other fundamental beliefs) in biasing perceptions to such a degree that the beliefs serve to maintain or reinforce themselves (Hamilton and Sherman 1994).

[17] See Soss (1999) for evidence of a similar "learning" process by which welfare recipients' experiences with the welfare system affect their more general orientations toward government.

5

The Consequences of Fairness

Support for Punitive Crime Policies

The vignettes we focused on in the last chapter were designed to allow us to examine the impact of fairness judgments on respondents' perceptions of agents of the criminal justice system – namely the police, and how these perceptions differ across the race of the respondent and the race of the civilian in the vignette. We now turn to another potential consequence of generalized fairness beliefs: anticrime-policy attitudes. We take up the matter of the racial divide toward policies that have become, in the eyes of many individuals, highly racialized. Specifically, what accounts for the high degree of racial polarization in the anticrime-policy domain? How is differential support for policies such as the death penalty, three-strikes laws, and spending for prison construction influenced by the way the policy is framed by elites? Finally, to what degree is support for such punitive policies related to assessments of fairness toward the justice system? Are those who believe that Blacks are to blame for their harsh treatment more supportive of policies that are disproportionately used against African Americans?

THE MASS ELITE LINKAGE

On September 13, 1994, President Clinton signed into law the Violent Crime Control and Law Enforcement Act of 1994. The legislation appropriated more than $30 billion, mostly earmarked for state and federal law enforcement efforts, prisons, and crime-prevention programs. It also imposed a ten-year ban on new assault weapons, revived the death penalty as a federal sentencing option, and mandated a sentence of life imprisonment for violent three-time federal offenders.

It is important to understand the dynamics behind this policy: between July 1990 and January 1994, the proportion of Americans regarding crime and violence as the most important problem in the Gallup poll had increased by an extraordinary degree, from 1 to 37 percent.[1] The legislation, not surprisingly, has been extolled as the prototypical example of governmental responsiveness to a public mandate for change.

Crime control policy, in general, has been regarded as the poster child of the instructed delegate model of representation, at all levels and across all branches of government. There are numerous studies finding an impact of public opinion on state death-penalty statutes (e.g., Nice 1992; Mooney and Lee 2000) and state implementation rates (e.g., Norrander 2000). In states with citizens who are more supportive of capital punishment, supreme court justices have been found to be significantly more likely to uphold the death sentence (or less likely to dissent from a prodeath majority), especially in a more competitive electoral environment (Hall 1992; Brace and Hall 1997).

At the national level, there is considerable evidence that elites are hyperresponsive to citizen beliefs, and especially fears, pertaining to crime. In her study of six policy domains, ranging from abortion to welfare to social security, Sharp (1999) found levels of mass-elite congruence to be particularly strong in the crime-policy domain, meaning that a heightened sense of punitive beliefs among citizens typically leads policy makers to enact more punitive policies. Further evidence is provided by Canes-Wrone and Shotts (2004), who analyzed eleven policy areas and the relationship between public opinion on government spending (more, same, or less in any given area) and presidents' proposed budgetary authority for a given year. Other than social security, in no other policy domain did she find a higher level of presidential responsiveness to public preference. Evidence clearly suggests, therefore, that elites pay an inordinately high level of attention

[1] See http://www.albany.edu/sourcebook/pdf/t212007.pdf (accessed January 3, 2010).

to citizen concerns in the area of crime. As with any policy area, public opinion has its greatest effects on public policy when salience is high (Burstein 2003); when the public is frightened, political elites are bound to take notice.

However, before we accept the conclusion that the public is necessarily well served by these tendencies, we must find evidence for two necessary conditions. First, we must find that the citizens have an accurate assessment of the policy environment, and second, we must find that elites have an accurate assessment of mass preferences. As we will show, it is nearly impossible to demonstrate that both, let alone one, of these conditions are met.

In the first place, the environment for crime (and punishment) is replete with mistaken assumptions and misunderstandings. According to Roberts and Stalans (1997, 37):

> In the early to mid-1990s, official crime statistics showed a decline [in crime rates]. For example, the rate of index crimes reported by the FBI dropped 4 percent from 1991 to 1992, 3 percent from 1992 to 1993, and 2 percent from 1993 to 1994 (Federal Bureau of Investigation 1995). Violent crime rates also declined over the same period. By 1995, the U.S. crime rate had fallen to its lowest level in a decade. The American public, however, continued to believe that crime rates were rising inexorably.

One decade later, statistics from the U.S. Department of Justice (1999, 116, 339) documented that each year from 1996 to 1998, a substantial majority of Gallup poll respondents believed that crime had increased since the previous year, despite evidence from the County Crime Index that rates had decreased steadily during this time period. So out of sync are actual and perceived crime rates that it takes very little to convince large numbers of individuals that the world is becoming a far more dangerous place. A dramatic upsurge among senior citizens in New York City believing that there had been an increase of crimes against the elderly during the 1970s was attributed to a single overzealous news editor exploiting the muggings of two senior citizens (Fishman 1978).

It is not only the levels of crime about which citizens are mistaken, but also individuals tend to be badly misinformed about the nature and efficacy of extant policies. For instance, a 1997 survey administered by the Florida Department of Corrections found that Floridians assumed prison inmates served only 40 percent, on average, of their original sentences – while the actual expectation is 85 percent of the original sentence (*Corrections Journal*, 1997, 5–6). Citizens also have grossly misinformed beliefs regarding incarceration rates, the frequency of the insanity defense, and more.

Not only are citizens often mistaken about the reality of the crime environment, but also elites are often mistaken about public preferences in this domain, and for a number of reasons. It is likely that they give inordinate weight to certain election results, as in 1968 when Richard Nixon ran, and won, at least partly on his law-and-order platform; twenty years later, George H. Bush may have made the same assumption.

Just as importantly, the nature of the survey, which typically relies on simple questions to tap complex beliefs, leads to erroneous conclusions, inasmuch as respondents are frequently forced to declare support or opposition to a particular policy, without the benefit of expressing opinions under particular conditions (Roberts 1992). Yet individuals are much less willing to execute those convicted of murder when the criminals are female, mentally retarded, juvenile, or when imprisonment without the possibility of parole is an option (McGarrell and Sandys, 1996). Applegate et al. (1996) and Callanan (2005) make much the same argument regarding the three-strikes laws, the support for which varies depending on the characteristics of the convict and, especially, the perceived severity and type (violent vs. property or drug) of the crime.

Question format, on top of question simplicity, doubtless contributes to an elite misperception of public punitiveness. Media surveys, in particular (the source of most information), almost always rely on one-sided agree-disagree policy statements, while only rarely providing policy alternatives to allow respondents to declare their relative preferences for punitive versus preventative measures. Given the climate during the 1980s and 1990s, when most policy initiatives were designed to toughen penalties and minimize the importance of crime prevention, survey questions generally gave Americans only an option to respond to a punitive statement – likely inflating the expression of public support for such policies.

The ubiquitous government spending item ("Are we spending too much, too little, or about the right amount on ....") provides, perhaps, the greatest opportunity to misinterpret the public mood. In a 2002 survey, 57 percent of respondents indicated a belief that we are spending "too little" on crime (compared to 30% believing we are spending "about right" and only 9% believing we are spending "too much").[2] Quite reasonably, elites could interpret these results as supportive of greater funding for police, prison construction, and more punitive law enforcement methods. At roughly the same time, however, respondents overwhelmingly (69% to 29%) expressed the view that the best way to lower the crime rate is to "attack social and economic problems that lead to crime" rather than "improving law enforcement with more prisons, police, and judges."[3]

Regardless of the reason, elites are far from accurate in their assessments of public attitudes.[4] More specifically, elites understand neither the nuance nor the complexity of citizen preferences. Neither do they appreciate the reality that the public is substantially less punitive than public policy would reflect (Cullen et al., 1998). In 1985, for example, public concerns with crime were beginning to escalate. Clark (1985) found that Michigan policy makers, on average, estimated support for alternative sentencing to be 12 percent, compared to the actual level of 66 percent.

More strikingly, policy makers do not seem to have heeded the more recent shifts in public opinion. A recent influential Pennsylvania State University survey of Pennsylvania adults found, for instance, that 42 percent of respondents consider rehabilitation, rather than incapacitation (20%) or retribution (only 11%), to be the most important purpose of prison (Sims and Johnston 2004, 283). Even more tellingly, by a ratio of 81 to 11 percent, more individuals believe that "early intervention," rather than "more prisons," is the best way to spend money on reducing crime (285). "Policymakers," according to Sims and Johnston (290),

[2] *Source*: National Opinion Research Center, General Social Survey, 2002.

[3] *Source*: The Gallup Organization, Inc., 2004.

[4] Even when the public and policy makers reach the same conclusion, they may do so for quite different reasons. Doble (2002), e.g., notes that the majority of Americans favor a balanced sentencing protocol, meaning that the most violent and dangerous offenders should be treated punitively and harshly, while other, less dangerous offenders should be subjected to extensive rehabilitative policies. Although elites also support this approach, they tend to do so only because it alleviates prison overcrowding and the high costs of incarceration, not because, as citizens believe, it is simply the more humane and logical way to treat individuals.

often are sure they know what the public wants, and much of what they do know about public opinion comes from well-organized special interest lobbying groups (massive letter-writing campaigns or their offices being inundated with telephone calls). Survey data have clearly been telling us, for some time now, that the public is not as conservative as policymakers think them to be.[5] Findings from both national and local studies now point toward a public that has backed away from an entrenched punitive mind-set when it comes to crime and measures to control it.

One such national survey, conducted by Peter D. Hart Research Associates (2002)[6] clearly demonstrates the changing nature of public opinion over the past several decades. In early 1994, a slim plurality of Americans (48%) agreed with the statement "We need a tougher approach to dealing with the causes of crime with an emphasis on improving job and vocational training, providing family counseling, and increasing the number of neighborhood activity centers for young people" rather than "We need a tougher approach to crime with an emphasis on stricter sentencing, capital punishment for more crimes, and fewer paroles for convicted felons" (42%). By September 2001 the ratio of respondents preferring the less punitive approach had swelled to 65 (vs. only 32% supporting the more punitive option) – a margin virtually unaffected by the terrorist attacks on September 11th.

To the degree that elites misperceive public opinion (or, to the degree that they fail to enact policies that are consistent with it), the consequences are curiously asymmetrical – at least based on an admittedly truncated three-decade track record. The trend in the late 1980s and early 1990s led to a host of punitive measures such as mandatory minimum sentencing. The public movement during the late 1990s and

[5] Matthews (2005) refers to this phenomenon as "the myth of punitiveness." A group of scholars (e.g., Bottoms 1995) characterized the public sentiment of one of "populist punitiveness" – a sentiment that Matthews convincingly argues to be wholly unsupported. Garland (2001), e.g., has written that this "punitive turn" has led not only to harsher and more frequent sentencing but also to three-strikes laws, parole release restrictions, "no frills" prisons, and retribution in juvenile courts (including the imprisonment of children). Pratt (2000) contends that an increasingly fearful and emotional public has led to various forms of stigmatization such as the reintroduction of chain gangs and boot camps, as well as pedophile registers. Matthews, however, notes that not only are such claims based on a faulty reading of public opinion, but also that these policies are far less common than is popularly perceived.

[6] Survey conducted for The Open Society Institute.

into the 2000s toward more leniency and supportive of preventative approaches, however, was not heeded by policy makers.

To a certain extent, this asymmetry is explained by the "autoregressive effects" (Nicholson and Meier 2003) of criminal justice policies. The increasingly punitive procedures of the 1980s and 1990s required expenditures for more prisons and more personnel. Once implemented, bureaucratic politics made it highly unlikely that expenditures or personnel could be curtailed.

But there is another dynamic at work. As public fears of, and concerns with, crime escalated into the 1980s and early 1990s, politicians (especially candidates) responded by giving the mass public what it supposedly wanted – that is, more prisons, more police officers, and far higher incarceration rates. Candidates continued to use crime as a "hot button," or wedge issue, best exemplified by the infamous Willie Horton ad run against Democratic Party presidential candidate Michael Dukakis in 1988, which suggested that Dukakis was "soft on crime." It soon became politically suicidal for candidates to promote less punitive solutions to crime, and, feeling pressures to converge (Sigelman and Buell 2004), candidates seemingly tried to "out tough" their opponents. So widespread did this tendency become that Democrat Bill Clinton, whose previous political career was not diagnostic of a tough, law-and-order politician, interrupted his 1992 presidential campaign to travel to his home state of Arkansas to witness the execution of a convict.

THE IMPACT OF ELITES ON MASS BELIEFS

Thus, whether a function of faulty perception, a function of bureaucratic inertia, or simply the presumed need to appear more punitive than one's campaign opponent, criminal justice policies of the last decade have not been informed by the preferences of the U.S. public. This does not mean, however, that mass preferences are not informed (loosely speaking) by elites – both in politics and the media.

Although many individuals hold strong opinions on matters such as capital punishment, and although fear of crime can become a visceral lens through which the world is interpreted, it is also the case that attitudes regarding crime are somewhat flimsy, or, as labeled by Cullen et al. (2000), "mushy." It is this very mushiness that renders such beliefs susceptible to the influence of others.

The most blatant consequence of crime media consumption, by which we primarily mean local television news, as well as "docudrama" crime shows, is a dramatic increase in fear and in the perception of the seriousness of crime as a problem (e.g., Altheide 2002). For example, Lowry et al. (2003, 61), examining the extraordinary increases in the percentage of Americans naming crime as the most important problem from 1992 to 1994, conclude that "the 1994 'Big Scare' was more a network TV news scare than a scare based upon the real world of crime." But there is a ripple effect of television beyond the mere escalation of fear: as carefully documented by Callanan (2005, Chapter 6), heightened levels of fear strongly encourage support for punitive crime policies – at least for the three-strikes laws.

No less powerful is the effect of political leaders on mass attitudes toward crime and punishment. To be sure, the effects are often dramatic. Beckett (1997, 14) provides the example of an antidrug campaign executed by the Bush administration in 1989. During the period between July and September of that year, the percentage of Americans citing drugs as the nation's biggest problem increased from 15 to 64 percent, a change far in excess of reported drug use during this period. When drug-related emergency room visits peaked to record levels in 1992, only 10 percent of respondents considered drugs to be the biggest problem. Clearly, an initiative from the White House, not the crime level itself, was driving these dramatic changes in public perceptions. In a more systematic analysis, Oliver (1998) determined that the more attention a president gives to the issue of crime (as indicated in *The Public Papers of the President of the United States*), the more concerned the American public becomes with the issue (at least by the barometer of the Gallup most important problem index), even after controlling for crime rate, unemployment, and media influences.

The lability of crime-related attitudes not only can but also frequently does lead individuals to bend in a more "liberal" direction in response to persuasive messages and additional information. In their study of undergraduate criminology majors, for example, Cochran and Chamlin (2005) found knowledge about the death penalty to be inversely related to attitudes supportive of the policy. In a clever experiment, Gilens (2001) found that providing a random half of respondents in a national survey with correct information about the crime rate, which, in contrast to the belief of most respondents, had actually decreased over the previous decade, ended up reducing support for government spending to build prisons by nearly 20 percent.

A quite different study of the impact of information, and discussion, is provided by the "deliberative poll," the first of which was conducted in Manchester, England, in 1994 and, fortuitously, focused on the issue of crime and crime reduction. The deliberative poll relies on probability samples but, unlike conventional polls, respondents (or participants) are subjected to several days of intensive discussion and information. Participants first complete a pretest, followed by hours of facilitated discussion, information sharing, and conversation among individuals. At the end, the same attitudes are assessed with a posttest. This quasi-experiment provides an effective, albeit imperfect means to examine the impact of discussion and information flow on attitude change.

At the end of the Manchester poll, as reported by Luskin et al. (2002; see also Hough and Park 2002), four significant net attitudinal changes were observed: individuals 1) became more aware of the limitations of prison as a tool for fighting crime (meaning that they were less likely to favor tough prison sentences); 2) became more sensitive to defendants' procedural rights (as exemplified by a growing hesitation to support police who "bend" the rules); 3) became less appreciative of the value of policing; and 4) became more interested in ameliorating the root causes of crime. In all, participants showed substantially less punitiveness as a result of the conversations and the information that was conveyed during these discussions.

There is considerable evidence, therefore, that the lability of crime-related attitudes often results, as a consequence of new information, discussion, or persuasion, in more liberal, or less punitive, beliefs. However, in practice, most of the messages that citizens receive about crime are likely to be one-sided inasmuch as virtually all elites in recent years have been advocates for more, rather than less, punitive approaches to the war on crime. When crime rates rose during the 1970s and 1980s, and when elites led the charge to ever more punitive policies, the malleability of citizen attitudes afforded elites an opportunity to shape public opinion. However, when crime rates began to decline and policy makers turned to other matters, punitive attitudes either declined as a function of the falling crime rate or else returned to an equilibrium. But because of the decisions reached, allegedly in response to public demands, we are left with more prisons, extraordinarily high incarceration rates, and the budgetary burdens necessary to pay for them.

THE RACIALIZATION OF CRIME

But there is another consequence of the steady drumbeat of elite cues of the past decades (and one could legitimately insert any number of decades): crime, to a great extent, has become heavily racialized in the mind of the American public, largely due to the ways that the media, and political elites, have chosen to portray the issue, and because of the malleability of the public opinion in this area.

A major culprit is the mass media, which routinely conflates race and crime in its coverage. There are any number of ways in which African Americans are represented disproportionately in crime coverage, most blatantly by portraying them as violent offenders far more frequently than Whites are so portrayed (e.g., Peffley et al. 1996; Dixon and Linz 2000; Gilliam and Iyengar 2000; Entman and Rojecki 2001). But there are more subtle practices that have the same effect. Oliver (1994) has found that Blacks are substantially more often shown resisting arrest and/or assaulting police officers, and are also more likely to be shown in a mug shot (Chiricos and Eschholz 2002). Entman and Rojecki (2001), moreover, have also argued that African Americans are more often shown in the grip of a police officer than are Whites, who are often shielded by attorneys, and that White officers speak of Black offenders while the reverse is virtually never portrayed in the media. The result of such practices is that Blacks are depicted as violent, disproportionately responsible for crime, and dehumanized to the degree that audiences see very little about African Americans other than their criminality.

Although the media can, and have been, involved in the racialization of crime, political elites are also implicated in the distortion. Sometimes, this tendency stems from blatant attempts to manipulate public opinion – usually for electoral purposes. Even though the most obvious example is the Willie Horton spot aired during the 1988 presidential campaign (see Mendelberg 1997, 2001 for explanations of the effectiveness of such ads), studies have shown that it takes relatively innocuous cues (e.g., describing criminals as "inner city") to encourage individuals to conceptualize culprits as African American (Hurwitz and Peffley 2005).

Equally responsible for the conflation of race and crime are the decisions that policy makers make – decisions that eventuate in the arrest, prosecution, and incarceration of African Americans to a disproportionate extent. We have alluded previously to the 100-to-1 law, which imposes the same penalty for the possession of one gram of crack cocaine (used primarily by Blacks) as for one hundred grams of powder cocaine (used primarily by Whites) – despite the gram-for-gram pharmacological equivalence of the two drugs.

But racial disproportionalities even creep into ostensibly race-neutral laws, best exemplified by felon disenfranchisement statutes. Currently, forty-eight states disenfranchise felons, albeit to differing degrees: the more draconian states impose permanent prohibitions against felons even after their punishment has been fulfilled, while other states restore voting rights upon release from prison. According to Manza and Uggen (2006), 5.3 million Americans – or more than 2 percent of the entire voting age population – were denied the right to vote in the 2004 presidential election. This number has increased dramatically over the decades due to the expansion of offenses deemed felonies and to an unprecedented escalation of criminal punishment in the country.

Although, on its face, felony disenfranchisement laws appear to be race-neutral, in practice they at least have the appearance of being racially discriminatory. More than two million (of the 5.3 million) disenfranchised citizens are African American. More suggestively, the percentage of non-Whites incarcerated in a state's penal system has been found to be a strong and consistent predictor of the passage of a more restrictive disenfranchisement law (Behrens et al. 2003).

We have argued that public attitudes regarding crime seem to matter to decision makers, who attempt to respond to citizen preferences – even if mass preferences are based on faulty information and elites have an inaccurate read of public opinion, as appears to be the case over much of the past decade as the public has become less punitive without an in-kind response from political leaders. What is most relevant to our purpose, however, is the lability of public attitudes regarding crime and punishment, for a malleable public is highly susceptible to the manipulative efforts of elites. The manipulation that concerns us most pertains to race or, more accurately, attempts to racialize public-policy attitudes. Given the consequential nature of crime-policy attitudes, and the strong likelihood that they influence political decision makers, it is essential to understand the degree to which such attitudes are driven by racial considerations.

Our purpose in this chapter is to explore crime-policy attitudes, first focusing on the degree to which Blacks and Whites differ in their opinions regarding the most important crime policies on the public agenda: the death penalty, the degree to which crime should be addressed through punishment rather than through tackling underlying social and economic problems, three-strikes laws, racial profiling, and juvenile justice. Second, we will focus on the conditions under which racial policies become polarized, and, in particular, the ease with which often subtle messages can drive the races even further apart. Finally, we examine more intensively two policies with very high levels of racial polarization, focusing particularly on the determinants of such attitudes, and the degree to which determinants differ between Blacks and Whites.

RACE AND CRIME-POLICY ATTITUDES

As a component of the National Race and Crime Survey (NRCS), approximately equal numbers of African-American and White respondents were asked about their views regarding a host of crime and punishment policies – policies of the sort that are in the news on a regular basis. We have not inquired about policies that are arcane or about which respondents should be expected to know very little. Doing so would have essentially guaranteed a respondent pool that is easily manipulatable – something we wished to avoid.

Figure 5.1 displays the marginal responses of Whites and African Americans to seven crime-policy questions: capital punishment,[7] whether crime is best reduced through stiff punishment or through addressing underlying social problems,[8] racial profiling,[9] whether illegal drug use is best curtailed by imposing stricter prison sentences or

[7] "Here is a question about the death penalty. Do you strongly oppose, somewhat oppose, somewhat favor, or strongly favor the death penalty for persons convicted of murder?"

[8] Some people say that the best way to reduce crime is to address the social problems that cause crime, like poverty and joblessness. Other people say the best way to reduce crime is to make sure that criminals are caught, convicted, and punished harshly. What about you? If you had to choose, which is the better way to reduce crime – to address social problems or to catch and punish criminals harshly?

[9] In many areas of the country, police officers use a practice known as racial profiling, in which they stop and question Black motorists because the officers believe Blacks are more likely to commit certain types of crime. Do you strongly approve, somewhat approve, somewhat disapprove, or strongly disapprove of racial profiling?

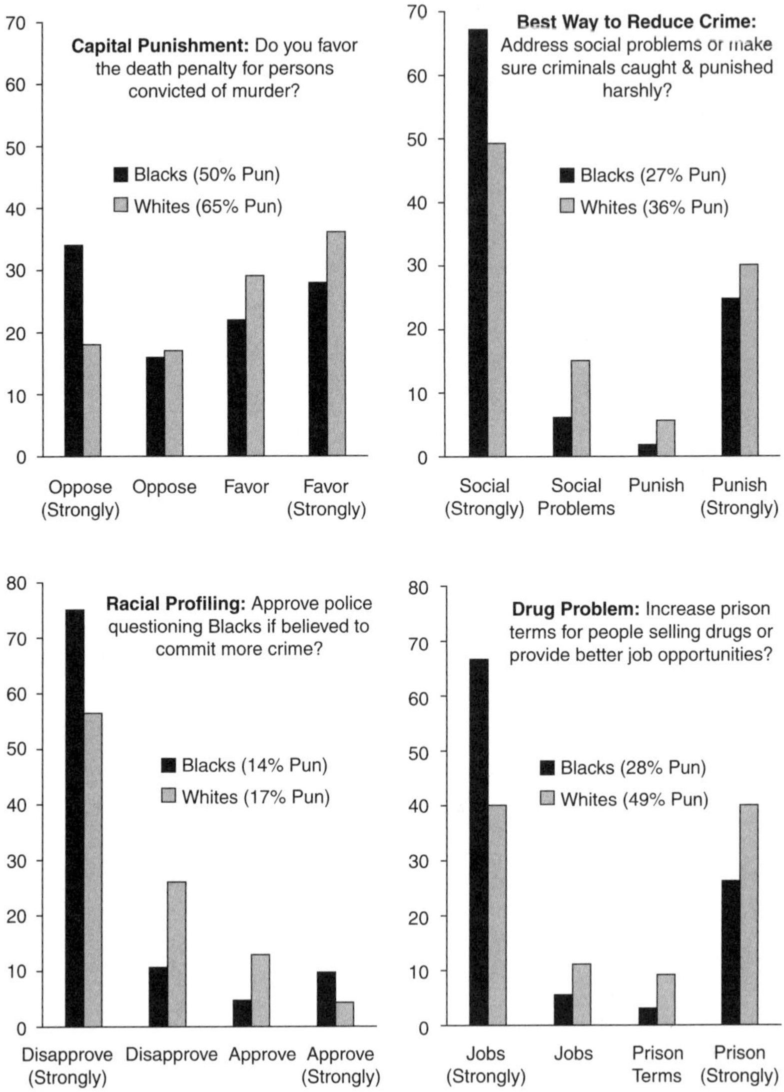

FIGURE 5.1. White-Black percentage differences in crime-policy attitudes.
Note: The graphs display percentage differences in Blacks' and Whites' support for various crime policies, with overall support (e.g., adding strongly approve + approve) for the punitive (abbreviated as "Pun") policy options listed in the legend of each graph. All interracial differences on the preceding (4-point) scales are significant at the .05 level or lower.
Source: NRCS data.

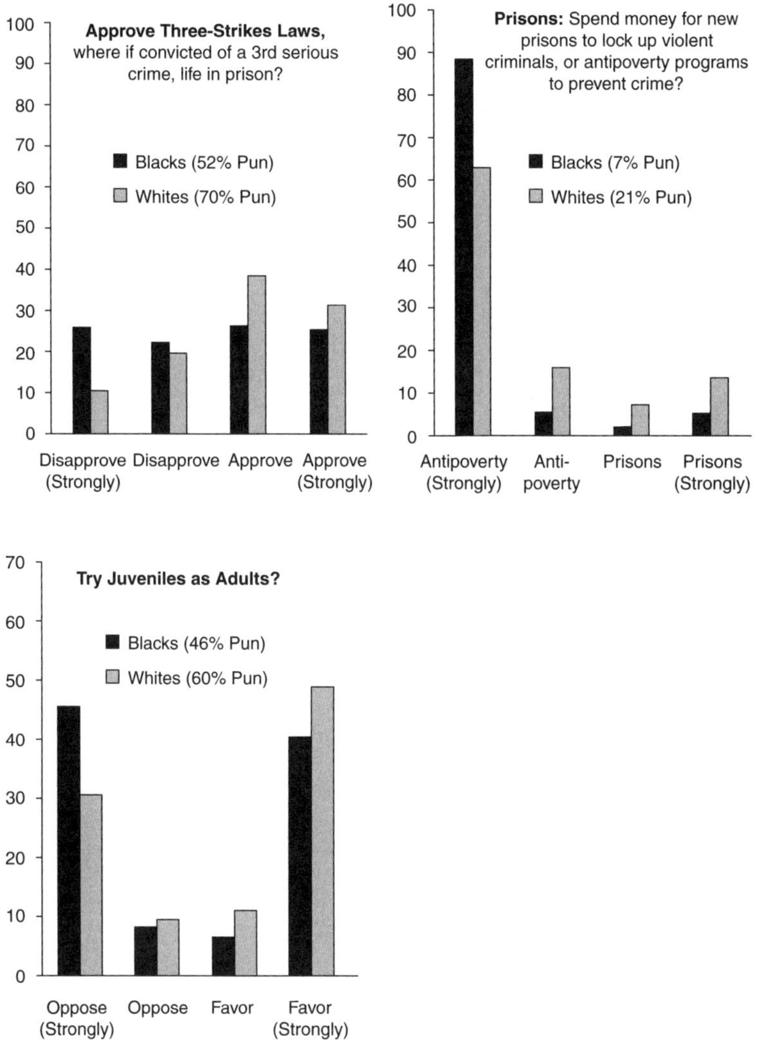

FIGURE 5.1. *continued.*

by providing more job opportunities,[10] three-strikes laws,[11] spending money for prison or for antipoverty programs to combat crime,[12] and whether juveniles should be tried as adults.[13] (In all cases, respondents were asked whether they felt strongly or not strongly about their position. The percentages adjacent to the race legend in each graph reflect the proportion of respondents [of each race] who provide punitive answers – regardless of whether their position is strongly held or not.)

Two clear findings emerge from Figure 5.1. First, consistent with more recent evidence such as that provided by the Pennsylvania State University (2004) and Peter H. Hart (2002) surveys, Americans are not particularly punitive in their orientations. By strong majorities, Whites support the death penalty for persons convicted of murder and, by smaller margins, three-strikes laws and trying juveniles as adults. Although African Americans are less punitive, sizeable minorities agree with the majority of Whites in both instances. However, in every case where respondents were presented with a clear choice between punitive and preventative measures, majorities of both races – and typically substantial majorities – indicate support for the less punitive option: believing that crime is most effectively decreased by addressing underlying social problems, job programs are the preferred method for combating illegal drug use, and money is more effectively used to fund antipoverty programs than to construct prisons.

More germane to our purposes, however, is the notable gap between Whites and African Americans. Without exception, Whites

[10] Some people think that the best way to deal with the drug problem is to increase prison terms for people who sell drugs. Others think that the best way to deal with the drug problem is to provide better job opportunities. What about you? Do you think that the drug problem is better solved by longer prison terms or more job opportunities?

[11] Let me ask you [about] three-strikes laws, in which anyone convicted of a third serious crime is sent to prison for the rest of their life. Do you strongly approve, somewhat approve, somewhat disapprove, or strongly disapprove of these three-strikes laws?

[12] Some people want to increase spending for new prisons to lock up violent criminals. Other people would rather spend this money for antipoverty programs to prevent crime. What about you? If you had to choose, would you rather see this money spent on building new prisons or on antipoverty programs?

[13] Some people think that if juveniles commit serious crimes they should be tried as an adult and have to serve the same punishment adults do. Others think that juveniles committing crimes should not be treated as adults because there needs to be more emphasis on rehabilitation. What about you? Do you think juveniles should be tried as adults or not?

advocate more punitive solutions than do Blacks. In some cases, the difference is modest – most notably with the racial profiling question where substantial majorities of both races are in opposition. But even in this case, the intensity of opposition from African Americans is stronger than from Whites.

In other important instances, interracial differences are profound. By large margins, Blacks are more oppositional to capital punishment, more likely to support job programs to address drug use, and more opposed to the three-strikes laws. We believe that some of the Black-White differences are muted due to ceiling effects: there would, doubtless, be even more racial polarization if not for the fact that overwhelming majorities of African Americans selected the most extreme response option (the least punitive one) for the racial profiling and prisons questions.

THE ENVIRONMENT OF POLARIZATION

Our purpose, however, is more ambitious than merely documenting interracial differences of opinion. Additionally, we believe it is important to focus on the environment of these differences, or the conditions that serve to widen or narrow the race gap. With this goal in mind, we devised the NRCS to accommodate a series of survey experiments, each designed to enable us to manipulate various properties of crime policies – properties that could potentially further polarize an already polarized country.

Ultimately, almost all studies of influence and persuasion focus on the message and/or the messenger. The audience may respond to various cues – explicit or implicit – in the persuasive communication or, alternatively, may respond to various properties of the individual or group (i.e., the source) delivering the communication. In the following text, we manipulate both message and messenger characteristics.

Capital Punishment

We have noted previously the conditionality of attitudes toward the death penalty, inasmuch as public support varies greatly and that proponents of the policy are quite affected by new information. Longmire (1996, 103), in his analysis of data from the National Opinion Survey on Crime and Justice (1995), determined that 23 percent of original death-penalty supporters indicate that they are more likely to oppose it when informed that capital punishment is not a deterrent to murder. Additionally, he found large percentages of proponents to be more likely to oppose the death penalty when informed that the poor are more likely to be executed (38%), innocent people are executed (45%), a life sentence is less expensive than execution (28%), a murderer is under eighteen years old (25%), and a murderer is severely retarded (61%). When supporters are informed that "minorities are more likely to receive the death penalty," 35 percent become oppositional.[14] Clearly, even with this most emotional of issues, individuals can, and often are, swayed by the message to which they are exposed.

We compare the efficacy of two very different messages – one racial and one nonracial – looking particularly at how the impact of the two messages differ across the race of the audience. Our methodology differs substantially from that used in the National Opinion Survey on Crime and Justice, which asked all respondents to respond to all messages. Respondents to the NRCS, in contrast, are randomly assigned to one of three groups: a baseline condition, in which individuals are asked the question in Figure 5.1: "Here is a question about the death penalty. Do you strongly oppose, somewhat oppose, somewhat favor, or strongly favor the death penalty for persons convicted of murder?"; a racial argument condition, in which individuals are asked the same question, only preceded by the statement "Here is a question about the death penalty. Some people say that the death penalty is unfair because most of the people who are executed are African Americans"; and a nonracial argument condition, in which the baseline question is preceded by "Some people say that the death penalty is unfair because too many innocent people are being executed." We believe this protocol reduces the consistency pressures on respondents to provide comparable answers regardless of the facts presented (e.g., whether the individual executed is unidentified or African American), thereby minimizing any social desirability bias inherent in the survey context. Because the experimental manipulation is restricted to the preface to the stem (i.e., whether it is the racial or the innocent treatment), any

[14] Although 35% become more oppositional in response to the information that minorities are more likely to receive the death penalty, 16% become more supportive, resulting in a net change of 19% who shift in the direction of opposition.

differences between groups can only be attributed to the inclusion and nature of the preface.

Table 5.1 displays the results across the three experimental conditions (baseline [column 1] vs. racial argument [column 2] vs. innocent argument [column 3]) separately for White and African-American respondents. Most obviously, the data confirm the consensual finding in the literature: Whites (in all three conditions) are more supportive of the death penalty than are African Americans.

But it is the magnitude of this difference and what happens to this magnitude across experimental treatments that are of greatest interest. African Americans respond to the anti-death-penalty argument in the fashion that one would predict based on the direction of the message – that is, they become more opposed. Although half of the Black respondents support capital punishment in the baseline, support drops to approximately one-third of respondents in the two treatment conditions. Somewhat surprisingly, the innocent argument has a modestly greater impact on them (causing a decrease of 16%, vs. 12.1% in response to the racial argument). Quite possibly, African Americans do not need to be reminded of the racial discrimination inherent in the death sentence, and, consequently, the message provides less in the way of new information.

It is the response of White respondents, however, that is most noteworthy. Although the innocence argument makes virtually no difference, Whites in the racial condition, upon hearing of the discriminatory properties of the death penalty, actually become more, rather than less, supportive, to the point where more than three out of four individuals favor capital punishment in this treatment group.

This finding is surprising not only because of what is revealed about White respondents, but also because it is so unexpected based on the extant literature. The Longmire (1996) analysis noted in the preceding text, for example, found respondents to become less supportive of capital punishment upon hearing that it is used more frequently against minorities.[15] We believe that, more than anything, the discrepancy reflects differing methodologies. In particular, because respondents in the Longmire survey are asked to respond to several

[15] Although the sample used also included minority respondents, more than 80% were White.

TABLE 5.1. *Percentage support for the death penalty, by race and experimental condition*

	Baseline Condition (No Argument)	Racial Argument	Innocent Arugment
	Do you favor or oppose the death penalty for persons convicted of murder?	Some people say that the death penalty is unfair because most of the people who are executed are African-Americans. Do you favor or oppose the death penalty for persons convicted of murder?	Some people say that the death penalty is unfair because too many innocent people are being executed. Do you favor or oppose the death penalty for persons convicted of murder?
Whites			
Strongly Oppose	17.95%	11.38%	20.09%
Somewhat Oppose	17.09	11.79	15.63
Somewhat Favor	29.06	25.20	29.46
Strongly Favor	35.90	51.63	34.82
Total % Favor	**64.96%**	**76.83%**	**64.28%**
% Favor vs. Baseline		+12% favor	–.68% favor
N	117	246	224
Blacks			
Strongly Oppose	34.17%	43.60%	45.98%
Somewhat Oppose	15.83	18.48	20.09
Somewhat Favor	22.50	17.54	18.75
Strongly Favor	27.50	20.38	15.18

TABLE 5.1. *(continued)*

	Baseline Condition (No Argument)	Racial Argument	Innocent Arugment
Total % Favor	50%	37.92%	33.93%
% Favor vs. Baseline		−12% favor	−16% favor
N	120	211	224
Interracial Difference	15.0%	38.9%	30.3%

Note: The experiment also randomly manipulated the source of the argument as either "some people" or "FBI statistics show that," which had no discernible influence on support for the death penalty. Differences across baseline and argument conditions, and across respondent race, are significant at $p < .05$.
Source: NRCS data.

death-penalty questions across multiple conditions, they are likely to feel pressure to decrease their support for the death penalty when told it is used more frequently against minorities in order to avoid appearing racially insensitive or bigoted. By contrast, because respondents in the NCRS are assigned to only one of the three versions of the question, social pressures are minimized, and individuals who are informed of the racial bias of the death penalty likely feel more free to express increased levels of support for capital punishment without the fear of exposing any prejudice.[16]

Most important is the net result of the racial argument, which serves to augment the race gap to an astonishing degree. The 15 percent race gap in the baseline condition essentially doubles (to 30.3%) in the innocent condition, but this change is due entirely to the change

[16] Some experimental studies find no difference in support for the death penalty across different argument conditions. Such results are readily explained by the rather bland form of the arguments used in the experiments. Bobo and Johnson (2004), e.g., provided respondents with information suggesting (but not explicitly stating) that the death penalty is racially unfair (e.g., "Blacks are about 12% of the US population, but they are almost half (43%) of those currently on death row"). Similarly, Edwards and Smith (1996) found that syllogistic arguments such as "Implementing the death penalty means that there is a chance that innocent people will be sentenced to death ... [t]herefore, the death penalty should be abolished" had little effect on participants' attitudes in their study. Consistent with research on motivated reasoning (e.g., Taber, Cann, and Kucsova 2007), our more direct and argumentative statement that the death penalty is "unfair" appears essential for moving support for capital punishment in either direction.

among Black respondents, who become substantially less supportive. In the racial condition, however, the gap widens to an extraordinary 40 percent, as 77 percent of Whites, but only 38 percent of Blacks, support the death penalty. Interestingly, this expansion is due to an almost identical movement of White and Black respondents, albeit in opposite directions, as the 12 percent of the former become more supportive and 12 percent of the latter become less supportive of the policy.

Prison versus Antipoverty Spending

Without doubt, the message in the capital punishment experiment is explicitly racial in nature – that is, individuals offered differential levels of support in response to an argument with an unambiguously racial dimension. There is evidence, however, that far more subtle cues can be equally efficacious, particularly regarding issues such as race in which many individuals resist appeals that are blatantly race related in nature. Several studies have investigated the impact of racially coded language on candidate preferences and vote intentions (e.g., Mendelberg 2001; Valentino et al. 2002) and on a slew of race-related policy attitudes.[17] Yet little is known about the power of such language to affect policy attitudes in the one domain in which, intuitively, it should have its most profound impact – crime.[18]

Public debate pursuant to "playing the race card" – or using racially coded language – began with the airing of the aforementioned Willie Horton ad. As meticulously detailed by Jamieson (1992, Chapter 1), the narrator of the spot states that Horton, a convicted murderer, received multiple weekend furlough passes from prison, during the last of which, the narrator informs us, he "fled, kidnapping a young couple, stabbing the man and repeatedly raping his girlfriend." Although the ad could have conveyed exactly the same information without graphics, the sponsor elected to superimpose the most menacing possible picture of Horton, an African American, over the narrative.

[17] See Nelson and Kinder (1996) regarding affirmative action attitudes and Valentino (1999) regarding welfare.

[18] Cf. Valentino (1999), who found that exposure to crime news depicting minority suspects lowered subjects' evaluations of Clinton's performance ratings, and Mendelberg (2001), who found that exposure to news about the Horton ad strengthened the connection between racial attitudes and opposition to economic policies (e.g., welfare) but not crime policy.

Tali Mendelberg (2001) convincingly argues that the Horton ad, as well as other racially coded spots such as the George Bush 1988 "revolving door" and the 1990 Jesse Helms "White hands" spots against Harvey Gantt, is effective because of its implicitness. White Americans, despite their resentment toward Blacks, are committed to a "norm of equality." This egalitarian streak causes individuals to reject blatantly racial appeals but not those that are implicit – that is, not recognized as racial. Horton fulfills the implicitness requirement in the sense that it never explicitly mentions that the subject is African American, nor does it make an explicit linkage between candidate Dukakis, his policies, and the Black recipient (i.e., Horton) of his policy.

Our prison spending experiment (the 6th item in Figure 5.1) was designed for the purpose of examining the impact of implicit racial coding. In the experiment, respondents were asked about the preferred way to prevent crime (spending money for prisons or for antipoverty programs), while randomly asking one-half about "violent criminals" and the other half about "violent *inner-city* criminals."

> Some people want to increase spending for new prisons to lock up violent [inner city/XXX] criminals. Other people would rather spend this money for antipoverty programs to prevent crime. What about you? If you had to choose, would you rather see this money spent on building new prisons, or on antipoverty programs?

As always, a branched format required individuals to indicate if they held the belief strongly or not strongly. Most importantly, for our purposes, is the fact that the manipulation is restricted to a single phrase (inner city) – a phrase that, for many, conjures up images of African-American inhabitants.[19]

In Table 5.2, the results are displayed separately for White and African-American respondents, broken down by experimental treatment groups. We once again note that, in both conditions, Blacks are less punitive than Whites. We also note that the inner-city cue plays a subtle but significant role in the polarization process. In the baseline condition, the interracial percentage difference in support for prison

19 When asked to estimate the "percentage of all Americans who live in inner cities who are Black," the median guess of White respondents was 60%.

TABLE 5.2. *Percentage support for prisons, by race and experimental condition*

	Baseline		Inner City
White			
Prisons (strongly)	12.4%		15.2%
Prisons (somewhat)	6.6		8.0
Antipoverty (somewhat)	19.0		12.8
Antipoverty (strongly)	62.0		64.0
Total % Support Prisons	**19.0%**		**23.2%**
% Change from Baseline to Inner City		4.2%	
N	137		125
Black			
Prisons (strongly)	5.2%		4.7%
Prisons (somewhat)	3.7		0.0
Antipoverty (somewhat)	4.5		5.4
Antipoverty (strongly)	86.6		89.9
Total % Support Prisons	**8.9%**		**4.7%**
% Change from Baseline to Inner City		−4.2%	
N	134		148
Interracial Difference	**10.1%**		**18.5%**

Note: Interracial differences between baseline and inner-city condition are significant at $p < .05$.
Source: NRCS data.

spending is 10.1 percent – a difference that is nearly doubled in the treatment condition.

The relatively modest impact (+4.2% for Whites and −4.2% for Blacks) of the inner-city cue, we believe, must be considered alongside several important details. First, the cue is particularly interesting because it has encouraged Whites to move in one (i.e., more punitive) direction and African Americans to move in the opposite direction. Clearly, it conveys a fundamentally different meaning to the races. A second and related point is that the cue is extremely subtle, thereby supporting our contention that messages can be framed in such a way that the race gap widens even without explicit mention of race. Third, any shift among Blacks is doubtless constrained by a ceiling effect – that is, the vast majority, even in the baseline condition, is so supportive of antipoverty programs that there is little room for additional movement in that direction. Finally, as we have reported elsewhere

(Hurwitz and Peffley 2005), the inner-city cue does more than merely prompt a small aggregate shift of Whites to become more supportive of prison spending. In addition, it leads to a large change in the evaluative criterion used by Whites – prompting them to link their support for punitive policies to their racial attitudes. Although there is virtually no relationship between White's stereotypes of Blacks and their support for prison construction in the baseline condition, there is a sizeable and significant association in the inner-city condition. Quite clearly, this prompt, though subtle, has the capacity to encourage Whites to bring race into the calculation when prompted to do so.

Three Strikes

To this point, we have only examined the potential of the message to influence the interracial chasm. In the three-strikes experiment, we explore both the properties of the message and of the messenger. In this experiment, we employed two independent treatments – one to manipulate the source ("some people" vs. Colin Powell vs. Jesse Jackson) and the other to manipulate the message ("_____ oppose these laws because prosecutors are more likely to use them against Blacks than against Whites" vs. "many people are sent to prison for life for committing three less serious crimes like drug possession"). Respondents, therefore, were randomly assigned to one of the six treatments. In its entirety, the question reads:

> Let me ask you another question about three strikes laws, where anyone convicted of a third serious crime is sent to prison for the rest of their life. [Some people/Some people like Jesse Jackson/Some people like General Colin Powell] oppose these laws because [prosecutors are more likely to use them against Blacks than against Whites/many people are sent to prison for life for committing three less serious crimes like drug possession]. Other people favor these laws because they keep repeat offenders in prison for life where they can't commit more crimes. What about you? Do you strongly approve, somewhat approve, somewhat disapprove, or strongly disapprove of these three strikes laws?

We therefore employ two arguments against the three-strikes laws, one of which is racialized (the policy is racially biased) and the other of which is not (the policy is too harsh), and three sources of this message – one of which is entirely race-neutral (some people), an African

American known primarily for his military service and who is widely regarded as politically moderate (Powell), and an African American who has acquired the reputation as a racially polarizing figure known for his outspoken endorsement of racial causes (Jackson).

The results are displayed, across treatment group and race, in Figure 5.2. Because of the six conditions, we cannot break respondents into response categories as we have for the other policy items due to the small number of cases in each cell.[20] We instead report means rather than percentages, where 1 = strong disapproval for three-strikes laws and 4 = strong approval. Responses at the far left are from the baseline condition, in which neither the anti-three-strikes argument (too harsh) nor the source ("some people") are racialized.

Whites are clearly more punitively oriented: in each of the six conditions, they are more supportive of the three-strikes laws. Of greater interest, however, is the response to experimental treatments and how such responses differ interracially. Virtually no interracial difference exists in the first, baseline condition – that is, when neither the source nor the argument is in any sense racialized. As we introduce either an African-American opponent to the law or introduce an argument that the laws are racially discriminatory (or both), however, interracial differences become pronounced, such that mean differences climb to .62 (3.06 – 2.44) in the racial bias/Jackson condition. The Black-White gap, although clearly noticeable under both of the too harsh conditions (.40 in both cases), increases substantially under the racial bias conditions.

Closer inspection of the figure, along with statistical analysis (not shown), reveals why the race gap is most pronounced when respondents are presented with an African-American source (like Jackson) questioning the racial fairness of the three-strikes policy.[21] Whites are moved more by the nature of the argument than the source; they move sharply and significantly away from the racial bias argument. That is,

[20] The small number of cases per condition also precludes an individual-level analysis of attitudes toward the three-strikes policy.

[21] Ordered probit was used to regress approval of the three-strikes laws on dummy variables representing the experimental manipulations in the following equation estimated for Blacks and Whites: Approval = Race of Source + Argument Type, where Race of Source = 1 when the source is Jackson or Powell and 0 for "some people." Argument type = 1 for the racial bias argument and 0 for the too harsh argument. We experimented with interactions between source and argument, and with different contrasts between sources, but none were significant.

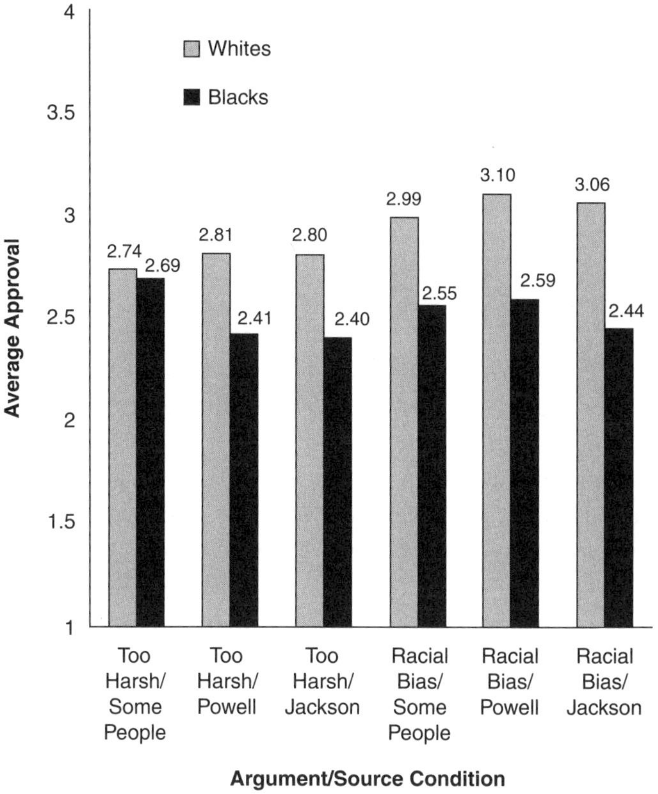

FIGURE 5.2. Mean approval of the three-strikes laws by race and experimental condition.

Note: 1 = strongly disapprove, 4 = strongly approve. Interracial differences are significant at the .05 level or lower for all argument/source conditions except the nonracialized, baseline condition (i.e., too harsh/some people).

Source: NRCS data.

we find the same backlash effect as with the capital punishment experiment, inasmuch as antipunitive arguments actually encourage Whites to become more, not less, punitive upon learning of evidence of racial discrimination. Blacks, by contrast, are more responsive to the source of the argument (at least in the too harsh condition); they are more accepting of arguments against the three-strikes laws when Powell or Jackson is the messenger instead of the generic "some people." It is the conjunction of an African-American source like Jackson (that Blacks respond to) and a racial argument against the three-strikes laws (that

Whites reject) that creates the most dramatically polarized responses in the racial bias/Jackson condition at the extreme right-hand side of the figure.

ANTECEDENTS OF POLICY ATTITUDES AND RACIAL DIFFERENCES

We turn now to an in-depth look at the antecedents of two policy questions, selected for their salience (capital punishment) and their generality (preferences for preventative vs. punitive approaches to fighting crime). Our examination of crime-policy attitudes has, to this point, focused on "raw" interracial differences in support for various anticrime measures and how support levels are shaped by external stimuli, such as the characteristics of the policy (e.g., prevention vs. punishment), question wording, and persuasive appeals (e.g., the source and the message). To gain a more complete understanding of why the races differ in their crime-policy views, however, it is necessary to expand our focus to include the characteristics of the individual.

Predicting Support for Capital Punishment

We take up capital punishment first, for no other single issue in the criminal justice sphere has occupied as prominent a place in public debate, and deservedly so, in light of the strong feelings this ultimate punishment conjures up. In addition, racial differences in support for the death penalty have historically been exceptional, doubtless because people of color account for a disproportionate number of executions and of those currently on death row. In Figure 5.1 and Table 5.1, we saw not only that the races differ markedly in their support for capital punishment, but also, even more importantly, that their susceptibility to arguments against the death penalty is strikingly dissimilar, with Blacks moving in the direction of both the racial and nonracial counterarguments and Whites either standing pat when presented with the nonracial argument (i.e., "Some people say that the death penalty is unfair because too many innocent people are being executed") or becoming more supportive of the death penalty when presented with a racial argument against it ("Some people say that the death penalty is unfair because most of the people who are executed are African Americans"). Because the death-penalty persuasion experiment is designed to mimic elite debate on this issue, investigating why the races diverge in their responses to arguments against capital punishment potentially has important implications for the future of the policy in the United States, which is the only advanced Western democracy that carries out executions.

To explain the susceptibility of the races to arguments against the death penalty, it is necessary to understand how elites have framed more recent arguments against the policy, as well as how such frames can promote either resistance or responsiveness from the public. Although arguments against the death penalty have ranged from the biblical to the economic, two have been particularly prominent. In their examination of *New York Times* abstracts from 1960 to 2004, Baumgartner et al. (2004) found that the death penalty underwent a dramatic new issue-redefinition beginning in the mid-1990s from a focus on morality and constitutionality to charges that innocent people may be on death row and, later, a focus on charges of racial bias in the application of the death penalty. The first of the newly salient antipunishment arguments hinges on the question of fallibility. Particularly with the availability of DNA testing, which has exonerated a number of death row inmates (Liebman 2000), we know the legal system is flawed to the point where an unknown proportion of individuals on death row are innocent. According to Haines (1992), such "flawed convictions" seriously erode public support for capital punishment.

Second, capital punishment, according to critics, is rife with racial and ethnic discrimination, so much so that, as of this writing, thirty-eight states have empanelled commissions to investigate these biases. Although the disproportionate numbers of Blacks on death row do not, by themselves, prove the system to be racially discriminatory, they do lead to the all important perception of discrimination on the part of many, particularly those within the African-American community. Further, there is by now a virtual consensus that Black assailants convicted of murdering Whites are far more likely to face the death penalty than those convicted of murdering minorities (e.g., Pasternoster 1991; Keil and Vito 1995). Much of the bias is more subtle, such as the practice of "jury bleaching," whereby district attorneys dismiss African Americans from jury pools in capital cases for reasons other than cause. The discriminatory nature of capital punishment is more than a mere perception. It is a reality.

Clearly, the new ways of framing arguments against the death penalty are made with some frequency by elites and can be expected to have some resonance with public opinion. But although we can demonstrate that Whites and Blacks respond differently to capital punishment, as well as to arguments against it (Figure 5.1 and Table 5.1), how can we explain these dramatic interracial differences? Research on political persuasion and issue framing tells us that arguments or issue frames can elicit either responsiveness or resistance from an intended recipient, depending on the characteristics of the message and the recipient. Studies of issue framing show that people often respond differently to messages that contain alternative frames of an issue. As Nelson and Oxley (1999, 1041) explain, "framing effects work by altering the *importance* that individuals attach to certain beliefs." If, for example, an argument against affirmative action is framed as an "undeserved advantage" for Blacks, then Whites' opposition to the policy is more likely to be based on their racial attitudes than when the issue is framed as "reverse discrimination" against Whites, in which case other criteria are used (Kinder and Sanders 1996). Because cues contained in the message can have a major impact on what prior beliefs are used by individuals to evaluate the message, issue frames or persuasive appeals can potentially exert a powerful impact on people's attitudes.

There is no guarantee that people will react mindlessly by simply accepting an issue frame or an argument. As we saw in the three-strikes experiment, people may end up resisting frames from less trustworthy sources (e.g., Druckman 2001a) or, most importantly for current purposes, resisting frames that conflict with their prior beliefs and predispositions (e.g., Brewer 2001; Haider-Markel and Joslyn 2001). Thus, frames (and persuasive messages more generally) can precipitate either persuasion or resistance, depending on the degree to which the frame is either consonant or dissonant with the prior predispositions that are activated.

We have already noted two of the most important ways of framing arguments against capital punishment – that is, raising questions about its fallibility and its racially discriminatory application. But what prior predispositions of Whites and Blacks should influence reactions to these frames? There is evidence that, at least for Whites, racial beliefs play an important role. It has been shown that prejudice renders individuals more punitive (e.g., Cohn et al. 1991), as does merely living in areas with higher concentrations of African Americans (e.g., Smith 2004). More specifically, pertaining to death penalty attitudes, Soss et al. (2003) found that race was an important predictor of Whites' support for the death penalty in 1992 – contextually (living among African Americans) and attitudinally (being racially prejudiced, as measured by racial stereotypes). Bobo and Johnson (2004) also found that racial resentment is a more important determinant of White respondents' support for the death penalty than for Black respondents.

There seems to be little doubt that, at least for Whites, racial attitudes can affect their support for capital punishment. But racial attitudes, as measured by global predispositions like prejudice and stereotyping, present several limitations as determinants of death-penalty support. First, many measures of racial attitudes are afflicted to some degree by social desirability bias because many Whites with negative views of Blacks censor their true attitudes in an interview for fear of being labeled a racist (e.g., Kuklinski and Cobb 1998; Feldman and Huddy 2005). Second, because the connection between global racial attitudes (e.g., stereotypes and prejudice) and policy attitudes is so indirect and circuitous, any observed relationship may be viewed as suspect and potentially spurious unless a range of stringent controls are included in the analysis (e.g., Gilens 1999). Third, any relationship between global racial attitudes and policy attitudes should depend upon a variety of factors, including characteristics of the policy (e.g., type and intended recipient) and of the individual (e.g., Hurwitz and Peffley 1997; Peffley, Hurwitz, and Sniderman 1997).

For these reasons, we prefer to focus on determinants that not only have important racial connotations but also have a more obvious connection to justice policy attitudes, such as our measure of attributions of Black treatment, or the degree to which people think the more punitive treatment of Blacks in the justice system is due to their internal failings or the biases of the system (see Chapter 3 for a more detailed description). Although such a predisposition has received almost no prior attention in the criminal justice literature, more general attributions of the causes of crime have consistently been found to influence support for crime policies, in general, and capital punishment, in particular (e.g., Young 1991; Grasmick et al. 1993; Grasmick and McGill 1994; Roberts and Stalans 1997; Cochran et al. 2003). Thus, there is a clear expectation that our measure of general attributions of crime, described in Chapter 3, will be tied to support for capital punishment among Whites and Blacks.

Additionally, and more importantly, attributions of Black treatment should be an especially telling explanation of why Whites and Blacks respond so differently to arguments against the death penalty, as revealed in Table 5.1. Among Whites, attributions of Black treatment should most strongly predict support for capital punishment in the racial argument condition but play a much weaker role in the baseline and innocent conditions where such beliefs are much less germane. By contrast, because most Blacks do not need any reminder of the racially discriminatory nature of the death penalty, the relationship between attributions of Black treatment and support for the policy should be much less affected by experimental condition. Regardless of whether Black respondents are in the baseline, innocent, or racial argument conditions, we expect those who attribute Black treatment to structural sources (i.e., discrimination) to be less likely to endorse the punishment relative to those who hold dispositional explanations.

In Table 5.3, we report the results of an ordered probit analysis, in which we investigate the antecedents of support for the death penalty in the three conditions for Whites and Blacks. Although our primary interest is in the impact of attributions of Black treatment, we include a range of additional "control" variables because support for the death penalty is doubtless shaped by a variety of confounding (attitudinal and demographic) factors, all of which have been described previously and in Appendix A.[22]

Our principal focus is on the first row of coefficients representing the impact of attributions of Black treatment on support for the death penalty across different argument conditions. Ignoring the differences across columns, individuals who hold dispositional beliefs about the causes of Black treatment are substantially more supportive of capital punishment relative to those who attribute this treatment to a biased justice system. As expected, however, the influence of Black treatment is markedly different for Whites and Blacks. Among Whites (top panel

[22] We also estimated equations that included system fairness, unfair treatment, and contextual variables (e.g., racial composition and county crime) as control variables, but because the results did not change and the effects of the control variables rarely achieved statistical significance, we do not report the more fully specified equations here.

TABLE 5.3. *Predicting support for the death penalty across race and experimental condition*

Table 5.3.A. Whites	Baseline (No Argument)		Racial Argument		Innocent Argument	
Attributions of Black Treatment	.03	(.08)	$.22^{***a}$	(.06)	.09	(.06)
General Attributions of Crime	$.14^{*}$	(.08)	$.17^{**c}$	(.06)	.03	(.09)
Anti-Black Stereotype	.02	(.03)	.03	(.02)	−.02	(.02)
Fear of Crime	−.15	(.13)	.09	(.09)	.06	(.09)
Punitiveness	$.20^{**c}$	(.09)	$.19^{***}$	(.06)	$.18^{***}$	(.06)
Party ID	$-.09^{c}$	(.07)	$.07^{a}$	(.04)	$.08^{*}$	(.05)
Ideology	.10	(.08)	$-.06^{b}$	(.05)	$.13^{***}$	(.05)
Education	$-.15^{*}$	(.08)	$-.15^{***}$	(.06)	$-.08^{c}$	(.07)
Female	$-.58^{**}$	(.23)	$-.52^{***c}$	(.17)	$-.32^{**c}$	(.16)
Income	$.17^{**}$	(.08)	$.14^{***b}$	(.06)	−.01	(.05)
Age	−.01	(.01)	−.003	(.004)	−.003	(.005)
Cutpoint 1	−2.38	(.76)	−3.44	(.58)	−2.60	(.57)
Cutpoint 2	−1.76	(.75)	−2.85	(.57)	−2.05	(.56)
Cutpoint 3	−.83	(.73)	−1.97	(.56)	−1.20	(.55)
N	117		240		223	

Table 5.3.B. Blacks	Baseline (No Argument)		Racial Argument		Innocent Argument	
Attributions of Black Treatment	$.15^{*}$	(.08)	$.15^{***}$	(.06)	$.16^{***}$	(.06)
General Attributions of Crime	.08	(.09)	−.03	(.06)	$.10^{*}$	(.05)
Anti-Black Stereotype	−.02	(.02)	−.01	(.01)	−.01	(.01)
Fear of Crime	.09	(.11)	−.02	(.02)	.05	(.07)
Punitiveness	.01	(.07)	$.15^{***a}$	(.05)	$.11^{**}$	(.05)
Party ID	.10	(.07)	.08	(.05)	.03	(.05)
Ideology	.03	(.06)	−.02	(.04)	.03	(.04)
Education	−.02	(.09)	$-.04^{b}$	(.07)	$.20^{***}$	(.07)
Female	$-.46^{**}$	(.23)	$.42^{***a}$	(.18)	−.12	(.18)
Income	.01	(.08)	.04	(.06)	−.08	(.06)

(continued)

TABLE 5.3. *(continued)*

Table 5.3.A. Whites	Baseline (No Argument)		Racial Argument		Innocent Argument	
Age	−.005	(.01)	.004	(.005)	.002	(.006)
Cutpoint 1	−1.34	(.64)	−.57	(.49)	−.21	(.56)
Cutpoint 2	−.87	(.66)	−.06	(.49)	.34	(.56)
Cutpoint 3	−.19	(.66)	.52	(.49)	1.01	(.57)
N	118		210		218	

*p < .10, **p < .05, ***p < .01

[a] Coefficient is statistically different across baseline and racial argument conditions (≤ .05).

[b] Coefficient is statistically different across innocent and racial argument conditions (≤ .05).

[c] Coefficient is statistically different across race of respondents (≤ .05).

Note: Entries are ordered probit regression coefficients with standard errors in parentheses. Higher values on the preceding variables indicate greater support for death penalty, more dispositional attributions of crime, more negative stereotypes of Blacks than Whites, more fear of crime, more punitive, more Republican, conservative, educated, male, higher income, and older. Statistical significance across the race of the respondent is based on models estimated for each condition pooled across race that included a race dummy and interactions between race and each of the predictors.

Source: NRCS data.

of Table 5.3A), the influence of views of attributions of Black treatment has only a small and statistically insignificant effect on death-penalty approval in the baseline and innocent conditions. When presented with the argument that capital punishment is racially unfair, however, Whites who feel that Black arrest rates are more attributable to the criminal dispositions of Blacks are substantially more likely to support the death penalty than those who attribute blame to a biased justice system.

Among African-American respondents, we find a very different pattern. As demonstrated by the coefficients in the first row of Table 5.3.B, attributions of Black treatment emerges as a robust and statistically significant predictor of death-penalty support in all three experimental conditions. Whether Blacks receive no argument, the innocent argument, or the racial argument, support for the death penalty is significantly lower among those who attribute Black punishment more to a racially biased justice system than to the characteristics of Blacks. Blacks apparently need no explicit prompting to view questions about the death penalty as a racial issue. Their support for the death penalty, regardless of how the issue is framed, is affected substantially by their beliefs about the causes of Black punishment.

Table 5.3 reveals a number of other interesting findings concerning the determinants of death-penalty attitudes.[23] First, anti-Black stereotypes are not significant predictors of death-penalty attitude among either race, which is contrary to the finding of Soss et al. (2003) that prejudice against Blacks is a powerful determinant of death-penalty approval among Whites. One likely reason for the difference is that we include several predictors that Soss et al. do not, namely attributions of Black treatment, which carries the effects of racial stereotyping, as demonstrated in Chapter 3 (Table 3.2).

Another important, though less surprising, finding is that support for the death penalty among both races emanates from a more general desire to punish wrongdoing. In every case but the baseline condition for Blacks, punitiveness plays a statistically significant role in conditioning higher levels of support for capital punishment. Also, consistent with other studies (Tyler and Weber 1982), fear of crime does not significantly elevate death-penalty approval, a result that is constant across all three conditions for Blacks and Whites.

Finally, although the impact of partisanship and ideology is only occasionally significant, various demographic factors play a more reliable and substantial role, even after controlling for a host of attitudinal measures. One is struck, for example, by the powerful role that gender plays in shaping approval of capital punishment – a role that is fully consistent with findings from much of the extant literature (Hurwitz and Smithey 1998; Bohm 2003). Among Whites, males are consistently more supportive of the death penalty than are females, regardless of the presence or type of argument involved. Among Blacks, however, we find a very different pattern for gender. Although Black men express greater support for executing convicted murderers in the baseline condition, when presented with the argument that the death penalty is racially unfair, they become much less supportive of capital punishment than Black women. Although any explanation of this reversal of gender effects is necessarily post hoc, one could speculate that because

[23] Given the modest correlations between attributions of Black treatment, on the one hand, and general attributions of crime and anti-Black stereotypes, on the other (.30 and .22 for Whites; .30 and .26 for Blacks), collinearity has not reduced the precision of the probit estimates, as is confirmed by calculating the Variance Inflation Factor (VIF) for the independent variables of the 6 equations in Table 5.3. The highest VIFs are for control variables and never exceed 2.0, which is well below problematic thresholds for this statistic (e.g., Fox 1991).

Black men receive the brunt of discriminatory treatment in the justice system – whether in the form of racial profiling (see Chapter 2, Table 2.3), police brutality, or death sentencing, when they are explicitly reminded of the racial bias in the system, they are much less supportive of the ultimate punishment relative to Black women.[24]

But what accounts for the "boomerang" or "backlash" effect in response to the racial argument among Whites observed in Table 5.1? As indicated, one likely source of Whites' strong resistance to the racial argument against the death penalty is the tendency for most Whites to believe that Black criminal behavior is caused by dispositional factors. Figure 5.3, designed to better document the power of these beliefs to affect death-penalty support in the racial argument condition, displays a bar chart of the predicted probabilities of Whites' support for the death penalty across the entire range of the attributions of Black treatment scale.[25] One is struck by the steep ascent in strong support for the death penalty as Whites' views on the attributions of Black treatment shift from more structural (i.e., environmental) to more dispositional (i.e., personal). Moving from the lowest (most structural) to the highest (most dispositional) points on the scale, expressions of strongly favoring the death penalty dramatically climb from 28 percent to 64 percent, suggesting a strong negative reaction to the racial argument among many Whites.

Because Whites tend to fall heavily toward the dispositional end of the attributions of Black treatment scale, it is no small wonder that

[24] Although Black women are also subject to numerous forms of negative encounters with police and discriminatory treatment by the justice system, Black men clearly bear the brunt of this treatment (e.g., Miller 1996; Walker et al. 2004), as suggested in Chapter 2 (Table 2.3), where we found that Black men were almost twice as likely to report being treated unfairly by the police than Black women (41% vs. 23%), though the numbers are staggering regardless of gender. Thus, it is not surprising that, when computing the predicted probability of Blacks' approval of the death penalty across gender and argument (baseline vs. racial argument), the changing coefficient for gender in Table 5.5 turns on the drop in support among Black men from 60% in the baseline condition to only 26% in the racial argument condition, while the support of Black women is essentially unchanged (at 43 and 41%, respectively).

[25] Predicted probabilities were generated based on the ordered probit results in Table 5.5, using the Spost program (Long and Freese 2006) for Stata 9.0 by varying attributions of Black treatment and holding other predictors at their sample means.

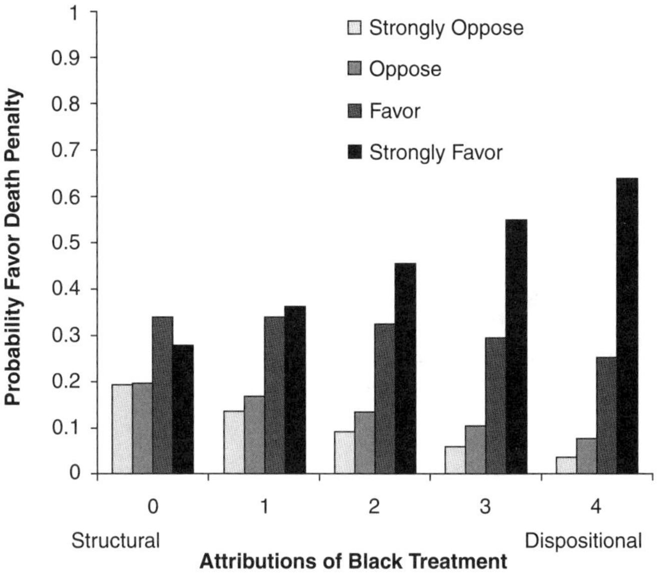

FIGURE 5.3. Whites' probability of death-penalty support for racial argument across attributions of Black treatment.

Note: The figure shows evidence of a "backlash" effect among Whites – that is, how strong support for the death penalty increases in the racial argument condition among Whites with more dispositional attributions of Black treatment.

Source: NRCS data.

when such views are activated (as in the racial argument), Whites collectively are highly resistant to the argument that the death penalty is racially unfair. Many Whites begin with the belief that the reason Blacks are punished is because they deserve it, not because the system is racially biased against them. So when these Whites are confronted with an argument against the death penalty that is based on race, they reject it with such force that they end up expressing more support for the death penalty than when no argument is presented at all. This result is entirely consistent with studies in motivated reasoning and persuasion (e.g., Johnson and Eagly 1989; Taber et al. 2002) that find when people with strong convictions (or who are otherwise highly involved) are presented with arguments that are inconsistent with their prior beliefs, they are likely to reject such arguments so strongly that a negative change occurs – that is, attitude change runs in the direction opposite to the argument.

Predicting Preferred Approaches to Fighting Crime

In the final portion of this chapter, we shift our attention from the specific issue of capital punishment to a more general policy orientation captured by the NRCS question asking respondents to choose which approach they think is "the better way to reduce crime" – by focusing on prevention ("addressing the social problems that cause crime") or punishment ("making sure that criminals are caught, convicted, and punished harshly"). This is an important orientation that presumably underlies attitudes toward a range of specific crime policies. As noted earlier, the public's preference for prevention versus punishment has shifted over time, from a lopsided emphasis on punishment in the mid-1990s to rough parity in support for the two approaches today. More germane to our purposes, when asked to choose, Blacks express more support for prevention versus punishment than Whites do (Figure 5.1).

But what accounts for these interracial differences and, more generally, how can we explain the antecedents of Whites' and Blacks' preferred approach to fighting crime? What attitudinal and social forces push people to more punitive or more preventive strategies? On the attitudinal side, we naturally focus on the two sets of causal beliefs found to influence support for capital punishment: general attributions of crime and attributions of Black treatment. Although it is a safe bet that generic beliefs about the causes of crime influence one's preferred approach to fighting crime, given research cited earlier, anticipating the role of attributions of Black treatment is more difficult. In contrast to the highly racialized issue of the death penalty, general preferences for punishment versus prevention are not necessarily viewed through a racial lens by Blacks and Whites. For many Blacks and Whites, concerns about criminal justice issues exist independently of any associations with race. However, it would be surprising to find that preferences for punitive versus preventative policies have no connection with racial attitudes. The question, then, is how important are attributions of Black treatment for policy attitudes that are not, a priori, linked to race in the public's mind?

Compared to the death-penalty experiment, the format of the "better way" question has advantages and disadvantages for investigating this question. On the one hand, we lack the additional analytic leverage an experiment provides, which makes responses to the question more difficult to interpret in some respects, inasmuch as people were asked only a single, "baseline" variant of the question. On the other hand, we now have the luxury of being able to examine the full sample (rather than subsamples that had been asked different versions of the question), which makes it easier to detect more subtle or complex effects of antecedents that smaller samples are likely to obscure.[26] Specifically, prior research suggests that the influence of racial attitudes varies across social context for both Blacks and Whites. Among Whites, support for more punitive crime policies (e.g., the death penalty and "getting tough" policies) has been linked to a higher concentration of Blacks living in the area (Baumer et al. 2003; Soss et al. 2003), similar to the "racial threat" hypothesis that has been the object of so many studies, reviewed briefly in Chapter 2. Among Blacks, although there has been less research on crime attitudes, living in predominantly Black neighborhoods has been linked to substantially elevated levels of racial consciousness among African Americans (Gay 2004). Among both races, a more "muscular" anti-crime focus should be tied to higher crime rates in the areas where people live (e.g., Baumer et al. 2003; Soss et al. 2003).

For our purposes, we are particularly interested in the various ways that social context influences the strength of the connection between attributions of Black treatment and support for punitive versus preventive strategies to reduce crime. In the same way that varying the argument condition affected the weight of racial attitudes in determining support for capital punishment, so should the social context influence the salience of racial attitudes in shaping responses to the "best way" item.

In Table 5.4, we display the results of an ordered probit analysis, in which we investigate the antecedents of support for preventive versus punitive policies for Blacks and Whites. Our central concern is in the impact of attributions of Black treatment (row 1), percent Black

[26] In prior chapters, one constant has been that when survey experiments were the focus of analysis, we were unable to detect any influence of social context, such as crime rates and census characteristics. Only when pooling death-penalty attitudes over experimental conditions, e.g., do we find that higher county crime rates are associated with greater support for the death penalty among Whites (not reported). The other instances where social context affected responses were analyses of unfair treatment and neighborhood discrimination (Tables 2.3 and 2.4), which utilized the full samples of Whites and Blacks.

TABLE 5.4. *Predicting a better way to reduce crime: prevention vs. punishment*

	Blacks	Whites
Attributions of Black Treatment	.172** (.044)	.185** (.042)
General Attributions of Crime	.242** (.044)	.202** (.039)
Punitiveness	−.078* (.038)	−.115** (.040)
Fear of Crime	.029 (.056)	−.071 (.063)
Anti-Black Stereotype	.005 (.009)	.012 (.012)
Party ID	.045 (.037)	−.021 (.031)
Ideology	−.013[a] (.031)	.119** (.034)
Education	−.122* (.055)	−.095* (.043)
Female	.185[a] (.129)	−.165 (.111)
Age	.005[a] (.004)	−.005 (.003)
Income	−.059[a] (.045)	.076 (.039)
South	.108 (.140)	.086 (.133)
Social Context		
Percent Black (Zip Code)	−.006*[a] (.003)	.002 (.005)
Percent Black*Attributions of Black Treatment	.005**[a] (.002)	.006 (.004)
County Crime Index	.00006*[a] (.00003)	−.00009** (.00003)
Large Metropolitan Area[c]	−.032 (.146)	.095 (.113)
Cutpoint 1	.903 (.449)	−.497 (.410)
Cutpoint 2	1.124 (.450)	−.012 (.410)
Cutpoint 3	1.200 (.450)	.194 (.410)
N	552	557

* $p < .05$, ** $p < .01$

[a] Coefficient is statistically different across race of respondents (≤ .05).

Note: Entries are ordered probit regression coefficients with standard errors in parentheses. Higher values on the preceding variables indicate greater support for punitive policies, more dispositional attributions of crime, more punitive, greater fear of crime, more negative stereotypes of Blacks than Whites, more Republican, conservative, educated, female, higher income, older, living in Deep South, higher percent Black in Zip Code, higher crime rate in county, living in a county with a large metropolitan area. Black treatment and percent Black are centered at their mean value for Whites and Blacks.

Source: NRCS data.

(row 13), and their interaction (row 14). In addition to the predictors included in the capital punishment equations, we include measures of social context and selected interactions with Black treatment, all of which are described in Appendix A.[27]

[27] Prior to forming the multiplicative terms, attributions of Black treatment and percent Black were centered (by subtracting the mean of each variable) so that the coefficients associated with these two variables are identical to those obtained before including the interaction term.

As can be seen by the first row of coefficients, the attributions of the Black treatment variable are an important predictor of preferences for reducing crime, even in the face of stringent controls for more general beliefs about crime (general attributions of crime), punitiveness, and various other attitudinal and demographic predictors. Individuals of both races are much more likely to prefer punitive over preventive policies if they blame Blacks for their harsher treatment, independently of whether they attribute crime in general to dispositional instead of systemic causes. Given the fact that the average White and Black respondent are at opposite ends of the attributions of Black treatment scale (Chapter 2), it is probably more accurate to say that Whites who blame Blacks for their harsher treatment are much less likely to support preventive policies, while Blacks who blame the justice system are much more likely to prefer prevention to punishment as a way to reduce crime.

Overall, judging from the coefficients, the antecedents of preferences for fighting crime are similar for Whites and Blacks, with a few important exceptions. Most critically, among Blacks, but not among Whites, the impact of attributions of Black treatment on crime policy is much greater for Blacks living in predominantly African-American communities.

The interaction is displayed graphically in Figure 5.4, where the predicted probability of strongly preferring prevention versus punishment is plotted across the attributions of Black treatment scale for Blacks who reside in communities (i.e., Zip Codes) of low, average, and high concentrations of African Americans, which correspond to 25, 50, and 75 percent Black. As depicted in Table 5.4, at average levels of percent Black, the impact of attributions of Black treatment (row 1) is comparable for White and Black respondents, though it should be stressed that the average White respondent lives in a Zip Code area where only 8 percent of the residents are Black, whereas the average Black respondent resides in Zip Codes that are 50 percent Black. The important point, however, is that in predominantly Black communities attributions of Black treatment has an even stronger impact in moving African Americans to favor prevention over punishment as the favored method for fighting crime. As one moves from the "blame Blacks" to the "blame system" ends on the Black treatment scale, for example, the percentage of Whites favoring prevention increases from 38 to 66 percent, while comparable percentages for Blacks (in predominantly Black neighborhoods) are 48 and 88 percent. Among African

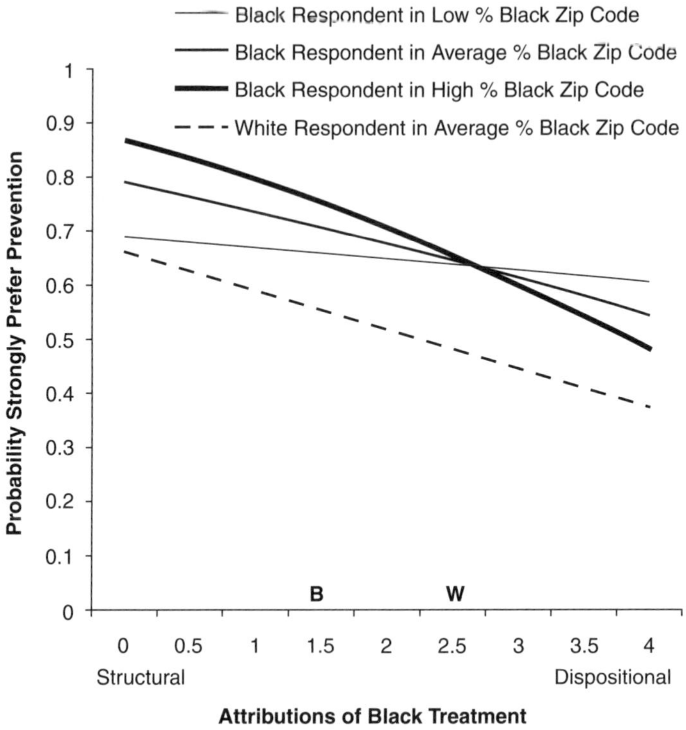

FIGURE 5.4. Probability of strong preference for prevention vs. punishment in order to reduce crime across percent Black.

Note: The figure shows how attributions of Black treatment are more predictive of support for prevention vs. punitive crime policies for Blacks living in neighborhoods (Zip Codes) with higher levels of percent Black. Among Black respondents, low, average, and high percent Black are 25%, 50%, and 75%, respectively. Among Whites, average percent Black = 8%. "B" and "W" indicate group means of Black treatment for Black and Whites. Predicted probabilities are based on ordered probit results in Table 5.4.

Source: NRCS data.

Americans living in neighborhoods with average or low concentrations of Blacks, however, Black treatment is much less consequential, with percentages of Blacks strongly favoring preventive policies rising from 54 to 79 percent (average) and 61 to 69 percent (low).

This interaction is consistent with studies showing that Blacks living in predominantly Black neighborhoods have a higher degree of racial consciousness in the way they approach political issues (e.g., Bledsoe et al. 1995; Gay 2004). They are more likely to share a feeling of common fate with other Blacks, perceive discrimination (Chapter 2), and respond accordingly on criminal-justice issues. By all appearances, African Americans in our survey are acutely aware of the way punitive policies have impacted Black communities, and they have responded by moving away from such punitive measures. Notably, the predispositions of African Americans living in mostly Black neighborhoods are not significantly different from other Blacks; on average, they score about the same on Black treatment (as well as other predispositions) as other Blacks. Rather, it is the weight of attributions of Black treatment on policy preferences that changes.

Another measure of social context – the county crime rate – moves Black respondents in the opposite direction. As expected, Blacks who live in counties with higher crime rates are less likely to support preventive strategies than Blacks who live in lower crime areas, an effect that is depicted graphically in Figure 5.5. Among Whites, however, we find the reverse effect of reported county crime rates. *Ceteris paribus*, Whites who live in counties with lower crime rates are less supportive of preventive policies. This relationship is not entirely unexpected, however. Whites' support for punitive policies has seldom been tied explicitly to realistic fears of crime (Tyler and Boeckmann 1997). Rather, Whites living in safe, predominantly White suburbs may hold the most punitive attitudes, irrespective of any realistic fears about being victimized by crime. For example, Gilliam, Valentino, and Beckmann (2002) found that Whites from predominantly White neighborhoods in Los Angeles were more likely to endorse negative racial stereotypes and more punitive crime policies after watching local television news stories about violent crime featuring Black perpetrators than Whites who were from racially mixed neighborhoods. Although the results of our study are slightly different, in that neither the racial mix of Whites' neighborhoods nor watching local television news were implicated, our findings are certainly consistent, in that social context matters and safe neighborhoods are certainly no guarantee of lower support for punitive crime policies among Whites.

CONCLUSIONS

Although crime-control policy is often regarded as the poster child for the instructed delegate model of policy making, there is abundant

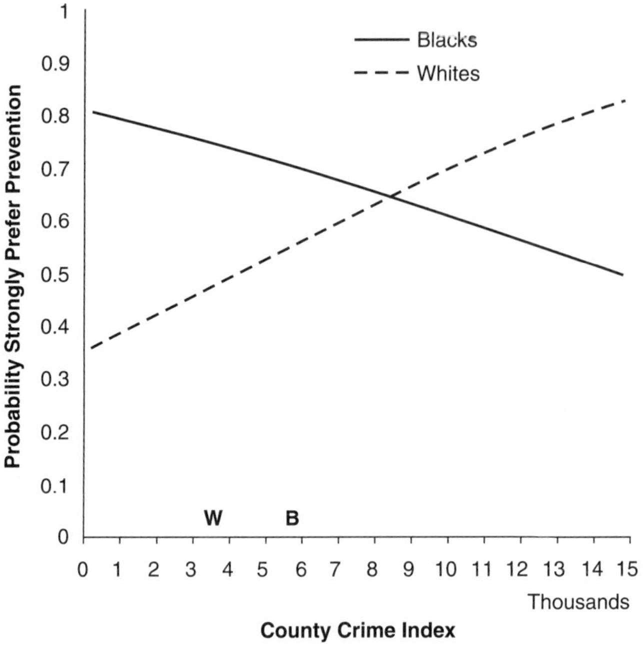

FIGURE 5.5. Probability of strong preference for prevention vs. punishment across county crime rate.

Note: The figure shows how crime rates affect preferences for preventive vs. punitive crime policies differently for Whites and Blacks. "B" and "W" indicate group means of county crime rate. Predicted probabilities are based on ordered probit results in Table 5.4.

Source: NRCS data.

evidence that when crime rates rose during the 1970s and 1980s, elites (i.e., politicians and the mass media) led the charge to even more punitive crime policies, and public opinion followed. When crime rates began to decline in the mid-1990s, public opinion recalibrated, but policy makers have not responded to the decline in support for punitive crime policies. The contemporary public, as represented by our 2001 survey (along with other studies), does not single-mindedly support punitive anticrime policies and reject preventative measures. To the contrary, when people are given a choice between punitive versus preventative instruments for fighting crime, majorities of both races believe that crime is more effectively decreased by addressing underlying social problems, job programs are the preferred method for combating illegal drug use, and money is more effectively used to fund antipoverty programs than to construct prisons. To be sure, support for social programs could wither in the face of conservative invectives about intrusive government programs, or charges of wasteful spending on "midnight basketball" or "welfare" programs. But when asked to choose between balanced alternatives, our respondents expressed a clear preference for prevention versus punishment.

More germane to our purposes, however, is the clear evidence for a racial divide on crime-policy attitudes. For each and every policy examined, Whites advocate more punitive measures than do Blacks. In many instances, the degree of polarization is profound. By large margins, for example, Blacks are more opposed to the death penalty, more supportive of job programs to address drug use, and more disapproving of the three-strikes laws. But what accounts for the high degree of racial polarization in the anti-crime-policy domain? And how is differential support for policies such as the death penalty, the three-strikes laws, and spending for prison construction influenced by the way the policy is framed by elites?

The prison spending experiment showed how an extremely subtle racial cue – the phrase *inner city* – can influence Whites' support for punitive crime policies. When asked whether they favored building prisons to lock up "violent criminals *in the inner city*," Whites were more supportive than if the inner-city reference was omitted, in part, because the implicit racial cue activated Whites' negative stereotypes of Blacks as violent and lazy. In the aggregate, White respondents became more punitive, while Black respondents became less so. The experiment shows not only how easy it is for politicians to inject race into the subtext of political discourse about crime, but also how the same racial cues can move Whites' and Blacks' crime-policy opinions in opposite directions.

In the death-penalty and three-strikes experiments, the opinion divide between Whites and Blacks again increased when the policy was framed along racial lines. What distinguishes these two experiments from the prison experiment, however, is the use of explicit racial frames in which respondents are presented with the argument that the policies are unfair because they are biased against African Americans. In this condition, Blacks move in a direction consistent with the argument, expressing more opposition to the policies, but Whites move in backlash fashion, voicing greater support for punitive policies after hearing that the policies are biased against African Americans.

Across the three experiments we find evidence for a political asymmetry in the power of elites to shape crime preferences by manipulating issue frames. Although it is possible for racial conservatives to "fly under the radar" using implicit racial messages and racially coded phrases, as in the prison spending experiment, racial liberals using explicit racial arguments, like those used in the three-strikes and capital punishment experiments, are likely to encounter a good deal of resistance among White audiences.

The more detailed individual-level analysis of crime-policy attitudes revealed how individuals' prior predispositions contribute to racially polarized opinions regarding two important issues: the death penalty and preferred approaches to fighting crime. One lesson from the individual-level analysis is that interracial divisions in assessments of fairness help drive polarization at the policy level. In the same way that beliefs about system fairness were found to shape differential reactions to crime scenarios in Chapter 4, beliefs about the fairness of Black punishment drive differential support for punitive crime policies. When asked to choose between punitive and preventative approaches to fighting crime, for example, one of the reasons Blacks are more supportive of preventative policies than Whites is that Blacks largely blame Black punishment on the biases of the justice system, while Whites largely blame Blacks for their harsh treatment.

The role of Black punishment is not invariant, however. Rather, its impact on policy attitudes varies across social context and question frames in theoretically explicable ways. For example, the effect of Black punishment on preferred ways to fight crime is much greater for African Americans living in predominantly Black neighborhoods, presumably because racial attitudes are more salient and accessible in highly concentrated Black communities. As a consequence, Blacks diverge more sharply from Whites in their stronger support for preventative (vs. punitive) approaches to fighting crime.

Observing change or constancy in the impact of Black punishment across question frames in the death-penalty experiment also helped to explain interracial differences in support for capital punishment. In contrast to Whites, African Americans connect their policy support regarding this issue to their general views of the way Blacks are treated in the justice system regardless of the way the death penalty is framed. They need no explicit prompting to view questions about the death penalty as a racial issue. In light of their deep suspicions about the fairness of the justice system, it comes as no surprise that African Americans are persuaded by either argument (racial or non-racial) questioning the fairness of the death penalty.

The backlash effect among Whites is also tied to their beliefs about Black punishment. Because most Whites blame Blacks instead of biases in the justice system for their harsh treatment, when such beliefs are activated in the face of an explicitly racial argument against the death penalty, they reject it so strongly they end up expressing more support for the death penalty than when no argument is presented at all.

Our explanation of the backlash effect is rooted in theories of persuasion that implicate people's reactions to arguments that run counter to their strong prior convictions – in this case, the belief that the justice system is not unfairly biased against Blacks. Other interpretations of the backlash effect are possible. The racial argument could activate stereotypes of Black offenders as particularly violent or beyond redemption, thus prompting a more punitive, pro-death-penalty response. Although plausible, this interpretation implicitly assumes that Whites react more to racial stereotypes that are activated than to the argument that the death penalty is unfair. But if Whites were reacting to their images of Black offenders, as suggested by this alternative explanation, surely anti-Black stereotypes would play a more direct role in shaping Whites' responses to the racial argument than we found to be the case.

Still another interpretation of the backlash effect is that it is a "principled" reaction driven by the conservative beliefs held by many Whites about the causes of Black punishment (e.g., Sniderman and Carmines 1997; Feldman and Huddy 2005). As we noted in Chapter 3, however, Whites' beliefs about Black punishment are based more on their anti-Black stereotypes and living in the Deep South than ideology or partisanship. We argued that the popular belief among Whites that Black punishment is attributable to the failings of Blacks, with no real weight given to biases in the criminal justice system, is more appropriately viewed as a form of "laissez-faire racism" (Bobo, Kluegel, and Smith 1997). By denying the discrimination that Blacks face in the justice system, Whites are free to "blame the victim" or turn a blind eye to the many injustices that Blacks suffer at the hands of the police and the courts. Thus, Whites' resistance to racial arguments against the death penalty is likely motivated, at least in part, by racial animus, or at the very least, a mixture of racial insensitivity and ignorance about the reality of discrimination in the justice system.

One important practical implication of our findings is that groups (or politicians) who attempt to mobilize opposition to punitive crime policies, such as the death penalty, the three-strikes laws, and stiffer prison sentences, face an acute political dilemma. Although such groups clearly need the support of Blacks, who are likely to comprise an important part of any reform coalition, direct appeals based on the claim that the policy discriminates against African Americans are likely to create a backlash among Whites who see no real discrimination in the criminal justice system. Because most Whites do not see widespread racial bias in the justice system (or any other domain, see Sigelman and Welch 1991), direct appeals based on claims of discrimination are unlikely to win their support.

The results of the death-penalty experiment suggest that a more effective argument for encouraging opposition to punitive crime policies is one that frames the unfairness of the policy more generally, without focusing on race, thereby avoiding Whites' resistance to more direct racial appeals. For example, in the case of capital punishment, the argument that many innocent people are being executed may not move Whites in great numbers toward opposition, but neither does it precipitate a White backlash. In addition, as we have seen, nonracial arguments (against the death penalty) can and do elicit Blacks' opposition to the policy because many Blacks already have a deep suspicion about the fairness of the legal system. Thus, making more general arguments against the lack of fairness of punitive crime policies without making a direct reference to race may constitute a successful "stealth" strategy that appeals to Blacks but does not produce countermobilization among Whites.

6

Conclusions

Throughout this book, we have recounted multiple and varying instances of African Americans and Whites responding to real-world events (or in some cases vignettes designed to mimic real-world events) in profoundly differing ways. We have documented ways in which the races evaluate the conduct of police officers, see the racial bias of certain policies, and judge the fairness of the criminal justice system so differently.

Perhaps most dramatically, if for no other reason than people read about such things in the papers and see such accounts on television, we have offered example after example of Whites and Blacks differentially interpreting actual events in the justice system, finding that the races almost seem to be responding to different realities. Abner Louima. Amadou Diallo. Reginald Denny. Rodney King. O. J. Simpson. The Jena Six. Time after time, African Americans perceive such instances using one interpretive lens, while Whites use another. Time after time, they come to dramatically different conclusions about the treatment that such individuals received at the hands of the criminal justice system.

The settings and the cast of characters in each of these episodes have doubtless served to racialize the public's responses: before citizens began to interpret the events, the scenarios had largely been defined in racial terms. Louima and Diallo were obvious victims of racial profiling. Denny and King were involved, in different ways, in an instance of race-related police brutality. In the Simpson case, his defense counsel did everything possible to frame the trial as an unfair accusation against an innocent African American made by a racist justice system, insisting that the police, against whom charges of bigotry were leveled, had planted evidence against him. In the tiny town of Jena, Louisiana, the crimes for which the six Blacks were charged were analyzed against the backdrop of the ultimate symbol of racial discrimination and animosity – nooses hanging from a tree.

Nevertheless, even though these instances had been racially defined in various ways, such definitions would have been meaningless had the public not been predisposed to process them racially. Our purpose, throughout this book, has been to address the reasons behind such predispositions – the reasons why Blacks and Whites perceive such wholly different realities in the world of criminal justice, why Whites believe the scales of justice to be balanced and fair, and why African Americans believe them to be so heavily tilted that they cannot possibly receive fair treatment from the police, courts, jury, or White American public. Why has the climate in the United States served to make such racialized interpretations almost inevitable and so utterly dramatic? Criminal justice, after all, is an ostensibly race-neutral domain.

THE TWO PERCEPTUAL REALITIES

In Chapter 3, we distinguished between three different levels at which individuals appraise the fairness of the criminal justice system: at the individual (or neighborhood level), systemic level, and group level. In the first instance, citizens evaluate the degree to which the justice system has treated them (and their neighbors) fairly. In the second, they take a more global perspective, formulating an overall assessment of the performance of the justice system. In the third, they rely on evidence regarding the evenness with which the system has treated various groups (particularly minority groups) in society. We have provided compelling evidence throughout this analysis that, regardless of the level at which fairness is evaluated, African Americans are consistently more cynical relative to Whites.

Individual Fairness

The most likely source of knowledge for individuals evaluating the justice system is personal experience. Citizens can acquire information about the discriminatory nature of the system of the sort discussed in Chapter 2, but such information is likely to pale in comparison with anything encountered firsthand. Given the voluminous evidence that the justice system is riddled with racial discrimination – from the laws to the police enforcement to the treatment of juveniles to the sentencing decisions – it is wholly unsurprising that African Americans often report race-based discriminatory treatment from the police. Thus, we take quite seriously the findings from Table 2.1, documenting a large interracial difference in the occurrence and the frequency in encounters with police officers. Almost 30 percent of African Americans (compared to 13% of Whites) reported unfair encounters – a difference that is surely conservative given the fact that Black respondents were asked only about racially discriminatory treatment while Whites were asked about *any* unfair situation. Not only are Black respondents more likely to report unfair treatment by the police, but they are also more likely to report that such encounters happened on more than one occasion. These data parallel numerous studies of racial profiling of pedestrians and drivers.

These experiences matter for a number of reasons, the most important of which is that they spill over into the evaluations that African Americans form of the criminal justice system in their communities. We asked respondents about the seriousness of problems such as police stopping and questioning Blacks more often than Whites, courts giving harsher sentences to Blacks than to Whites, and police caring more about crimes against Whites than against Blacks in the neighborhood of the respondent. The racial divide could not be more striking: on average (across these 3 questions), fully 70 percent of African Americans, but only 18 percent of Whites, rated these as "serious" problems in the neighborhood. When asked whether "African Americans in your community are treated less fairly than Whites" in dealing with the police, Blacks are more than twice as likely to respond affirmatively (77% vs. 35%).

What is most relevant for our purposes is the close link between the personal experiences of our respondents and perceptions of racial discrimination in the community: African Americans who reported being treated unfairly by the police are substantially more likely to see police discrimination as problematic in the neighborhood. We argue, moreover, that these personal experiences are not merely the biased interpretations of encounters among individuals who have already formed the opinion that there is rampant discrimination in the community. To the contrary, as reported in Appendix B (Table B.1), these personal encounters with the police are independently evaluated as unfair, and such evaluations then spill over into the judgments that African Americans make of law enforcement in the community.

Systemic Fairness

To what extent do personal experiences with the law, or perceptions of fairness in the local community, influence how individuals perceive justice at the system level? As we have shown in Chapter 3, a great deal. We find a strong tendency for individuals of both races to generalize their personal experiences and local perceptions into judgments of the global justice system. As might be expected, African Americans are almost twice as likely as Whites to believe the justice system does not treat everyone "fairly and equally," and substantially more believe that the courts do not provide fair trials to all, the two sentiments comprising our measure of system fairness.

Interestingly, we found that both personal and vicarious experiences are better predictors of Whites' than Blacks' global views of system fairness. On reflection, this makes perfect sense insofar as many Whites doubtless begin with a fairly positive view of the justice system, so relatively rare negative experiences have a jarring effect on their views of the wider system. Among Blacks, however, negative interactions with the police provide only one of many pieces of evidence confirming the discriminatory nature of the justice system. Even Blacks who have not been the target of "driving while Black" or "stop and frisk" encounters, therefore, are likely to have enough information acquired vicariously through family, friends, the media, or community leaders to help them formulate cynical judgments of the broader criminal justice system.

The most important finding, however, is that what happens in the community profoundly influences the evaluations that both races offer of the criminal justice system. When individuals feel that they, personally, have been mistreated by the police, they are substantially more likely to distrust the system as a whole. They are likely to come to similar conclusions when they believe their neighborhoods to be fraught with discrimination.

Group Fairness

Perceptions of the justice system "back home" are doubly consequential: not only do they drive judgments of the broader justice system, but they also influence beliefs about the evenness with which the system treats groups – in this case, African Americans.

There are a number of ways to assess the concept of group fairness, but we took the approach of asking respondents to explain the reasons why African Americans are arrested and imprisoned far more often than Whites (attributions of Black treatment). It is possible to attribute this fact to the disposition of Blacks (they are just more likely to commit crimes, or they do not respect authority) or to the environment – that is, the perception that the criminal justice system is biased against African Americans. Not surprisingly, Blacks are far more likely to attribute higher arrest and incarceration rates to discrimination in the justice system than Whites, who attach much more weight to the characteristics of Blacks, per se (i.e., their criminal nature).

In Table 3.2, we examine the antecedents of attributions of Black treatment. For present purposes, the salient finding is that respondents who perceive discriminatory treatment in the community (most of whom are Black) are more likely – far more likely – to attribute the higher arrest and incarceration rates of African Americans to external rather than internal factors. Conversely, those who do not believe there is much of a problem of police and court discrimination in the neighborhood (most of whom are White) are much more likely to explain the patterns in the justice system as due to the lawless, disrespectful attributes of Blacks, as a group.

We also find that anti-Black stereotypes are strongly associated with a tendency to blame Blacks for their harsher treatment in the justice system and to downplay the role of discrimination, particularly among White respondents, though we noted that these attributions are the product of a variety of beliefs and orientations that are not, on their face, strongly tied to prejudice.

For present purposes, we emphasize three basic conclusions from our analysis of respondents' perceptions of fairness. First, it is difficult to exaggerate the degree to which perceived (and real) bias within the community affects the more global judgments that individuals formulate about the criminal justice system – how it treats African Americans and how, in general terms, the system applies justice in an even-handed manner.[1]

Second, to a certain extent we take issue with the voluminous literature examining citizen evaluations of the justice system (mainly associated with Tom Tyler), which underscores the almost single-minded focus on procedure. Relying mainly on studies of dyadic interactions between citizens and legal authorities, these studies conclude that citizens are more likely to base their evaluations of fairness on the process (e.g., did the police officer treat them fairly and courteously?) than on the outcome (e.g., did they receive a citation?).

We have argued, however, that citizen evaluations of fairness are not based exclusively on police-civilian interactions that are experienced personally but, additionally, are informed by the media, community leaders, educators, and other sources. Among Blacks, for example, along with negative encounters with the police, perceptions of community discrimination and higher education are strong predictors of the belief that the justice system is unfair in general and biased against African Americans in particular. At least for Blacks, therefore, a narrow focus on dyadic relationships misses a great deal of the information to which citizens attend when evaluating the justice system.

Our attributions of Black treatment measure essentially asks respondents to explain the substantially higher levels of Black arrest and incarceration rates (an outcome), and we have shown that Black respondents do so by questioning the process by which such disparate outcomes are generated. Although we are limited in our conclusions because of the correlational nature of our data, the following scenario seems entirely plausible to us: when confronted with such staggering disparities in outcomes, Black respondents frequently attribute these disparities to a justice system that is replete with procedural discrimination. It therefore seems highly likely that evidence of distributive injustice can be used to formulate evaluations of procedural justice, thus

[1] The fact that so many Whites are oblivious to the discrimination that is so widely recognized and experienced by Blacks can be viewed as yet another consequence of hypersegregation in the United States (Massey and Denton 1993; Oliver 2010).

demonstrating how assessments of procedural justice and distributive justice are often inextricably linked in the minds of citizens.[2]

Third, the different "realities" of justice between Blacks and Whites could not be more dissimilar. Blacks far more often have encounters with law enforcement officers, see rampant discrimination in their communities, see the legal system as fraught with bias, and attribute the distribution of legal outcomes to inherent bias in the justice system. By any benchmark in the public opinion literature – whether studies of the gender gap, or even Black-White differences in the economic domain – this chasm is enormous.

THE CONSEQUENCES OF RACIAL DIVISION

Evaluating Actors and Events

Most importantly, these different conceptions of justice in the United States are, to say the least, consequential, for they provide lenses through which Blacks and Whites process information about the criminal justice system in this country. In Chapter 4, we addressed the question of how fairness beliefs shape respondents' reactions to vignettes of police brutality and racial profiling designed to mimic "real-world" incidents in the United States that are highly controversial and potentially incendiary. Specifically, we constructed two vignettes in order to determine whether respondents' were more sympathetic to, and trusting of, the police officer or the civilian in the encounter, and whether such sympathies depend on the race of the latter (which we explored by randomly varying the race of the civilian). In the first (the police brutality experiment), an officer is accused of brutally beating a man, and respondents are asked: 1) if the police will conduct a fair investigation; and 2) the severity of the sentence the officer should receive if found guilty. In the second (the stop-and-search experiment), the police stop and arrest two young men for carrying drugs. Here, we ask whether: 1) the search for drugs is reasonable; and 2) the respondent believes the police (who alleged that

[2] Such a conclusion is consistent with more recent studies in social psychology that find people use outcome as well as process information to form impressions of fairness (e.g., Van den Bos, Lind, and Wilke 2001).

the men were carrying drugs) or the men (who alleged that the police planted the drugs on them).

As expected, for respondents of both races, a general belief in the fairness of the justice system translates into higher levels of trust in, and support for, the police officers: believing the police will conduct a fair investigation in the brutality case and supporting a harsh sentence for the offending officer, viewing the police search of the men as reasonable, and believing the officers (rather than the civilians, who argued that the police had planted drugs on them).

What stood out in the analysis, however, is the way that fairness beliefs were used so differently by Blacks and Whites in interpreting the scenarios. Among African Americans, systemic fairness perceptions do not influence attitudes toward the police when the civilians (those who have been brutalized or subjected to drug searches) are White. However, when the civilian is Black, respondents at the most cynical end of the system fairness scale have difficulty believing that Blacks can be treated fairly and civilly by the police.

Whites exhibit a wholly different set of tendencies. In each case, sympathy for the police officer increases along with a respondent's belief in the fairness of the justice system. Notably, however, Whites make virtually no distinction between Black and White citizens, essentially assuming that the police officers respond to all civilians identically, regardless of color. Collectively, these findings suggest that "fairness" often takes on a radically different meaning for the races. When Blacks are asked about their general assessments of the fairness of the justice system, even though no mention is made of race, they are much more likely to interpret such questions as an evaluation of whether the system is fair and equal to African Americans. Consequently, such beliefs are more likely to be activated when Black respondents are asked about scenarios involving confrontations between the police and Black civilians. White respondents naively think about the fairness of the system and the police in a racial vacuum, as if it is possible to evaluate the justice system without reference to race.

Policy Attitudes

In the subsequent chapter, we examined anti-crime-policy attitudes. We found, on issue after issue, Whites to be significantly more punitive than Blacks – more likely to support the death penalty, believe that the best way to reduce crime is to punish criminals harshly (rather than to address social problems), advocate increasing prison terms (rather than creating better job opportunities) as the preferred way to address the drug problem, support the three-strikes laws, prefer spending money on prisons rather than on antipoverty programs, and favor trying juveniles as adults.

Not surprisingly, policy attitudes are closely linked to perceptions of fairness, at least in the case of the death penalty. In our capital punishment experiment respondents were randomly assigned to one of three groups. All three groups were asked about the death penalty, but those in the "race" condition were informed that it is racially discriminatory, and those in the "innocent" condition were informed that innocent people are sometimes executed.

African Americans, we found, do not need to be reminded of the racially discriminatory nature of the justice system, as evidenced by the fact that those who attribute the higher arrest and incarceration rates for Blacks to bias in the justice system are substantially more oppositional to capital punishment than are those who attribute such outcomes to the unlawful and disrespectful characteristics of African Americans. This is true regardless of the condition to which Black respondents are assigned – that is, regardless of whether they have been reminded of the disproportionate application of the sentence. Whites evaluate capital punishment more selectively, basing their judgments on beliefs about the bias of the justice system only when informed that the penalty is racially discriminatory.

Given the greater distrust of African Americans for the justice system and the tendency of Blacks to link their policy attitudes to this generalized distrust (at least in regard to the death penalty), it would be surprising if we did not find such large interracial differences with respect to policy attitudes. What did surprise us, however, is the ease with which attitudes on seemingly race-neutral policies become racialized. Most dramatically, we saw this in the capital punishment experiment: what began as a 15 percent difference in approval for the death penalty between Black and Whites almost tripled (to 40%) once respondents were informed that the death penalty, according to "some people," is used in a racially discriminatory fashion. African Americans, predictably, became even more oppositional to the penalty, while, shockingly, a nontrivial number of Whites became more supportive once informed that the punishment is administered disproportionately to Blacks.

But we saw polarization effects with other policies, as well, often resulting from extremely subtle cues. When we asked respondents about the preferred way to deal with violent crime, approximately 10 percent more Whites than Blacks selected the more punitive option of building more prisons (rather than funding antipoverty programs). When we asked about the preferred way to deal with inner-city crime, a phrase selected because of its association with African Americans, the interracial difference almost doubles to 19 percent. When we asked about support for the three-strikes laws, which impose mandatory life sentences for individuals convicted of three crimes that meet certain criteria, interracial differences again widened merely by attributing opposition to such laws to certain African Americans (Colin Powel or Jesse Jackson) or by presenting an argument that the laws are racially discriminatory. Thus, not only do Whites tend to be more punitive than Blacks, but also this racial chasm tends to expand as a result of various cues – cues that are a standard part of ordinary political discourse.

Our conclusions become crystal clear against the backdrop of our analyses and findings: what happens to the individual in his or her neighborhood matters. The impressions that are formed from these encounters are generalized to broader views of fairness – that is, whether the citizen believes the system to administer justice fairly to all, and whether she or he believes the system to administer justice fairly to African Americans, in particular. We strongly believe, furthermore, that these perceptions are crucial in understanding the racial chasm in response to incendiary events and to crime policies. Those who are most cynical about justice in America (primarily African Americans) will interpret events in a much more distrusting manner and will be far less willing to endorse certain policies that they believe to be racially discriminatory. To continue the spiral, as they see more of these events and hear more about the bias behind certain policies, their beliefs about the fairness of the justice system become even more negative in nature.

But what of the role of Whites? After all, a chasm can exist only insofar as two parties diverge. Throughout this book, we have used words and phrases such as *naïve* and *color blind* to describe Whites in their evaluations. We used these terms to describe how, in the face of overwhelming (social scientific) evidence to the contrary, many Whites perceive the American justice system as fair and impartial, in large part because such views are consistent with their (personal and vicarious) experiences with the justice system. The terms were used to explain how Whites – at least when evaluating the conduct of police officers in their confrontations with civilians – made almost no distinction depending on whether the civilian was White or African American.

Does this mean that Whites harbor racial prejudice and base their evaluations of justice on a bigoted belief system? To be sure we (and others) have, at a minimum, reasons to wonder – at least in certain cases. Jennifer Eberhardt and her colleagues (2004), for example, have amassed considerable evidence that when Whites are primed to think about African Americans, they will readily see weapons, which is clearly suggestive of a tendency for many Whites to link Blacks with crime – a linkage that doubtless leads to the belief that Blacks are worthy of a more punitive response from our justice system. Further, we found that anti-Black stereotypes are a significant (though not the dominant) source of Whites' overwhelming tendency to attribute the harsh treatment Blacks receive in the justice system to the Blacks, with no real weight given to biases in the system. These attributions – that is, the refusal to acknowledge racial biases in the justice system – were strongly implicated in the "backlash" reaction of Whites to the racial argument against the death penalty that prompted greater support for capital punishment. In some important respects, then, the reactions of some Whites cannot be construed as anything short of blatant bigotry.

However, we are also in agreement with Bobo, Kluegel, and Smith (1997), who have argued that "Jim Crow racism" has been largely replaced by what they term "laissez faire racism." Whites no longer believe that Blacks are biologically inferior, just as they no longer support strict segregation and open discrimination. In the contemporary environment, however, Blacks are still "stereotyped and blamed as the architects of their own disadvantaged status." Although Bobo et al. apply the concept of laissez faire racism primarily to the economic system, it is also eminently applicable to the justice system.

Because most Whites believe the justice system is fair and equitable, no remedial policies are necessary to correct racial disparities or restore an imbalance in racial justice.[3] Believing that the justice system provides equal treatment to all, that it punishes only those individuals who deserve to be punished, and that the punishment fits the crime allows Whites to turn a blind eye toward the many forms of racial injustice that are so pervasive in the Black community. It allows many Whites to be morally offended by staggering rates of Black incarceration because they are seen as further evidence of Black proclivities toward crime. The mere suggestion that the system is racially unfair creates an indignant response among many Whites, who take it as an article of faith that they system is largely color blind.

THE CURRENT POLITICAL CLIMATE

Almost everything about the criminal justice domain is unstable, largely because the ingredients are so fluid. Crime rates, public attitudes, elite responses, consequent policies, and population characteristics change. Additionally, given our argument that the criminal justice arena in the United States is characterized by an extraordinarily high level of racial division, it is essential to add that racial attitudes change.

Given this volatility, we must consider the question of time-boundedness – that is, whether our results are only descriptive of the late twentieth century and very early twenty-first century or, instead, are descriptive of a more general condition in this country. We see three reasons to wonder about the generalizability of our results. First, it is quite possible that crime stories less frequently saturate the news today, having become less salient for several reasons. For one thing, the crime rate has been inching downward over the last decade and the American public may be consequently less worried about crime. For another, since the attacks of September 11, 2001 and the recession of 2008 and 2009, other, more pressing concerns may have pushed crime toward the back burner on the

[3] There is an obvious, though imperfect, parallel between Whites' opposition to measures designed to address racial economic inequality (e.g., affirmative action) and their opposition to proposals to reforming racial disparities in the justice system.

political agenda. To the degree that crime has become less salient, Whites may be less often bombarded with news images associating race and crime, and Blacks may be less concerned with the problems of racial profiling and discrimination in the justice system.[4] Additionally, it is possible that some of the anticrime legislation enacted (or more rigorously enforced) during preceding years, much of which disproportionately punished African Americans, may be reconsidered in the presence of declining rates of crime. If so, the extraordinarily high levels of cynicism we have found among Blacks may begin to abate.

The second and third reasons are made salient by the elections of 2008, which not only gave citizens their first real opportunity to vote for an African-American presidential candidate but also propelled into office Barack Obama, Joe Biden, and a democratically controlled bicameral legislature. The second potential catalyst for change, therefore, may have been afforded by this historic event. As we have argued repeatedly, Whites and African Americans are so polarized because many Whites believe the system to be fair (choosing to attribute the higher arrest and incarceration rates of Blacks to their personal failings) and because many Blacks profoundly distrust a justice system that they believe to be biased against them. Although the meaning of the 2008 election remains unclear, it is worth asking whether: 1) Whites have begun to shed some of their racial stereotypes and prejudices, as evidenced by their willingness to vote for an African-American presidential candidate;[5] and 2) as a consequence

[4] The premise of this question – that the crime rate has declined – is undeniably true. The violent crime rate, e.g., has been edging downward in the United States since 1994 and hit a two-decade low in 2004 (see, e.g., http://www.ojp.usdoj.gov/bjs/homicide/hmrt.htm), with much smaller increases thereafter (http://www.fbi.gov/ucr/prelim2007/table3.htm). Criminologists agree that the decline in crime was real, not some statistical artifact; debate among scholars has centered on parsing the relative contribution of several factors implicated in lowering crime rates, such as the expanding prison population, a smaller youth population, economic prosperity, and changes in policing. According to Zimring (2007, 197), "the crime decline of the 1990s was a classic example of multiple causation, with none of the many contributing causes playing a dominant role."

[5] To be precise, 43% of Whites voted for Obama vs. John McCain in the 2008 general election, up from 41% who voted for Kerry vs. Bush in 2004 and 42% for Gore vs. Bush in 2000. The point is that many more Whites voted for an African-American presidential candidate than anyone thought possible just a decade earlier.

of the outcome, the high levels of Black cynicism will gradually wane with an African American at the highest level of power. If either of these transpires, it is likely that the racial chasm will begin to narrow.

Third, even if the public remains largely unmoved by the changing salience of crime and if the 2008 electoral results reveal little about shifting public sentiments, the elections may well serve another function – that is, providing a wholesale turnover in the policy environment and the new cast of characters charting public policy in the country. When he was governor of Texas, for example, George W. Bush took pride in presiding over a state with, by far, the highest use of capital punishment in the country.[6]

President Obama, by contrast, has come from a background in community organizing – a background that exposed him to the realities of life in the inner city. Vice President Biden has acknowledged his regret for supporting the Anti-Drug Abuse Act of 1986, which "contributed to the incarceration of more than a half-million people in state and federal prisons for drug offenses" (Fears 2009, A04).[7] With both chambers controlled by more liberal and more democratic legislators, who are also more likely to represent minority constituents and metropolitan areas, the possibility of meaningful policy change is real. Because current anticrime policies almost surely fuel the discontent of so many African Americans, meaningful changes to these policies have the potential to spur significant reductions in their levels of cynicism and despair.

Thus, with the declining salience of crime, a public that has perhaps begun (or will soon begin) to modify its beliefs, and the election of elites who have shown tendencies toward less punitive orientations, we must address the question of whether our results are time-bound to the last years of the twentieth century and the very early years of the twenty-first century. We take up each of these three possibilities, in turn.

[6] In 1999 and 2000, George W. Bush's last two full years as governor, nearly half (47%) of all executions in the United States were carried out in Texas (Snell 2001).

[7] This is in contrast to the 40,000 jailed for such offenses in 1980. At the time of the passage of the bill, Biden was the ranking minority member on the Senate Committee on the Judiciary.

Changing Salience of Crime?

We do not expect falling crime rates to serve as a catalyst for change for, as noted in Chapter 5, public concern about crime tends to remain high even in the face of falling levels. In every year since Gallup first asked the questions, the percentage of Americans who thought there was "more crime in the U.S. than a year ago" outnumbered those who felt there was less crime (1989–2007), and a majority of the public described crime in the United States as either a "very" or "extremely" important problem (2000–7). Inasmuch as public concerns and fears about crime are shaped more by local news coverage than actual crime rates (Lowry et al. 2003; Romer et al. 2003), the salience of crime is likely to continue as long as it remains the most heavily covered topic on local broadcast news,[8] which is still the most popular news source in the United States (Prior 2007).[9] Although, as we contend in the following text, anticrime policies may be in transition, there is little if any evidence that such changes are attributable to actual crime statistics.

But what about the contemporary experience of African Americans, for whom police misconduct and racial profiling doubtless contributed to declining support for the justice system? In the post-9/11 environment, with the nation's collective attention focused on broader security concerns, and with the late-decade recession spotlighting severe economic problems, are Blacks more trusting of the police? The available evidence, though sporadic, suggests that the racial divide in attitudes toward law enforcement is as severe today as a decade ago. Barely a year after 9/11, for example, Blacks were markedly less trusting of the police than Whites, with only 42 percent of non-Whites saying they have a "great deal" or "quite a lot" of confidence in the police, compared to 62 percent of Whites.[10] In their study of attitudes toward the police conducted in late 2002, Weitzer and Tuch (2006)

[8] Taken from "Local TV Content, A Day in the Life, Annual Report 2006." http://www.journalism.org/node/536 (accessed December 7, 2009).

[9] In addition, recall that in Chapter 5 we found that Whites living in counties with lower crime rates were more, not less, supportive of using punitive vs. preventive measures to reduce crime.

[10] See http://www.gallup.com/poll/7078/Racial-Divide-Crime-Police-Protection.aspx (accessed January 3, 2010).

found huge racial differences in the tendency for Blacks (44%) versus Whites (4%) to report "being stopped by the police because of their race." For Blacks and Whites, then, we do not expect changes in the salience of crime – due either to declining crime rates or to the emergence of other more pressing issues onto the national agenda – to play a significant role in narrowing the race gap in the justice system.

A Shift in Public Attitudes?

Is it reasonable to assume significant changes in public attitudes either before or after the 2008 election – changes that would serve to narrow the race gap? Put differently, is there reason to assume that Whites demonstrated with their vote that they had begun to abandon some of the stereotypes (or perhaps prejudices) that predispose them to blame African Americans, rather than a biased justice system, for the enormous differences in punitive outcomes? Or do we have reason to predict that Blacks will become less cynical about the criminal justice system given the electoral outcome?

As for African Americans, we have repeatedly documented the sense of frustration and even anger expressed by many Blacks, who simply feel that the justice system is discriminatory, which is based largely on their experiences with the police and courts at the local level. Although it is certainly possible that Obama's electoral victory may have a ripple effect in ameliorating such feelings directed toward the justice system, such a possibility is purely conjectural at this point. As we go to press, it is far too early to assess whether, or to what degree, Blacks may become more efficacious and less cynical given the outcomes of the 2008 elections. Simply, we do not yet know whether an African American in the White House will make much of a difference to the views of Black citizens about justice in America.

Can we take any comfort from the results of the election, when substantial numbers of Whites did something that would have been out of the question only decades ago – that is, vote for a Black man for the presidency? Again, it is too soon to tell. We do not, however, take much comfort from the preliminary evidence, which suggests that Whites' support for Obama was quite racialized: those who supported him exhibited significantly lower levels of prejudice than those who did not (Piston 2010; Tesler and Sears 2009).[11] Although we do not claim that the stereotypes and prejudices of Whites are unchanged, we do claim that, at least in the aggregate, the 2008 election did not provide much evidence of any meaningful shift.

Moreover, even if the percentage of the Whites endorsing anti-Black stereotypes has dipped slightly in recent years, what really matters is the extent to which the issue of crime is associated with race in the minds of Whites. Recent studies of Whites' policy attitudes toward welfare suggest that despite dramatic changes in the policy environment, timeworn associations between Whites' policy attitudes and racial stereotypes are remarkably resistant to change. What is so striking about the changes in welfare policy that took place in 1996, when then-President Clinton signed reform legislation designed to, in his words, "end welfare as we know it," is that many reformers hoped that by imposing stringent limits on lifetime benefits and adding work requirements to qualify for assistance, stereotyping of the poor and African Americans would decline and public support for welfare would increase. But despite these changes, public opposition toward welfare among Whites has remained high and is as rooted in racial attitudes as it was more than a decade ago (Soss and Schram 2007; Dyck and Hussey 2008). The strong implication is that the associations between race and crime in the public's mind are likely to be resistant to change.

The Changing Policy Environment

Even in the absence of any changes in the beliefs of the American public (fueled either by the declining salience of crime or by the 2009 election), we must address the question of time-bounded results as a consequence of changes in the elite policy environment. With the seismic change in state and national politics resulting from the 2008 elections, there are surely reasons to expect changes in the racialization of justice in America. It is crucial to note that policy change is often formulated almost independently of any alterations in mass preferences. As noted by Bartels (2008), there are numerous instances of

[11] These results are based on both conventional (i.e., racial resentment) and unobtrusive (i.e., list experiment) measures of prejudice.

policies in which elites have resisted public support for change, either by leaving somewhat unpopular programs intact (e.g., the estate tax) or by seriously eroding programs that the public strongly supports (e.g., an increase in the minimum wage).

Additionally, the 2008 election certainly provided no clear evidence to political elites that the American mass public wanted change in any policies that could be considered either crime or race related. In the general election, Barack Obama ran almost entirely on race-neutral issues, seldom even mentioning race except when necessary to do so.[12] When allegations emerged about Obama's association with the Reverend Jeremiah Wright, whose extremely controversial statements were labeled as anti-American and anti-Semitic, Obama denounced the statements and, eventually, the reverend. We do not believe, therefore, that the election could possibly be interpreted by the elite as anything even approaching a mandate for either racial or judicial change.

Nonetheless, there is no denying that the elite policy environment has changed considerably in recent years, essentially in the absence of any public catalyst. Even before the election one could find considerable evidence that policy makers at all levels had begun to take a fresh look at the draconian policies of previous eras, as then-Senator Biden was the lead sponsor of a bill (with the cosponsorship of then-Senator Obama) in the 110th Congress to eliminate the 100-to-1 sentencing disparity for using comparable quantities of powder and crack cocaine, respectively – a disparity built into the anti-Drug Abuse Act of 1986. Since the election, serious reform proposals are receiving attention, endorsement, and even, in notable cases, unilateral implementation. Senators Obama and Biden have assumed the positions as the leaders of their party and their government. The Obama administration has taken the most forceful position possible in its declaration that the sentencing discrepancy should be eliminated entirely. As expressed by Attorney General Eric Holder, in remarks to the Washington, D.C., Court of Appeals:[13] "It is the view of this Administration that the

[12] During the primaries in 2007, candidate Obama spoke about racial disparities in the incarceration of Black men ("we still have more young black men in prison than in college") to liberal and Black audiences (e.g., the NAACP and a fund-raiser in Harlem [Dobbs, *Washington Post*, December 14, 2007]), but such statements were noticeably absent in the general election.

[13] Delivered June 19, 2009.

100-to-1 crack-powder sentencing ratio is simply wrong. It is plainly unjust to hand down wildly disparate prison sentences for materially similar crimes. It is unjust to have a sentencing disparity that disproportionately and illogically affects some racial groups." Additionally, support for reform is increasingly bipartisan in nature, with even conservative Republicans agreeing on the need for sentencing equalization (Mauer 2009).[14]

It is not just the executive and legislative branches that are in the process of rethinking criminal justice policy. The U.S. Supreme Court ruled in 2005 that sentencing guidelines are not mandatory but, instead, advisory.[15] Two years later, it found that district judges could impose less severe sentences than recommended by such guidelines (Cose 2009).[16] Recently, these decisions have led to the beginnings of a trickle-down effect, with federal district court judges in Iowa and the District of Columbia citing the Supreme Court to justify imposing sentences for crack-cocaine users that were commensurate with those given to powder-cocaine users (*Washington Post* 2009).

Granted, much of the interest in reform is being driven by the view, as expressed by Attorney General Holder, that certain policies are "simply wrong" and "plainly unjust." But, as with any policy environment ripe for change, other factors have come into play. In large part, the federal government and, especially, state governments are forced to confront serious budgetary constraints, made far worse as a result of the deep recession that began in 2008. According to a study published by the Pew Charitable Trusts (2008), total spending on corrections topped $49 billion in 2007, up from $12 billion two decades earlier. Continued prison growth is expected to cost states an additional $25

[14] The federal government is poised to address more than just drug sentencing guidelines. During the same week in June 2009, two congressional committees held hearings on two important criminal justice bills. The House Committee on the Judiciary, Subcommittee on Crime, Terrorism, and Homeland Security held hearings on H.R. 2289, the Juvenile Justice and Accountability Improvement Act of 2009, which is designed to eliminate sentences of juvenile life without parole. Of even greater potential importance, only two days later the Senate Committee on the Judiciary, Subcommittee on Crime and Drugs held hearings on the National Criminal Justice Commission Act of 2009 (S. 714), which would establish a blue-ribbon commission to conduct an 18-month comprehensive review of the nation's criminal justice system, culminating in a report offering concrete recommendations.

[15] *U.S. v. Booker* 125 S.Ct. 738 (2005)

[16] *Kimbrough v. U.S.* 128 S.Ct. 558 (2007)

billion by 2011 (Pew Charitable Trusts 2007). California alone spent $8.8 billion on corrections in 2007, an inflation-adjusted 216 percent increase from its 1987 level.[17]

States are now responding by finding numerous ways to cut the costs of incarceration. Although there is no simple solution, approaches include alternate sentencing (e.g., community service and alcohol awareness programs), prisoner-reentry programs (e.g., job training and drug rehabilitation) in order to reduce high rates of recidivism, and early release to parole and probation officers (Richburg 2009).[18]

There is no guarantee that the justice system's approach to crime in the United States will undergo the types of changes that now look quite feasible. It will always be the case that elected officials will cower when they believe they may be labeled "soft on crime." Nonetheless, severe economic problems coupled with a wholesale change in national political leadership have set the stage for profound policy changes. To the degree that drug penalties are made more equitable and prison populations (which are now disproportionately African American) are reduced, the widespread cynicism on the part of so many Blacks that we have recorded may begin to decline.

[17] The lion's share of these increases are a consequence of the antidrug legislation passed during the 1980s. But cost considerations are causing policy makers to take a second look at other laws. It is not just that corrections facilities are spending more because they have so many more prisoners. They are also spending more because of prisoner lawsuits demanding everything from more sanitary conditions to dental care to more nourishing food and better libraries. But the largest single cost-per-prisoner increase is attributable to rising health care expenses, and these expenses are driven overwhelmingly by the aging prison population resulting from the three-strikes laws.

[18] Still another potential catalyst for change is the availability of new, and better, information about the causes and consequences of drug abuse today. As an example, the Anti-Drug Abuse Act of 1986, a key provision of which was the 100-to-1 cocaine-crack penalty, was passed with very little debate in Congress, and almost immediately signed into law by President Reagan. In large measure, the bill resulted from the shocking death of Len Bias, a collegiate basketball player whom the Boston Celtics drafted as their first-round choice that year – a death reported as due to a crack overdose. Tip O'Neill, the Speaker of the House and a devoted Celtics fan, used a myriad of parliamentary maneuvers to spearhead the bill through Congress, justifying it on the grounds that crack is a far more potent drug relative to powder cocaine. It is now known, however, that: 1) the two forms of cocaine are, gram-for-gram, pharmacologically equivalent; and 2) Bias died from an overdose of powder, not crack, cocaine.

Contemporary Racial Disparities

In short, the available evidence suggests that, although the criminal justice environment in the United States may be on the verge of change in some respects, we can make no predictions regarding either the possibility or the likelihood of such changes. We can only describe the reality that exists today: despite falling crime rates, incarceration rates in the United States have climbed to the highest level in the country's history. By almost any standard, the United States is the most punitive nation in the world. According to the 2008 Pew study,[19] "The United States incarcerates more people than any country, including the far more populous nation of China. At the start of the new year [2008], the American penal system held more than 2.3 million adults. China was second, with 1.5 million people behind bars, and Russia was a distant third with 890,000 inmates.... America is also the global leader in the rate at which it incarcerates its citizenry, outpacing nations like South Africa and Iran."[20] This same study reports (page 5) that, over the past thirty years, our inmate population has more than tripled, so that, as of this writing, more than one in one hundred Americans is now behind bars.

Although these data, taken alone, are staggering, they are germane to our study less because of what they reveal than because of what they obscure – namely, the astonishing racial disparities in the prison population. Among White men eighteen or older, one in 106 is imprisoned, while the comparable figure for Black men is one in fifteen. Among Black men between twenty and thirty-four years of age, fully one in nine are behind bars.[21] According to Mauer's (2006) projections, almost one-third of Black males born at the beginning of the twenty-first century will spend at least some time incarcerated (compared to 6% of White males).

[19] Pew Center on the States. "One in 100: Behind Bars in America 2008." http://www.pewcenteronthestates.org/uploadedFiles/One%20in%20100.pdf (accessed December 28, 2009).

[20] According to Pew (35), the total penal population of the United States (2,245,189) is far in excess of that found, combined, in all of the 26 countries in Europe with the largest inmate populations (1,842,115), despite the fact that our total population is more than 500 million residents smaller than theirs.

[21] Among females, the disparities are also enormous: in the 35 to 39 age group, e.g., 1 in 355 White women and 1 in 100 Black women are incarcerated (Pew 34).

How much of this racial discrepancy is due to unequal rates of law violation is unclear. What *is* clear, however, is that almost every aspect of law enforcement has had the effect of apprehending and punishing African Americans far more so than Whites. Equally disturbingly, these inequalities are worsening due, in large measure, to the draconian drug laws that went into effect in the mid-1980s – laws that launched the twenty-year increase in our prison population.

Even if such policies are modified or repealed, the problem does not begin to disappear. Although there may have been no intentional de jure discrimination in the drug policies, there is no denying the resultant de facto discrimination. In her compelling account of the impact of the war-on-drugs on racial disparities under the law, Provine (2007) argues convincingly that the 100-to-1 powder-crack cocaine provision only begins to describe the story. It is not just that crack (used disproportionately by Blacks) is punished much more severely than powder cocaine (used disproportionately by Whites),[22] it is, more importantly, that crack abuse has become targeted: with "the 1986 Anti-Drug Abuse Act and its 1988 counterpart ... Congress intended, and law-enforcement agencies received [strong economic incentives to] focus as many resources as possible on crack arrests, including arrest and prosecution of small-time users and sellers" (120).

But *targeting* does not mean merely targeting the drug; it also means targeting the underclass that tends to use the drug. Overwhelmingly, police resources are devoted to poor, inner-city neighborhoods (e.g., Beckett et al. 2006), a choice that makes little sense if, for no other reason, than cities and states seem to devote few other resources (e.g., infrastructure repair, hospitals, sanitation, libraries, or schools) disproportionately to such communities. Further, even though a larger percentage of African Americans than Whites may use crack rather than powder cocaine, the majority of documented crack users is White. Still, in 2003, 81 percent of all individuals sentenced for crack offenses were Black (Provine 2007, 5).[23]

Not only is the policy unjust in many ways, but the sheer financial considerations are staggering. According to the Pew Study (2008, 12),

[22] Provine (2007, 3) notes that "crack ... is punished more severely in the federal system, with an average term of ... almost nine years, than most violent offenses."

[23] Citing King (2006, 8).

inflation-adjusted state expenditures on corrections have more than doubled during this recent war on drugs, increasing (in 2007 dollars) from $19.38 billion in 1987 to $44.06 billion by 2007.[24] It is not surprising, therefore, that states are forced to cut back dramatically on other discretionary spending programs. To cite just one example, Pew estimates (32) that in 2007, for every dollar states spent on higher education, they spent sixty cents on corrections. By way of contrast, they spent thirty-two cents in 1987.

Tom Tyler's claims to the contrary, it would be astonishing if African Americans focused only on procedural justice in their perceptions of such realities. With one-third of African-American men likely to serve at least some prison time, it almost does not matter if the laws, and the enforcement of the laws, are procedurally unfair. The bottom line is that many Blacks see such outcomes and quite naturally come to the conclusion that the criminal justice system simply *is* unfair. But to most Whites, who believe that the system dispenses proportionate punishment to Blacks who break the law, the fairness of the system is seldom called into question.

BRIDGING THE RACIAL DIVIDE?

This leads us to an even more troubling question: just how enduring is the racial divide in the justice domain? Is the deep gulf separating the races likely to remain a permanent fixture in America? Or is there a way to somehow bridge the attitudinal divide? Most importantly, is there reason to hope that African Americans' faith in the fairness of the justice system can be restored? Is there reason to hope that Whites will begin to understand more of the concerns that Blacks face in their encounters with the courts and the police?

As will become clear, there are no easy answers to these questions. Because Black Americans' cynicism is based on real disparities in the way the races are treated by the justice system, only genuine policy changes can begin to restore their confidence that the system is fair.

[24] These figures are based only on direct costs, such as prison construction and mandatory health care for inmates. They do not include considerations such as state welfare expenditures to families required because the father is unable to pay child support while imprisoned.

At the same time, however, any wholesale change in criminal justice policies will likely require the support of the dominant White majority, and as we have seen repeatedly, Whites, until very recently, have not been terribly proactive in this respect.

One possible scenario for change would target procedural justice by changing the way police officers interact with civilians, especially Blacks who, far more often than Whites, are subject to demeaning, unfair, and discriminatory treatment. Because these confrontations are generalized to a more basic suspicion that the entire justice system is unfair, which then may "loop back" to bias perceptions of later encounters with the police, it is vital to break this spiral by implementing several policy changes at the national and local levels, such as placing restrictions on racial profiling, empowering civilian review boards, and the increasing the use of community-oriented policing. Although our study shows that an overwhelming majority of Whites and Blacks oppose the practice of racial profiling (Chapter 5), it is doubtful whether Whites would support a change in policing if it were opposed by local law enforcement. Although Weitzer and Tuch (2006) found that a majority of Whites support plans for more police accountability (e.g., civilian review boards and stronger punishment for misconduct) in the abstract, they also found that many Whites are staunch champions of the police and are more concerned with providing resources and removing restrictions so the police can "do their job."

We have argued that citizens do not define justice strictly in procedural terms. Other strategies for restoring Blacks' faith in the justice system must therefore focus on distributive justice by attempting to reduce the staggering incarceration rate of African Americans in the United States. It is hard to imagine Blacks ever concluding that the system is fair when one of every nine Black men in his twenties has been incarcerated. As our persuasion experiments in Chapter 5 clearly demonstrate, however, any appeals to Whites to reconsider punitive crime policies (e.g., three-strikes laws and capital punishment) based on the argument that Blacks are treated unfairly are destined to fall on deaf ears. The considerable evidence of criminologists notwithstanding, most Whites believe the harsher treatment Blacks receive is fully justified and even deserved. Because such racial arguments tend to create a "backlash" effect among Whites, they were found to be counterproductive, moving Whites in the aggregate to greater support for the three-strikes laws and the death penalty.[25]

If a multiracial coalition is essential to achieving a reduction in Black incarceration, and if Whites resist the claim that high incarceration rates are unfair to Blacks, we are left to consider a race-neutral argument that high rates of imprisonment are somehow unjust or unwise for all, not just Blacks. Such a "stealth" strategy can help Blacks disproportionately while at the same time steering clear of a White backlash. One possible scenario for change would capitalize on the significant shift in public support for anticrime policies documented in Chapter 5, where several surveys showed the public has backed away from its reflexive support for punitive crime measures. Faced with an altered climate of public opinion, as well as a policy environment that includes state budget crises, prison overcrowding, and a falling crime rate, policy makers are seemingly revisiting some of the more draconian policies passed in the 1980s and 1990s, such as the three-strikes laws and drug laws that send so many young Black men to prison.

Yet, despite the flurry of elite activity in the criminal justice arena, reform movements can only go so far. Most obviously, state and federal elites are quite clearly preoccupied with myriad other concerns that the public now considers more salient – concerns including two wars in the Middle East, the most serious economic crisis since the Great Depression, and attempts to overhaul the health care system.

Additionally, even though the public has clearly tempered its support for punitive anticrime measures, we have found that a significant portion of Whites, often a majority, still approves policies like the three-strikes laws (70%), increasing prison terms for people who sell drugs (49%), and capital punishment for convicted murderers (65%). Moreover, it is doubtful that the new political realities can, by themselves, move the public to decrease its support for punitive policies.

[25] It is also doubtful whether standard strategies for reducing prejudice (e.g., Monteith et al. 2002) could be applied successfully to correct the belief among Whites that Blacks deserve the harsher punishment they receive. Even though we found beliefs about Black treatment to be associated with anti-Black stereotypes, it seems clear, based on their responses to the persuasion experiments, that most Whites do not view their beliefs about Black treatment as either prejudicial or incorrect. Rather, Whites are likely to feel a degree of moral certitude in asserting that Black offenders, like anyone else, should "do time for the crime."

As mounting evidence in a variety of policy domains clearly indicates, mass policy attitudes seldom change in direct response to events (e.g., Zaller 1992; Berinsky 2009). Rather, events such as war casualties and domestic crises are "mediated" by elite reactions, interpretations, and messages.

In order to move public opinion decidedly on crime policy, elites must help lead the way. But contemporary reform attempts notwithstanding, it remains highly unlikely that elected officials are willing to shift from a fundamentally punitive orientation to one that is based on prevention, treatment, and rehabilitation. Such positions have not been taken up seriously by either major party since the 1988 presidential election, when Democratic Party candidate Michael Dukakis lost in a landslide, in part, it was believed, because his opposition to capital punishment allowed the Republicans to portray him as weak on crime. In every election since, national Democratic Party candidates have adopted the position that anything less than full-throated support for punitive policies is tantamount to political suicide.

It is hard to overemphasize how skewed and one-sided political discourse regarding criminal justice policies has been in the United States for the last twenty years. One striking example is the defeat of the ballot measure known as Proposition 66 in California in the general election in November 2004. Proposition 66 was an initiative designed to scale back significantly parts of California's three-strikes sentencing law – not to neuter it, but simply to bring it in line with the twenty-four other states that have three-strikes laws by making sure that the third offense, which triggers a twenty-five-year-to-life sentence, is limited to serious or violent crimes. Currently, even crimes not defined as serious or violent can count as a third strike, leading, for example, to the sentencing of an individual to fifty years without parole for stealing children's videotapes from Kmart (Murphy 2004).

According to veteran observers, the fact that Proposition 66 even got on the ballot in California was deemed remarkable, for "any two-sided debate about three strikes is a real novelty in California" (Murphy 2004). Despite the attraction of helping to alleviate the state's severe prison-overcrowding problem and saving the state hundreds of millions of dollars from being spent on warehousing nonviolent criminals, the ballot initiative failed after Governor Schwarzenegger and

California's county district attorneys actively opposed it. Although optimists might view Proposition 66 as evidence of a shift in the debate, we think it illustrates a more pessimistic conclusion: without more elite support for scaling back some of the most draconian and costly laws in the nation's legal system, there is little hope of moving the public to support more general reforms. It is hard for us to envision a workable stealth strategy for reducing the staggering rates of Black incarceration.

It is possible that our pessimism is unwarranted. Few would have anticipated sixty years ago, that, given the climate of public opinion at both mass and elite levels, the United States would enter and survive the tumult of the civil rights movement and elect an African-American president. Although much of the success of the movement came from the extraordinary leadership of individuals like the Reverend Martin Luther King Jr., as well as the tireless efforts of countless civil rights activists, much of it came from unexpected quarters: President Harry Truman who, as a descendent of members of the Ku Klux Klan, nevertheless integrated the uniformed armed forces after World War II; Hubert Humphrey, who electrified and alienated many of those attending the Democratic National Convention in 1948 with his speech imploring the party to take a prointegration stance; Earl Warren, a Republican governor nominated by a Republican president, who is largely credited with the accomplishments gained through the federal judiciary; and Lyndon Johnson, a Democrat mainly with ties to Southern Democrats, who oversaw more civil rights legislation than any other president in American history. There is no reason to discount the possibility that comparable leaders will make comparable contributions to reform in the U.S. criminal justice system. We are waiting.

Appendix A

National Survey and Survey Items

NATIONAL SURVEY

The survey data for the analysis are from the National Race and Crime Survey (NRCS), a nationwide random-digit telephone survey administered by the Survey Research Center (SRC) at the University of Pittsburgh. Between October 19, 2000 and March 1, 2001, the SRC interviewed 603 (non-Hispanic) Whites and 579 African Americans. White respondents were selected with a variant of random-digit dialing and an oversample of Black respondents was randomly selected using stratified sampling techniques. The number of completed interviews was 1,182 for an overall response rate of 48.64 percent.[1] The interviews, which averaged approximately thirty minutes, were conducted using Computer Assisted Telephone Interviewing (CATI) facilities, enabling the interviewers to randomize respondents into experimental treatment groups in an almost infinite number of configurations. For most respondents (90%), the race of the interviewer was matched to that of the respondent in an effort to minimize social desirability bias from race of interviewer effects (e.g., Davis 1997).

The survey instrument was subject to extensive pretesting, consisting of in-depth, face-to-face "cognitive interviews" with a small number of African-American respondents and telephone interviews with twenty-five White and twenty-five Black respondents.

[1] Response rate calculated by the Response Rate 3 formula (RR3) of the American Association of Public Opinion Research, http://www.aapor.org (accessed December 7, 2009).

SAMPLE

The NRCS sample roughly approximates the 2000 Census on key demographic characteristics, such as family income and educational attainment, as can be seen in Table A.1. The NRCS tends to overrepresent females among Blacks and Whites. Sample weights were applied, but the significance of the reported coefficients in the analyses was never altered. Thus, the unweighted sample is used throughout.

SURVEY ITEMS

FAIRNESS MEASURES

Unfair Treatment

African-American respondents: Was there any time in the last five years or so when you felt you were treated unfairly in dealing with

TABLE A.1. *NRCS sample characteristics and 2000 Census, percentages*

Family Income	Blacks NRCS	Blacks 2000 Census	Whites NRCS	Whites 2000 Census
	100%	100%	100%	100%
<10K	13.3	14.7	4.2	3.6
10K–20K	13.3	15.8	8.4	7.4
20K–30K	20.6	15	12.7	10.4
30K–50K	28.7	22.5	27.9	23.2
50K–75K	14	17	23.3	24
75K–100K	6.9	8	11	13.9
>100K	3.2	7	12.5	17.5
Education (25 yrs+)	100%	100%	100%	100%
< 9	1.3	8	1.1	4.6
9–12, No Grad	12.3	19.8	4	10
High School Grad	31.6	29.8	28	30
Some College, No Degree	28.6	28.2	28.9	28.5
BA Degree	15.7	9.5	22.8	17.2
Advanced Degree	8.05	4.8	12	9.8
Sex	100%	100%	100%	100%
% Male	36.6	47.4	40.6	48.9
% Female	63.4	52.6	59.4	51.1

the police, such as being stopped or followed while driving because you were African American? (If "yes": Did this happen once, two, or three times, or more?)
White respondents: Was there any time in the last five years or so when you felt you were treated unfairly in dealing with the police, such as being stopped or followed while driving? (If "yes": Did this happen once, two, or three times, or more?)

Neighborhood Discrimination

Perceived seriousness of neighborhood discrimination: Now I'm going to read you several statements that some people make about problems with the justice system in their community. As I read each one, please rate how serious it is in your community on a seven-point scale, where 1 means it is not a problem and 7 means it is a serious problem. The first statement is:

Police who stop and question Blacks far more often than they stop Whites.
Courts that give harsher sentences to African Americans than to Whites.
Police who care more about crimes against White people than crimes against minorities.[2]
Blacks treated less fairly?: Just your impression, do you feel that African Americans in your community are treated less fairly than Whites in the following situations? (Options: Yes, No, Don't Know, Refused)
In stores downtown or in the shopping mall?
On the job?
In dealing with the police, such as traffic incidents?

System Fairness

The justice system in this country treats people fairly and equally.[3]
The Courts can usually be trusted to give everyone a fair trial.

[2] Only items (a) and (b) were included in the neighborhood discrimination scale used as an independent variable in Chapter 3.
[3] This, and all Likert format items provide, as response options: strongly agree, somewhat agree, somewhat disagree, and strongly disagree. "Uncertain" was not an option offered to respondents, although we did record "don't know" or "uncertain" responses if volunteered.

Attributions of Black treatment

Statistics show that African Americans are more often arrested and sent to prison than are Whites. The people we talk to have different ideas about why this occurs. I'm going to read you several reasons, two at a time, and ask you to choose which is the MORE IMPORTANT reason why, in your view, Blacks are more often arrested and sent to prison than Whites. (Options: respondents were asked to select one or the other; although we did not provide "uncertain" or "can't decide" as options, we did record them if volunteered.)

The police and justice system are biased against Blacks, OR Blacks are just more likely to commit crimes.

The police and justice system are biased against Blacks, OR many younger Blacks don't respect authority.

GROUP PERCEPTIONS

Anti-Black stereotypes

(Ratings of "most Whites" are subtracted from ratings of "most Blacks"): Now I'll read a few words or phrases that people sometimes use to describe different groups in our society. First, I'll ask about words that are sometimes used to describe [Blacks/Whites]. Of course, no word fits absolutely everybody, but, as I read each one, please tell me using a number from 1 to 7 how well you think it describes MOST [BLACKS/WHITES]. If you think it's a VERY POOR description of MOST [BLACKS/WHITES], give it a 1. If you feel the word is a VERY ACCURATE description of MOST [BLACKS/WHITES], give it a 7. And, of course, you may use any number in between. First, what about lazy? Prone to violence? Prefer to live on welfare? Hostile? Dishonest?

Anti-Semitism

Now I'm going to read some statements different people have made about Jews. Please tell me how much you agree or disagree with each one (reverse coded).

Most Jews are more willing than other people to use dishonest practices to get ahead in life.

Most Jews don't care what happens to people who aren't Jewish.

POLITICAL PREDISPOSITIONS

Party identification

We used the standard seven-point scale ranging from "Strong Democrat" to "Strong Republican."

Ideology

We used the standard seven-point scale ranging from "Strong Liberal" to "Strong Conservative."

CRIME-RELATED ATTITUDES AND BEHAVIORS

General attributions of crime

The people we talk to have different reasons for crime in America these days. I am going to read you several reasons, two at a time, and ask you to choose the one you feel is the MORE IMPORTANT cause of crime.

First, do you feel crime is caused more by poverty and lack of opportunity, OR by people being too lazy to work for an honest living?

Poverty and lack of opportunity, OR because many younger people don't respect authority?

Punitiveness

Parents need to stop using physical punishment as a way of getting their children to behave properly (reverse coded).

One good way to teach certain people right from wrong is to give them a good stiff punishment when they get out of line.

Fear of crime

How worried are you about you or a family member of your family being a victim of a serious crime? Would you say you are: very worried, somewhat worried, only a little worried, or not worried (reverse coded)?

Local news

How often do you watch local television news? Do you watch local news every day, three or four times a week, once or twice a week, or hardly ever (reverse coded)?

DEMOGRAPHIC AND SOCIOECONOMIC INDICATORS

Education
What is the highest grade or level of education you have completed? Eighth grade or less, grades 9–11, high school graduate/GED, some college or postsecondary school, bachelor's degree (BA/BS/BSN), Some graduate study, master's degree (MA/MS/MSW/MSN), doctoral degree (Ph.D./MD/OD/DVM/JD)

Gender
Female = 0; Male = 1

Age

Marital Status:
Single = 0; Married = 1

Income
Which of the following best describes the combined yearly income of all members of your household before taxes? Just stop me when I get to the category that applies to your household: under $10,000; $10,000 to just under $20,000; $20,000 to just under $30,000; $30,000 to just under $50,000; $50,000 to just under $75,000; $75,000 to just under $100,000; over $100,000

South
0 = non-South; 1 = South, defined as residing in one of the following states: Alabama, Arkansas, Florida, Georgia, Louisiana, Mississippi, North Carolina, South Carolina, Texas, or Virginia

CONTEXTUAL VARIABLES

Percent Black (in Zip Code of respondent)

County crime index
Number of index crimes (murder, rape, robbery, aggravated assault, burglary, larceny, and automobile theft) reported in the Uniform Crime Report in 2000 per 100,000 residents of the county of respondent

Large metropolitan area
Whether respondent lives in a county located in a metropolitan area with a population of at least one million residents

Median income (in Zip Code of respondent)

POLICE VIGNETTES

Police brutality experiment

There was a recent incident in Chicago in which a police officer was accused of brutally beating a [White/Black] motorist who had been stopped for questioning. The police department promised to investigate the incident.

How likely do you think it is that the police department will conduct a fair and thorough investigation of the policeman's behavior? Would you say very likely, somewhat likely, somewhat unlikely, or very unlikely?

If he is found guilty of beating the motorist, how should the policeman be punished – should he be fired, sentenced to one year in prison, or be sentenced to two or more years in prison?

Stop and search experiment

In another incident, the police see two young [African-American/White] men about twenty years old. They are walking very near a house where the police know drugs are being sold. The police search the two men and arrest them for carrying drugs.

Do you think this is definitely a reasonable search, probably a reasonable search, probably not a reasonable search, or definitely not a reasonable search?

Who are you more likely to believe in this case – the police, who claim the two men were carrying drugs, or the two men, who claim the police planted the drugs on them? Are you much more or somewhat more likely to believe them [two men or police]?

ANTI-CRIME-POLICY ATTITUDES

Capital Punishment Experiment

Respondents randomly assigned to one of three conditions:

Baseline: Here is a question about the death penalty. Do you strongly oppose, somewhat oppose, somewhat favor, or strongly favor the death penalty for persons convicted of murder?

Racial argument: Baseline question preceded by: Some people say that the death penalty is unfair because most of the people who are executed are African Americans.
Nonracial argument: Baseline question preceded by: Some people say that the death penalty is unfair because too many innocent people are being executed.

Best way to reduce crime
Some people say that the best way to reduce crime is to address the social problems that cause crime, like poverty and joblessness. Other people say the best way to reduce crime is to make sure that criminals are caught, convicted, and punished harshly. What about you? If you had to choose, which is the better way to reduce crime – to address social problems, or to catch and punish criminals harshly?[4]

Racial profiling
In many areas of the country, police officers use a practice known as racial profiling, where they stop and question Black motorists because the officers believe Blacks are more likely to commit certain types of crime. Do you strongly approve, somewhat approve, somewhat disapprove, or strongly disapprove of racial profiling?

Drug Problem Experiment
Respondents are randomly assigned to one of two conditions:
Some people think that the best way to deal with the drug problem is to increase prison terms for people who sell drugs. Others think that the best way to deal with the drug problem is to provide better job opportunities. What about you?
Some people think that the best way to deal with the drug problem in inner-cities is to increase prison terms for people who sell drugs. Others think that the best way to deal with the drug problem in inner-cities is to provide better job opportunities. What about you (reverse coded)?

Three-Strikes Laws Experiment
Let me ask you a question about the three-strikes laws, where anyone convicted of a third serious crime is sent to prison for the rest of their

[4] Branch format: after question answered, respondent then asked if she or he feels "strongly or not so strongly" about answer.

life. (Respondents are now randomly assigned into one of three source cue groups [some people/Jackson/Powell] and, independently, into one of two argument groups [prosecutors are more likely to use them against Blacks than against Whites/many people are sent to prison for life for committing three less serious crimes like drug possession].) [Some people/Some people like Jesse Jackson/Some people like General Colin Powell] oppose these laws because [prosecutors are more likely to use them against Blacks than against Whites/many people are sent to prison for life for committing three less serious crimes like drug possession]. Other people favor these laws because they keep repeat offenders in prison for life where they can't commit more crimes. What about you? Do you strongly approve, somewhat approve, somewhat disapprove, or strongly disapprove of these three-strikes laws?

Prison Experiment

Respondents are randomly assigned to one of two conditions:
Some people want to increase spending for new prisons to lock up violent criminals. Other people would rather spend this money for antipoverty programs to prevent crime. What about you?
Some people want to increase spending for new prisons to lock up violent inner-city criminals. Other people would rather spend this money for antipoverty programs to prevent crime. What about you (reverse coded)?

Juvenile justice

Some people think that if juveniles commit serious or violent crimes they should be tried as an adult and have to serve the same punishment adults do. Others think that juveniles committing serious or violent crimes should not be treated as adults because there needs to be more emphasis on rehabilitation. What about you?

Appendix B

Examining Reciprocal Effects of Unfair Treatment and Neighborhood Discrimination

In our analysis in Chapter 2 (Table 2.4), we regard unfair treatment as exogenous to perceptions of neighborhood discrimination, even though perceptions of discrimination, or procedural unfairness, may conceivably influence interpretations of experiences with legal authorities (e.g., Lind and Tyler 1988). To determine whether our assumption of exogeneity is reasonable, we estimated a simultaneous equations model in which unfair treatment by police and neighborhood discrimination are reciprocally related. To identify the model, we excluded female, age, and married from the neighborhood discrimination equation and anti-Black stereotypes and anti-Semitism from the unfair treatment equation. We estimated this model using two-stage least squares. The estimates are shown in Table B.1. As can be seen, unfair treatment continues to have a significant impact on neighborhood discrimination (although the standard error for the coefficient increases), while the coefficient for neighborhood discrimination on unfair treatment is small and insignificant. Although estimating possible reciprocal effects is more critical for Blacks, we display similar estimates for Whites as well.

TABLE B.1. *TSLS analysis of unfair treatment and police stopping Blacks more*

	Blacks				Whites			
	Neighbor Discrimination		Unfair Treatment		Neighbor Discrimination		Unfair Treatment	
Neighbor Discrimination			.037	(.054)			.11	(.061)
Unfair Treatment	1.03*	(.50)			1.58	(.84)		
Anti-Black Stereotype	−.063**	(.021)			−.041	(.033)		
Anti-Semitism	−.28**	(.076)			−.24**	(.092)		
Party ID	−.40**	(.089)	.0074	(.035)	−.014	(.067)	.0067	(.012)
Ideology	.015	(.070)	−.051**	(.020)	−.27**	(.080)	.017	(.023)
Education	.21	(.12)	.060	(.036)	−.0058	(.094)	−.013	(.020)
Female			−.36**	(.086)			−.071	(.054)
Age			−.011**	(.0025)			−.0064**	(.0017)
Married			−.064	(.087)			−.11	(.063)
Income	−.32**	(.11)	.0091	(.035)	−.11	(.085)	.015	(.022)
South	−.048	(.32)	−.017	(.094)	−.21	(.30)	.041	(.068)
County Crime Index	−9.7e-05	(6.5e-05)	3.9e-05*	(1.8e-05)	.00015*	(7.4 e-05)	2.4e-06	(1.85e-05)
Percent Black (Zip Code)	.33*	(.16)	−.028	(.053)	.18*	(.074)	−.029	(.018)
Large Metropolitan Area	.21	(.33)	−.012	(.099)	.89**	(.26)	−.14	(.074)
Constant	12.0**	(1.00)	.67	(.74)	7.63**	(.85)	−.040	(.48)
F	10.87**		15.97**		8.46**		5.80**	
Partial R-squared	.046		.074		.066		.032	
N	561		561		593		593	

*p < .10, **p < .05, ***p < .001

Note: Coefficients are two-stage least squares estimates, with robust standard errors in parentheses. Anti-Semitism was assessed by agreement with two Likert items: "Most Jews are more willing than other people to use dishonest practices to get ahead in life" and "most Jews don't care what happens to people who aren't Jewish," coded so that higher values indicate greater anti-Semitism.

Source: NRCS data.

References

Controlled Substances Act.

Chicago v. Morales. 1997. In *NE 2d*: Illinois Supreme Court.

Chicago v. Morales. 1999. In *US*: U.S. Supreme Court.

Pratt v. Chicago Housing Authority. 1994. In *F. Supp.*: Northern District of Illinois.

"One in 100: Behind Bars in America 2008." 2008. Washington, D.C.: Pew Charitable Trusts.

"Public Safety, Public Spending: Forecasting America's Prison Population, 2007–2011." 2007. Washington, D.C.: Pew Charitable Trusts.

Abramson, Paul R., John Herbert Aldrich, and David W. Rohde. 1991. *Change and Continuity in the 1988 Elections.* Washington, D.C.: CQ Press.

Albonetti, Celesta A. 1997. "Sentencing under the Federal Sentencing Guidelines: Effects of Defendant Characteristics, Guilty Pleas, and Departures on Sentence Outcomes for Drug Offenses, 1991–1992." *Law and Society Review* 31 (4): 789–822.

Allen, Richard L., Michael C. Dawson, and Ronald E. Brown. 1989. "A Schema-based Approach to Modeling an African-American Racial Belief System." *American Political Science Review* 83 (2): 421–41.

Altheide, David L. 2002. *Fear: News and the Construction of Crisis.* New York: Aldine de Gruyter.

Applebaum, Lauren D. 2001. "The Influence of Perceived Deservingness on Policy Decisions Regarding Aid to the Poor." *Political Psychology* 22: 419–42.

Applegate, Brandon K., Francis T. Cullen, Michael G. Turner, and Jody L. Sundt. 1996. "Assessing Public Support for Three-Strikes and You're-Out Laws: Global versus Specific Attitudes." *Crime and Delinquency* 42: 517–34.

Asher, Herbert. 1980a. "Presidential Elections," in *Academic American Encyclopedia*. Princeton, NJ: Arete Publishing Company.

———1980b. *Presidential Elections and American Politics: Candidates, and Campaigns since 1952*. Rev. ed. Homewood, IL: The Dorsey Press.

Austin, James. 1995. "The Overrepresentation of Minority Youths in the California Juvenile Justice System," in *Minorities in Juvenile Justice*, ed. K. K. Leonard, C. E. Pope, and W. Feyerherm. Thousand Oaks, CA: Sage Publications: 153–78.

Azzi, Assaad E. 1992. "Procedural Justice and the Allocation of Power in Intergroup Relations: Studies in the United States and South Africa." *Personality and Social Psychology Bulletin* 18: 736–47.

Bachman, Ronet. 1996. "Victim's Perceptions of Initial Police Responses to Robbery and Aggravated Assault: Does Race Matter?" *Journal of Quantitative Criminology* 12: 363–90.

Baldus, David C., Charles Pulaski, and George Woodworth. 1983. "Comparative Review of Death Sentences: An Empirical Study of the Georgia Experience." *Journal of Criminal Law and Criminology* 74: 661–753.

Barrett-Howard, Edith, and Tom R. Tyler. 1986. "Procedural Justice as a Criterion in Allocation Decisions." *Journal of Personality and Social Psychology* 50: 296–304.

Bartels, Larry M. 2008. *Unequal Democracy: The Political Economy of the New Gilded Age*. Princeton, NJ: Princeton University Press.

Baumer, Eric P., Richard Rosenfeld, and Steven F. Messner. 2003. "Explaining Spatial Variation in Support for Capital Punishment: A Multi-Level Analysis." *American Journal of Sociology* 108: 844–75.

Baumgartner, Frank R., Suzanna De Boef, and Amber E. Boydstun. 2004. An Evolutionary Factor Analysis Approach to the Study of Issue-Definition. Paper presented at Annual Meeting of the Midwest Political Science Association, April 15–18, Chicago.

Beckett, Katherine. 1997. *Making Crime Pay: Law and Order in Contemporary American Politics*. New York: Oxford University Press.

Beckett, Katherine, and Theodore Sasson. 2004. "Crime, Politics and the Public: The Sources of Mass Incarceration in the U.S.A." *The Japanese Journal of Sociological Criminology* 29: 27–49.

Beckett, Katherine, Kris Nyrop, and Lori Pfingst. 2006. "Race, Drugs and Policing: Understanding Disparities in Drug Delivery Arrests." *Criminology* 44 (1): 105–38.

Behrens, Angela, Christopher Uggen, and Jeff Manza. 2003. "Ballot Manipulation and the 'Menace of Negro Domination': Racial Threat and Felon Disenfranchisement Laws in the United States." *American Journal of Sociology* 109: 559–605.

Berinsky, Adam. 2009. *In Time of War: Understanding American Public Opinion from World War II to Iraq*. Chicago: University of Chicago Press.

Black, Donald, ed. 1980. *The Manners and Customs of the Police*. New York: Academic Press.

Black, Donald J., and Albert J. Reiss Jr. 1970. "Police Control of Juveniles." *American Sociological Review* 35 (1): 63–77.

Bledsoe, Timothy, Susan Welch, Lee Sigelman, and Michael Combs. 1995. "Residential Context and Racial Solidarity among African Americans." *American Journal of Political Science* 39: 434–58.

Blumstein, Alfred. 1982. "On the Racial Disproportionality of United States' Prison Populations." *Journal of Criminal Law and Criminology* 73: 1259–81.

Bobo, Lawrence. 1997. "Race, Public Opinion and the Social Sphere." *Public Opinion Quarterly* 61 (1): 1–15.

Bobo, Lawrence D., and Devon Johnson. 2004. "A Taste for Punishment: Black and White Americans' Views on the Death Penalty and the War on Drugs." *Du Bois Review* 1: 151–80.

Bobo, Lawrence D., and James R. Kluegel. 1993. "Opposition to Race-targeting: Self-interest, Stratification Ideology, or Racial Attitudes." *American Sociological Review* 58: 443–64.

Bobo, Lawrence D., James R. Kluegel, and Ryan A. Smith. 1997. "Laissez Faire Racism: The Crystallization of a 'Kinder, Gentler' Anti-Black Ideology," in *Racial Attitudes in the 1990s: Continuity and Change*, ed. S. A. Tuch and J. K. Martin. Greenwood, CT: Praeger: 15–44.

Bobo, Lawrence, Camille L. Zubrinsky, James H. Johnson Jr., and Melvin L. Oliver. 1994. "Public Opinion before and after a Spring of Discontent," in *The Los Angeles Riots: Lessons for the Urban Future*, ed. M. Baldassare. Boulder, CO: Westview Press: 103–34.

Bodenhausen, Galen V. 1988. "Stereotypic Biases in Social Decision Making and Memory: Testing Process Models of Stereotype Use." *Journal of Personality and Social Psychology* 55: 726–37.

Bohm, Robert M. 2003. "American Death Penalty Opinion: Past, Present and Future," in *America's Experiment with Capital Punishment*, ed. J. Acker, R. Bohm, and C. Lanier. Durham, NC: Carolina Academic Press.

Bonczar, Thomas P. 2003. "Bureau of Justice Statistics Special Report: Prevalence of Imprisonment in the US Population, 1974–2001." Washington, D.C.: U.S. Department of Justice.

Borg, Sami. 1995. "Electoral Participation," in *The Impact of Values*, ed. J. W. V. Deth and E. Scarbrough. New York: Oxford University Press.

Bottoms, Anthony. 1995. "The Philosophy and Politics of Punishment and Sentencing," in *The Politics of Sentencing Reform*, ed. C. M. Clarkson and R. M. Clarkson. Oxford: Clarendon Press.

Brace, Paul, and Brent D. Boyea. 2008. "State Public Opinion, the Death Penalty, and the Practice of Electing Judges." *American Journal of Political Science* 52: 360–72.

Brace, Paul R., and Melinda Gann Hall. 1997. "The Interplay of Preferences, Case Facts, Context, and Rules in the Politics of Judicial Choice." *The Journal of Politics* 59 (4): 1206–31.

Brewer, Marilynn B., and Rupert J. Brown. 1998. "Intergroup Relations," in *The Handbook of Social Psychology*, ed. D. T. Gilbert, S. T. Fiske, and L. Gardner. Oxford: Oxford University Press.

Brewer, Paul R. 2001. "Value Words and Lizard Brains: Do Citizens Deliberate about Appeals to Their Core Values?" *Political Psychology* 22: 45–64.

Bridges, George S. 1997. "A Study on Racial and Ethnic Disparities in Superior Court Bail and Pre-Trial Detention Practices in Washington." Olympia: Washington State Minority and Justice Commission.

Bridges, George S., and Sara Steen. 1998. "Racial Disparities in Official Assessments of Juvenile Offenders: Attributional Stereotypes as Mediating Mechanisms." *American Sociological Review* 63: 554–70.

Bridges, George S., Darlene J. Conley, Rodney L. Engen, and Townsand Price-Spratlen. 1995. "Racial Disparities in the Confinement of Juveniles: Effects of Crime and Community Social Structure on Punishment," in *Minorities in Juvenile Justice*, ed. K. K. Leonard, C. E. Pope, and W. Feyerherm. Thousand Oaks, CA: Sage Publications.

Brokner, J., and B. M. Wiesenfeld. 1996. "An Integrative Framework for Explaining Reactions to Decisions: Interactive Effects of Outcomes and Procedures." *Psychological Bulletin* 102: 189–208.

Bureau of Justice Statistics. 1999a. "Capital Punishment 1997." Washington, D.C.: U.S. Department of Justice.

———1999b. "U.S. Department of Justice Sourcebook of Criminal Justice Statistics." Washington, D.C.: U.S. Department of Justice.

———2000. "National Crime Victimization Survey," in *National Crime Victimization Survey (NCVS) Series*. Washington, D.C.: U.S. Department of Justice.

——— September 2004. "Criminal Victimization, 2003." ed. U.S. Department of Justice (NCJ 205455). Washington, D.C.: U.S. Department of Justice.

Burstein, Paul. 2003. "The Impact of Public Opinion on Public Policy: A Review and an Agenda." *Political Research Quarterly* 56: 29–40.

Butler, Paul. 1995. "Racially Based Jury Nullification: Black Power in the Criminal Justice System." *Yale Law Journal* 105: 677–725.

———1997. "The Role of Race Based Jury Nullification in American Criminal Justice." *John Marshall Law Review* 30: 911–22.

Bynum, Timothy S., Gary W. Cordner, and Jack R. Greene. 1982. "Victim and Offense Characteristics: Impact on Police Investigative Decision-Making." *Criminology* 20: 301–18.

Callanan, Valerie J. 2005. *Feeding the Fear of Crime: Crime-Related Media and Support for Three Strikes*. New York: LFB Scholarly Publishing.

Campbell, Alec, Richard A. Berk, and James J. Fyfe. 1998. "Deployment of Violence: The Los Angeles Police Department's Use of Dogs." *Evaluation Review* 22: 535–61.

Canes-Wrone, Brandice, and Kenneth W. Shotts. 2004. "The Conditional Nature of Presidential Responsiveness to Public Opinion." *American Journal of Political Science* 48: 690–706.

Caplow, Theodore, and Jonathan Simon. 1980. "Understanding Prison Policy and Population Trends." *Journal of Criminal Law and Criminology* 64: 198–207.

———1999. "Understanding Prison Policy and Population Trends" in "Prisons," ed. Michael Tonry and Joan Petersilia, special issue, *Crime and Justice* 26: 63–120.

Cardwell, Diane, and Sewell Chan. November 28, 2006. "Mayor Calls 50 Shots by the Police 'Unacceptable.'" *New York Times.*

Carmines, Edward, and James Stimson. 1980. "The Two Faces of Issue Voting." *American Political Science Review* 74: 78–91.

Chiricos, Ted G., and Charles Crawford. 1995. "Race and Imprisonment: A Contextual Assessment of the Evidence," in *Ethnicity, Race, and Crime: Perspectives across Time and Place*, ed. D. F. Hawkins. Albany: State University of New York Press.

Chiricos, Ted G., and Sarah Eschholz. 2002. "The Racial and Ethnic Typification of Crime and the Criminal Typification of Race and Ethnicity in Local Television News." *Journal of Research in Crime and Delinquency* 39: 400–20.

Chiricos, Theodore G., and William D. Bales. 1991. "Unemployment and Punishment: An Empirical Assessment." *Criminology* 29: 701–24.

Chong, Dennis, and James N. Druckman. 2006. "Democratic Competition and Public Opinion." Paper presented at Annual Meeting of the American Political Science Association, August 31–September 3, Philadelphia.

Christopher, Warren, ed. 1991. "Report of the Independent Commission on the Los Angeles Police Department" (The Christopher Commission). Upland, PA: Diane Publishing Co.

Citizens for Independent Courts Task Force on the Role of the Legislature in Setting the Power and Jurisdiction of the Courts. 2000. "Uncertain Justice: Politics and America's Courts: The Reports of the Task Forces of Citizens for Independent Courts," in *Uncertain Justice: Politics and America's Courts.* New York: Century Foundation Press.

Clark, Patrick M. 1985. "Perceptions of Criminal Justice Surveys, Executive Summary." Lansing: Michigan Prison and Jail Overcrowding Project.

Cochran, John K., and Mitchell B. Chamlin. 2005. "Can Information Change Public Opinion?: Another Test of the Marshall Hypotheses." *Journal of Criminal Justice* 33: 573–84.

Cochran, John K., Denise Paquette Boots, and Kathleen M. Heide. 2003. "Attribution Styles and Attitudes toward Capital Punishment for Juveniles,

the Mentally Incompetent, and the Mentally Retarded." *Justice Quarterly* 20: 65–93.
Cohn, Steven F., Steven E. Barkan, and William E. Haltman. 1991. "Punitive Attitudes toward Criminals: Racial Consensus or Racial Conflict?" *Social Problems* 38: 287–96.
Conley, D. 1994. "Adding Color to a Black and White Picture: Using Qualitative Data to Explain Racial Disproportionality in the Juvenile Justice System." *Journal of Research in Crime and Delinquency* 31: 135–48.
Conover, Pamela. 1988. "The Role of Social Groups in Political Thinking." *British Journal of Political Science* 18: 51–76.
Conover, Pamela Johnston, and Stanley Feldman. 1981. "The Origins and Meaning of Liberal/Conservative Self-Identifications." *American Journal of Political Science* 25 (3): 617–45.
Converse, Philip E. 1964. "The Nature of Belief Systems in Mass Publics," in *Ideology and Discontent*, ed. D. Apter. New York: Free Press: 206–61.
Cose, Ellis. 2009. "Closing the Gap: Obama Could Fix Cocaine Sentencing." *Newsweek*, July 20, 25.
Crawford, Charles, Ted Chiricos, and Gary Kleck. 1998. "Race, Racial Threat, and Sentencing of Habitual Offenders." *Criminology* 36 (3): 481–511.
Crew, Keith. 1991. "Race Differences in Felony Charging and Sentencing: Toward an Integration of Decision-making and Negotiation Models." *Journal of Crime and Justice* 14: 99–122.
Crutchfield, Robert D., George S. Bridges, and Susan R. Pitchford. 1994. "Analytical and Aggregation Biases in Analyses of Imprisonment: Reconciling Discrepancies in Studies of Racial Disparity." *Journal of Research in Crime and Delinquency* 31: 166–82.
Cullen, Francis T., Bonnie S. Fisher, and Brandon K. Applegate. 2000. "Public Opinion about Punishment and Corrections." *Crime and Justice* 27: 1–79.
Cullen, Francis T., John Paul Wright, Shayna Brown, Melissa M. Moon, Michael B. Blankenship, and Brandon K. Applegate. 1998. "Public Support for Early Intervention Programs: Implications for Progressive Policy Agenda." *Crime and Delinquency* 44: 187–204.
Cureton, Steven R. 2001. "Determinants of Black-to-White Arrest Differentials: A Review of the Literature," in *The System in Black and White: Exploring the Connections between Race, Crime, and Justice*, ed. M. W. Markowitz and D. D. Jones-Brown. Westport, CT: Praeger: 65–71.
Curran, Barbara A. 1977. "The Legal Needs of the Public: The Final Report of a National Survey." Chicago: American Bar Foundation.
Dannefer, Dale, and Russell K. Schutt. 1982. "Race and Juvenile Justice Processing in Court and Police Agencies." *American Journal of Sociology* 87: 1113–32.
Davis, Darren W. 1997. "The Direction of Race of Interviewer Effects among African-Americans: Donning the Black Mask." *American Journal of Political Science* 41: 309–22.

Davis, Darren W., and Brian D. Silver. 2003. "Stereotype Threat and Race of Interviewer Effects in a Survey on Political Knowledge." *American Journal of Political Science* 47: 33–45.

Dawson, Michael C. 1994. *Behind the Mule: Race and Class in African-American Politics*. Princeton, NJ: Princeton University Press.

Delgado, Richard. 1994. "Rodrigo's Eighth Chronicle: Black Crime, White Fears: On the Social Construction of Threat." *Virginia Law Review* 80 (2): 503–48.

DeSantis, Andrea, and Wesley A. Kayson. 1997. "Defendants' Characteristics of Attractiveness, Race, and Sex and Sentencing Decisions." *Psychological Reports* 81: 679–83.

Devine, Patricia G., and Sara M. Baker. 1991. "Measurement of Racial Stereotype Subtyping." *Personality and Social Psychology Bulletin* 17: 44–50.

Dilworth, Donald C. 1996. "Jury Nullification: When Jurors Leave the Law Behind." *Trial* 32: 12–14.

Dixon, Jo. 1995. "The Organizational Context of Criminal Sentencing." *American Journal of Sociology* 100: 1157–98.

Dixon, Travis L., and Daniel Linz. 2000. "Race and the Misrepresentation of Victimization on Local Television News." *Communication Research* 27: 547–73.

Doble, John. 2002. "Attitudes to Punishment in the U.S.: Punitive and Liberal Opinions," in *Changing Attitudes to Punishment: Public Opinion, Crime and Justice*, ed. J. V. Roberts and M. Hough. Portland, OR: Willan Publishing.

Dovidio, John F., Jennifer K. Smith, Amy Gershenfeld Donnella, and Samuel L. Gaertner. 1997. "Racial Attitudes and the Death Penalty." *Journal of Applied Social Psychology* 27: 1468–87.

Druckman, James N. 2001a. "On the Limits of Framing Effects: Who Can Frame?" *The Journal of Politics* 63: 1041–66.

———2001b. "The Implications of Framing Effects for Citizen Competence." *Political Behavior* 23: 225–56.

Duke, Lynne. February 26, 2000. "Jury Acquits 4 N.Y. Officers; Panel Rules Police Acted Reasonable in Slaying of Amadou Diallo." *Washington Post*, A01.

Dyck, Joshua J., and Laura S. Hussey. 2008. "The End of Welfare as We Know It? Durable Attitudes in a Changing Information Environment." *Public Opinion Quarterly* 72 (4): 589–618.

Eagly, Alice H., and Shelley Chaiken. 1993. *The Psychology of Attitudes*. New York: Harcourt Brace.

Eberhardt, Jennifer L., Phillip Atiba Goff, Valerie J. Purdie, and Paul G. Davies. 2004. "Seeing Black: Race, Crime, and Visual Processing." *Journal of Personality and Social Psychology* 87: 876–93.

Edsall, Thomas B. May 11–17, 1992. "Two Steps Forward, One Step Backlash." *Washington Post National Weekly Edition*.

Edwards, Kari, and Edward E. Smith. 1996. "A Disconfirmation Bias in the Evaluation of Arguments." *Journal of Personality and Social Psychology* 71: 5–24.

Ellsworth, Phoebe C., and Samuel R. Gross. 1994. "Hardening of the Attitudes: Americans' Views on the Death Penalty." *Journal of Social Issues* 50: 19–52.

Entman, Robert M. 1992. "Blacks in the News: Television, Modern Racism, and Cultural Change." *Journalism Quarterly* 69: 341–61.

———1993. "Framing: Toward Clarification of a Fractured Paradigm." *Journal of Communication* 43: 51–8.

Entman, Robert M., and Andrew Rojecki. 2001. *The Black Image in the White Mind: Media and Race in America.* Chicago: University of Chicago Press.

Fears, Darryl. April 15, 2009. "A Racial Shift in Drug-Crime Prisoners." *Washington Post.*

Feder, Lynette. 1994. "Psychiatric Hospitalization History and Parole Decisions." *Law and Human Behavior* 18: 395–410.

Federal Bureau of Investigation. 1995. "Crime in the United States – 1994." Washington, D.C.: U.S. Government Printing Office.

———2000. "Crime in the United States," in *Uniform Crime Reports.* Washington, D.C.: U.S. Government Printing Office.

Fehr, Ernst, and Simon Gachter. 2002. "Altruistic Punishment in Humans." *Nature* 415: 137–40.

Feldman, Stanley. 1982. "Economic Self-interest and Political Behavior." *American Journal of Political Science* 26: 446–66.

———1988. "Structure and Consistency in Public Opinion: The Role of Core Beliefs and Values." *American Journal of Political Science* 31: 416–40.

———2003. "Values, Ideology, and the Structure of Political Attitudes," in *Oxford Handbook of Political Psychology*, ed. D. O. Sears, L. Huddy, and R. Jervis. New York: Oxford University Press.

Feldman, Stanley, and Leonie Huddy. 2005. "Racial Resentment and White Opposition to Race-Conscious Programs: Principles or Prejudice." *American Journal of Political Science* 49 (1): 168–83.

Feldman, Stanley, and John Zaller. 1992. "The Political Culture of Ambivalence: Ideological Responses to the Welfare State." *American Journal of Political Science* 36: 268–307.

Feldman-Barrett, Lisa, and Janet K. Swim. 1998. "Appraisals of Prejudice and Discrimination," in *Prejudice: The Target's Perspective*, ed. J. K. Swim and C. Stangor. San Diego, CA: Academic Press.

Fishman, Mark. 1978. "Crime Waves as Ideology." *Social Problems* 25: 531–43.

Florida Department of Corrections. 1997. "Florida Department Surveys Residents' Views of Its Prisons." *Corrections Journal* 7 (August): 5–6.

Fox, John. 1991. *Regression Diagnostics.* Newbury Park, CA: Sage Publications.
Frank, Robert H. 1990a. *Luxury Fever.* New York: Free Press.
———1990b. "Rethinking Rational Choice," in *Beyond the Marketplace: Rethinking Economy and Society*, ed. R. Friedland and A. F. Robertson. New York: de Gruyter.
Frazier, Charles E., and Donna M. Bishop. 1995. "Reflections on Race Effects in Juvenile Justice," in *Minorities in Juvenile Justice*, ed. K. K. Leonard, C. E. Pope, and W. Feyerherm. Thousand Oaks, CA: Sage Publications.
Gabbidon, Shaun L., and Helen Taylor Greene. 2005. *Race and Crime.* Thousand Oaks, CA: Sage Publications.
Gaines, Brian J., James H. Kuklinski, and Paul J. Quirk. 2007. "The Logic of the Survey Experiment Reexamined." *Political Analysis* 15: 1–20.
Gallup, George Jr., and Alec Gallup. December 1999. "The Gallup Poll Monthly (Number 411)." Princeton, NJ: The Gallup Poll.
Gallup Poll. 2005. "Death Penalty." Princeton, NJ: The Gallup Organization.
Garland, David. 2001. *The Culture of Control: Crime and Social Order in Contemporary Society.* Oxford: Oxford University Press.
Gaubatz, Kathlyn Taylor. 1995. *Crime in the Public Mind.* Ann Arbor: University of Michigan Press.
Gay, Claudine. 2004. "Putting Race in Context: Identifying the Environmental Determinants of Black Racial Attitudes." *American Political Science Review* 98: 547–62.
Geller, William A. 1982. "Deadly Force: What We Know." *Journal of Police Science and Administration* 10: 151–77.
Geller, William A., and Kevin J. Karales. 1981. *Split-Second Decisions: Shootings of and by Chicago Police.* Chicago: Chicago Law Enforcement Study Group.
Georges-Abeyle, Daniel. 1984. *The Criminal Justice System and Blacks.* New York: Clark Broardman.
Gilens, Martin. 1999. *Why Americans Hate Welfare: Race, Media, and the Politics of Anti-Poverty Policy.* Chicago: University of Chicago Press.
———2001. "Political Ignorance and Collective Policy Preferences." *American Political Science Review* 95 (2): 379–96.
Gilliam, Franklin D., and Shanto Iyengar. 2000. "Prime Suspects: The Influence of Local Television News on the Viewing Public." *American Journal of Political Science* 44: 560–73.
Gilliam, Franklin, Nicholas A. Valentino, and Matthew Beckmann. 2002. "Where You Live and What You Watch: Neighborhood Racial Context as a Moderator of News Exposure Effects." *Political Research Quarterly* 55 (4): 755–80.
Graham, Sandra, and Brian S. Lowery. 2004. "Priming Unconscious Racial Stereotypes about Adolescent Offenders." *Law and Human Behavior* 28 (5): 483–504.

Grasmick, Harold G., John Cochran Jr., Robert J. Bursik, and M'Lou Kimpel. 1993. "Religion, Punitive Justice, and Support for the Death Penalty." *Justice Quarterly* 10: 289–314.

Grasmick, Harold G., Charles R. Tittle Jr., Robert J. Bursik, and Bruce J. Arneklev. 1993. "Testing the Core Empirical Implications of Gottfredson and Hirschi's General Theory of Crime." *Journal of Research in Crime and Delinquency* 30: 2–29.

Greenberg, Jerald. 1986. "Reactions to Procedural Justice in Payment Distributions: Do the Means Justify the Ends?" *Journal of Applied Psychology* 72: 55–61.

Gregory, James F. 1995. "The Crime of Punishment: Racial and Gender Disparities in the Use of Corporal Punishment in U.S. Public Schools." *Journal of Negro Education* 64: 454–62.

Gross, Samuel R., and Robert Mauro. 1989. *Death and Discrimination: Racial Disparities and Capital Sentencing.* Boston: Northeastern University Press.

Hagan, John. 1974. "Extra-legal Attributes and Criminal Sentencing: An Assessment of a Sociological Viewpoint." *Law and Society Review* 8: 357–84.

Hagan, John, and Celesta Albonetti. 1982. "Race, Class, and the Perception of Criminal Injustice in America." *American Journal of Sociology* 88: 329–55.

Haider-Markel, Donald P., and Mark R. Joslyn. 2001. "Gun Policy, Opinion, Tragedy, and Blame Attribution: The Conditional Influence of Issue Frames." *Journal of Politics* 63: 520–43.

Haines, Herb. 1992. "Flawed Executions, the Anti-Death Penalty Movement, and the Politics of Capital Punishment." *Social Problems* 39 (2): 125–38.

Hall, Melinda Gann. 1992. "Electoral Politics and Strategic Voting in State Supreme Courts." *Journal of Politics* 54 (2): 427–46.

———1995. "Justices as Representatives: Elections and Judicial Politics in the American States." *American Politics Quarterly* 23: 485–503.

Hamilton, David L., and Jeffrey W. Sherman. 1994. "Stereotypes," in *Handbook of Social Cognition*, ed. J. Robert S. Wyer and T. K. Srul. Hillsdale, NJ: Lawrence Erlbaum: 1–68.

Harding, David J. 2003. "Counterfactual Models of Neighborhood Effects: The Effect of Neighorhood Poverty on Dropping Out and Teenage Pregnancy." *American Journal of Sociology* 109 (3): 676–719.

Harris, David A. 1999. "Driving While Black: Racial Profiling on Our Nation's Highways." New York: American Civil Liberties Union.

———2002. *Profiles in Injustice.* New York: New Press.

Hawkins, Darnell F. 1986. "Black and White Homicide Differentials: Alternatives to an Inadequate Theory," in *Homicide among Black Americans*, ed. D. F. Hawkins. Lanham, MD: University Press of America.

Haynes, Graeme A., and James M. Olson. 2006. "Coping with Threats to Just-World Beliefs: Derogate, Blame, or Help?" *Journal of Applied Social Psychology* 36: 664–82.

Helweg-Larsen, Marie. 1999. "The Lack of Optimistic Bias in Response to the 1994 Northridge Earthquake: The Role of Personal Experience." *Basic and Applied Social Psychology* 21: 119–29.

Hepburn, John R. 1978. "Race and the Decision to Arrest: An Analysis of Warrants Issued." *Journal of Research in Crime and Delinquency* 15: 54–73.

Hewstone, Malcolm D., Harmon M. Hosch, Howard C. Daudistel, Dolores A. Perez, and Joseph B. Graves. 1996. "Ethnicity, Legal Resources, and Felony Dispositions in Two Southwestern Jurisdictions." *Justice Quarterly* 13: 11–30.

Hibbing, John R., and John R. Alford. 2004. "Accepting Authoritative Decisions: Humans as Wary Cooperators." *American Journal of Political Science* 48: 62–76.

Hibbing, John R., and Elizabeth Theiss-Morse. 1995. *Congress as Public Enemy: Public Attitudes toward Political Institutions.* New York: Cambridge University Press.

——— 2002. *Stealth Democracy: Americans' Beliefs about How Government Should Work.* Cambridge: Cambridge University Press.

Hindelang, Michael J. 1978. "Race and Involvement in Common Law Personal Crimes." *American Sociological Review* 43: 93–109.

Hochschild, Jennifer L. 1981. *What's Fair? American Beliefs about Distributive Justice.* Cambridge, MA: Harvard University Press.

———1995. *Facing Up to the American Dream: Race, Class, and the Soul of the Nation.* Princeton, NJ: Princeton University Press.

Hough, Mike, and Alison Park. 2002. "How Malleable Are Attitudes to Crime and Punishment? Findings from a British Deliberative Poll," in *Changing Attitudes to Punishment: Public Opinion, Crime and Justice*, ed. J. V. Roberts and M. Hough. Portland, OR: Willan Publishing: 163–83.

Huckfeldt, Robert, Paul E. Johnson, and John Sprague. 2005. *Political Disagreement: The Survival of Diverse Opinions within Communications Networks.* New York: Cambridge University Press.

Huddy, Leonie. 2004. "Contrasting Theoretical Approaches to Intergroup Relations." *Political Psychology* 25 (6): 947–67.

Huddy, Leonie, and Stanley Feldman. 2009. "On Assessing the Political Effects of Racial Prejudice." *Annual Review of Political Science* 12: 423–47.

Huddy, Leonie, and Nayda Terkildsen. 1993. "Gender Stereotypes and the Perception of Male and Female Candidates." *American Journal of Political Science* 37: 119–47.

Huebner, Beth M., and Timothy S. Bynum. 2008. "The Role of Race and the Ethnicity of Parole Decisions." *Criminology* 46 (4): 907–38.

Human Rights Watch. 1998. *Shielded from Justice: Police Brutality and Accountability in the United States*. New York: Human Rights Watch.
Hurwitz, Jon, and Mark Peffley. 1997. "Public Perceptions of Race and Crime: The Role of Racial Stereotypes." *American Journal of Political Science* 41: 375–401.
———2005a. "Explaining the Great Racial Divide: Perceptions of Fairness in the U.S. Criminal Justice System." *The Journal of Politics* 67: 762–83.
———2005b. "Playing the Race Card in the Post-Willie Horton Era: The Impact of Racialized Code Words on Support for Punitive Crime Policy." *Public Opinion Quarterly* 69: 99–112.
Hurwitz, Jon, and Shannon Smithey. 1998. "Gender Differences on Crime and Punishment." *Political Research Quarterly* 51: 89–115.
Hutchings, Vincent, Walton Hanes Jr., and Andrea Benjamin. Forthcoming. "The Impact of Explicit Racial Cues on Gender Differences in Support for Confederate Symbols and Partisanship." *Journal of Politics*.
Hutchings, Vincent, Nicholas Valentino, Tasha Philpot, and Ismail K. White. 2004. "The Compassion Strategy: Race and Gender Gap in American Politics." *Public Opinion Quarterly* 68 (4): 512–41.
Inman, Mary L., and Robert S. Baron. 1996. "Influence of Prototypes on Perceptions of Prejudice." *Journal of Personality and Social Psychology* 70: 727–39.
Iyengar, Shanto. 1989. "How Citizens Think about National Issues: A Matter of Responsibility." *American Journal of Political Science* 33: 878–900.
Jaccard, James, Robert Turrisi, and Choi K. Wan. 1990. *Interaction Effects in Multiple Regression*. Newbury Park, CA: Sage Publications.
Jackman, Mary R., and Michael J. Muha. 1984. "Education and Intergroup Attitudes: Moral Enlightenment, Superficial Democratic Commitment, or Ideological Refinement?" *American Sociological Review* 49: 751–69.
Jackson, Pamela Irving. 1989. *Minority Group Threat, Crime, and Policing: Social Context and Social Control*. New York: Praeger.
Jacobs, David, and Robert M. O'Brien. 1998. "The Determinants of Deadly Force: A Structural Analysis of Police Violence." *American Journal of Sociology* 103: 837–62.
Jamieson, Kathleen Hall. 1992. *Dirty Politics: Deception, Distraction, and Democracy*. New York: Oxford University Press.
John, Richard St. 1997. "License to Nullify: The Democratic and Constitutional Deficiencies of Authorized Jury Lawmaking." *Yale Law Journal* 106: 2563–97.
Johns, Christina Jacqueline. 1992. *Power, Ideology, and the War on Drugs: Nothing Succeeds Like Failure*. New York: Praeger.
Johnson, Blair, and Alice Eagly. 1989. "Effects of Involvement on Persuasion: A Meta-Analysis." *Psychological Bulletin* 106: 290–314.
Johnson, Blair T., Aaron Smith-McLallen, Ley A. Killeya, and Kenneth D. Levin. 2004. "Truth or Consequences: Overcoming Resistance to

Persuasion with Positive Thinking," in *Resistance and Persuasion*, ed. E. S. Knowles and J. Linn. Mahwah, NJ: Lawrence Erlbaum: 215–34.

Johnson, Devon. 2001. "Punitive Attitudes on Crime: Economic Insecurity, Racial Prejudice, or Both?" *Sociological Focus* 34 (1): 33–54.

Johnson, W. Wesley, and Mark Jones. 1998. "Probation, Race and the War on Drugs: An Empirical Analysis of Drug and Non-drug Felony Probation Outcomes." *Journal of Drug Issues* 28: 985–1004.

Jost, John T., Mahzarin R. Banaji, and Brian A. Nosek. 2004. "A Decade of System Justification Theory: Accumulated Evidence of Conscious and Unconscious Bolstering of the Status Quo." *Political Psychology* 25 (6): 823–989.

Jost, John T., and Brenda Major, eds. 2001. *The Psychology of Legitimacy: Emerging Perspectives on Ideology, Justice, and Intergroup Relations.* Cambridge: Cambridge University Press.

Kahle, Lynn R., ed. 1983. *Social Values and Social Change: Adaptation to Life in America.* New York: Praeger.

Keil, Thomas J., and Gennaro F. Vito. 1995. "Race and the Death Penalty in Kentucky Murder Trials: 1976–1991." *American Journal of Criminal Justice* 20: 17–36.

Kempf-Leonard, Kimberly, and Henry Sontheimer. 1995. "The Role of Race in Juvenile Justice in Pennsylvania," in *Minorities in Juvenile Justice*, ed. K. K. Leonard, C. E. Pope, and W. Feyerherm. Thousand Oaks, CA: Sage Publications: 98–127.

Kennedy, Randall. 1997. *Race, Crime, and the Law.* New York: Pantheon Books.

Key, V. O. 1949. *Southern Politics in State and Nation.* New York: Alfred P. Knopf.

Kiewiet, D. Roderick. 1983. *Macroeconomics and Micropolitics: The Electoral Effects of Economic Issues.* Chicago: University of Chicago Press.

Kinder, Donald. 1993. "On Behalf of an Experimental Political Science," in *Experimental Foundations of Political Science*, ed. D. Kinder and T. R. Palfrey. Ann Arbor: University of Michigan Press.

Kinder, Donald R., and D. Roderik Kiewiet. 1981. "Sociotropic Politics: The American Case." *British Journal of Political Science* 11: 129–61.

Kinder, Donald R., and Tali Mendelberg. 1995. "Cracks in American Apartheid: The Political Impact of Prejudice among Desegregated Whites." *The Journal of Politics* 75: 402–24.

Kinder, Donald R., and Lynn M. Sanders. 1996. *Divided by Color: Racial Politics and Democratic Ideals.* Chicago: University of Chicago Press.

Kinder, Donald R., and David O. Sears. 1981. "Prejudice and Politics: Symbolic Racism versus Racial Threats to the Good Life." *Journal of Personality and Social Psychology* 40 (3): 414–31.

Kinder, Donald R., and Nicholas Winter. 2001. "Exploring the Racial Divide: Blacks, Whites, and Opinion on Nationality Policy." *American Journal of Political Science* 45: 439–56.

King, Ryan S. 2009. Testimony before the Standing Committee on Justice and Human Rights, House of Commons, December 6, 2006, Ottawa, Ontario (cited August 1, 2009). Available at http://www.sentencingproject.org/doc/publications/sl_canada_testimony.pdf (accessed January 3, 2010).

Kleck, Gary. 1981. "Racial Discrimination in Criminal Sentencing: A Critical Evaluation of the Evidence with Additional Evidence on the Death Penalty." *American Sociological Review* 46: 783–805.

Klein, Stephen, Joan Petersilia, and Susan Turner. 1990. "Race and Imprisonment Decisions in California." *Science* 247: 812–16.

Kluegel, James R., and Elliot R. Smith. 1986. *Beliefs about Inequality: Americans' Views of What Is and What Ought to Be.* New York: Aldine de Gruyter.

Koch, Jeffrey W. 2000. "Do Citizens Apply Gender Stereotypes to Infer Candidates' Ideological Orientations?" *Journal of Politics* 62: 414–29.

Kochar, Rakesh, Robert Suro, and Sonya Tafoya. 2005. "The New Latino South: The Context and Consequences of Rapid Population Growth." Pew Hispanic Center: A Pew Research Center Project. Available at http://www.pewhispanic.org/files/reports/50.pdf (accessed January 20, 2010).

Krosnick, Jon A. 1999. "Survey Research." *Annual Review of Psychology* 50: 537–67.

Kuklinski, James H., and Michael D. Cobb. 1998. "When White Southerners Converse About Race," in *Perception and Prejudice: Race and Politics in the United States*, ed. J. Hurwitz and M. Peffley. New Haven, CT: Yale University Press: 35–57.

Kuklinski, James H., Michael D. Cobb, and Martin Gilens. 1997. "Racial Attitudes and the 'New South.'" *Journal of Politics* 55: 323–49.

Kuklinski, James H., Paul J. Quirk, Jennifer Jerit, David Schwieder, and Robert Rich. 2000. "Misinformation and the Currency of Citizenship." *Journal of Politics* 62: 791–816.

Kunda, Ziva. 1990. "The Case for Motivated Reasoning." *Psychological Bulletin* 108 (3): 480–98.

Lane, Robert. 1962. *Political Ideology: Why the Common American Man Believes What He Does.* New York: The Free Press.

Langan, Patrick A. 1994. "No Racism in the Justice System." *The Public Interest* 117: 48–51.

Lauritsen, Janet L., and Robert J. Sampson. 1998. "Minorities, Crime, and Criminal Justice," in *The Handbook of Crime and Punishment*, ed. M. Tonry. New York: Oxford University Press: 54–84.

Leiber, Michael, and Jayne Stairs. 1999. "Race, Contexts, and the Use of Intake Diversion." *Journal of Research in Crime and Delinquency* 36: 56–86.

Leonard, Kimberly K., and Henry Sontheimer. 1995. "The Role of Race in Juvenile Justice in Pennsylvania," in *Minorities in Juvenile Justice*, ed. K. K. Leonard, C. E. Pope, and W. H. Feyerherm. Thousand Oaks, CA: Sage Publications: 98–127.

Lerner, Melvin J. 1980. *The Belief in a Just World: A Fundamental Delusion.* New York: Plenum Press.

Lerner, Melvin J., and Sally C. Lerner. 1981. *The Justice Motive in Social Behavior: Adapting to Times of Scarcity and Change.* New York: Plenum Press.

Leventhal, Gerald S. 1980. "What Should Be Done with Equity Theory?" in *Social Exchange Advances in Theory and Research*, ed. K. J. Gergen, M. S. Greenberg, and R. H. Willis. New York: Plenum.

Levin, Jack, and Alexander R. Thomas. 1997. "Experimentally Manipulating Race: Perceptions of Police Brutality in an Arrest: A Research Note." *Justice Quarterly* 14: 577–86.

Lewis, Peter W. 1979. "Killing the Killers: A Post-Furman Profile of Florida's Condemned: A Personal Account." *Crime and Delinquency* 25: 200–18.

Lewis-Beck, Michael, and Mary Stegmaier. 2000. "Economic Determinants of Electoral Outcomes." *Annual Review of Political Science* 3: 183–219.

Leyden, Liz. March 7, 2000. "N.Y. Police Convicted of Coverup in Beating; 3 Officers Conspired to Obstruct Probe." *Washington Post*, A03.

Liberman, Peter. 2006. "An Eye for an Eye: Public Support for War against Evildoers." *International Organization* 60: 687–722.

Lichtenstein, K. R. 1982. "Extra-legal Variables Affecting Sentencing Decisions." *Psychological Reports* 50: 611–19.

Lictblau, Eric. August 24, 2005. "Profiling Report Leads to a Demotion." *The New York Times.*

Lieber, Michael J., and Jayne M. Stairs. 1999. "Race, Contexts, and the Use of Intake Diversion." *Journal of Research in Crime and Delinquency* 36: 56–86.

Liebman, James. 2000. "The Overproduction of Death." *Columbia Law Review* 100: 2030–156.

Lind, E. Allan. 1982. "The Psychology of Courtroom Procedure," in *The Psychology of the Courtroom*, ed. N. Kerr and R. Bray. New York: Academic Press: 13–37.

Lind, E. Allan, and Tom R. Tyler. 1988. *The Social Psychology of Procedural Justice.* New York: Plenum Press.

Lind, E. Allan, Tom R. Tyler, and Yuen J. Huo. 1997. "Procedural Context and Culture: Variation in the Antecedents of Procedural Justice Judgments." *Journal of Personality and Social Psychology* 73: 767–80.

Lipset, Seymour Martin, and William Schneider. 1978. "The Bakke Case: How Would It Be Decided at the Bar of Public Opinion?" *Public Opinion* 1: 38–48.

Liska, Allen E., and Mitchell B. Chamlin. 1984. "Social Structure and Crime Control among Macrosocial Units." *American Journal of Sociology* 90: 383–95.

Long, J. Scott, and Jeremy Freese. 2006. *Regression Models for Categorical Dependent Variables Using Stata*. 2nd ed. College Station, TX: Stata Press.

Longmire, Dennis R. 1996. "Americans' Attitudes about the Ultimate Weapon: Capital Punishment," in *Americans View Crime and Justice: A National Public Opinion Survey*, ed. T. J. Flanagan and D. R. Longmire. Thousand Oaks, CA: Sage Publications: 93–108.

Lord, Charles G., Lee Ross, and Mark R. Lepper. 1979. "Biased Assimilation and Attitude Polarization: The Effects of Prior Theories on Subsequently Considered Evidence." *Journal of Personality and Social Psychology* 37: 2098–109.

Lowry, Dennis T., Tam Ching, Josephine Nio, and Dennis W. Leitner. 2003. "Setting the Public Fear Agenda: A Longitudinal Analysis of Network TV Crime Reporting, Public Perceptions of Crime, and FBI Crime Statistics." *Journal of Communication* 53: 61–73.

Luskin, Robert C., James S. Fishkin, and Roger Jowell. 2002. "Considered Opinions: Deliberative Polling in Britain." *British Journal of Political Science* 32: 455–87.

MacDonald, J. M. 2001. "Analytic Methods for Examining Race and Ethnic Disparity in the Juvenile Courts." *Journal of Criminal Justice* 29 (6): 507–19

Maclin, Tracey. 1998. "Race and the Fourth Amendment." *Vanderbilt Law Review* 51 (2): 333–94.

Major, Brenda, and Toni Schmader. 2001. "Legitimacy and the Construal of Social Disadvantage," in *The Psychology of Legitimacy: Emerging Perspectives on Ideology, Justice and Intergroup Relations*, ed. J. T. Jost and B. Major. New York: Cambridge University Press: 176–204.

Manza, Jeff, and Christopher Uggen. 2006. *Locked Out: Felon Disenfranchisement and American Democracy*. New York: Oxford University Press.

Martinez, Jr., Ramiro. 2005. "Moving Beyond Black and White Violence: African American, Haitian, and Latino Homicides in Miami," in *Violent Crime: Assessing Race and Ethnic Differences*, ed. Darnell F. Hawkins. Cambridge: Cambridge University Press: 22–43.

Massey, Douglas S., and Nancy A. Denton. 1993. *American Apartheid: Segregation and the Making of the Underclass*. Cambridge, MA: Harvard University Press.

Matthews, Roger. 2005. "The Myth of Punitiveness." *Theoretical Criminology* 9: 175–201.

Mauer, Marc. 1999. *Race to Incarcerate*. New York: The New Press.

———2009. *Support for Crack Cocaine Sentencing Reform Signals More Rational Approach to Public Safety*. Available at http://jurist.law.pitt.hotline/2009/06/support-for-crack-cocaine-sentencing.php (accessed January 3, 2010).

Maxfield, Linda D., and John H. Kramer. 1998. "Substantial Assistance: An Empirical Yardstick Gauging Equity in Current Federal Policy and Practice." Washington, D.C.: U.S. Sentencing Commission.

Mazzella, Ronald, and Alan Feingold. 1994. "The Effects of Physical Attractiveness, Race, Socioeconomic Status, and Gender of Defendants and Victims on Judgments of Mock Jurors: A Meta-Analysis." *Journal of Applied Social Psychology* 24: 1315–44.

McCann, Jay A. 1997. "Electoral Choices and Core Value Change: The 1992 Presidential Campaign." *American Journal of Political Science* 41: 564–83.

McCauley, Clark, Margo Durham, John B. Copley, and John P. Johnson. 1985. "Patients' Perceptions of Treatment for Kidney Failure: The Impact of Personal Experience on Population Predictions." *Journal of Experimental Social Psychology* 21: 138–48.

McClain, Paula D., Niambi M. Carter, Victoria M. DeFrancesco Soto, Monique L. Lyle, Jeffrey D. Grynaviski, Shala C. Nunnally, Thomas J. Scotto, J. Alan Kendrick, Gerald F. Lackey, and Kendra Davenport Cotton. 2006. "Racial Distancing in a Southern City: Latino Immigrants' Views of Black Americans." *Journal of Politics* 68: 571–84.

McConahay, John B. 1986. "Modern Racism, Ambivalence, and the Modern Racism Scale," in *Prejudice, Discrimination, and Racism*, ed. J. F. Dovidio and S. L. Gaertner. Orlando, FL: Academic Press: 91–125.

McGarrell, Edmund F., and Marla Sandys. 1996. "The Misperception of Public Opinion toward Capital Punishment." *American Behavioral Scientist* 39 (4): 500–13.

Meares, Tracey L. 1997. "Charting Race and Class Differences toward Drug Legalization and Law Enforcement: Lessons for Federal Criminal Law." *Buffalo Criminal Law Review* 1: 137–74.

Mendelberg, Tali. 1997. "Executing Hortons: Racial Crime in the 1988 Presidential Campaign." *Public Opinion Quarterly* 61: 134–57.

———2001. *The Race Card: Campaign Strategy, Implicit Messages, and the Norm of Equality*. Princeton, NJ: Princeton University Press.

Miller, Jerome G. 1996. *Search and Destroy: African-American Males in the Criminal Justice System*. New York: Cambridge University Press.

Monteith, Margo J., Leslie Ashburn-Nardo, Corrine Voils, and Alex M. Czopp. 2002. "Putting the Brakes on Prejudice: On the Development and Operation of Cues for Control." *Journal of Personality and Social Psychology* 83: 1029–50.

Mooney, Christopher Z., and Mei-Hsien Lee. 2000. "The Influence of Values on Consensus and Contentious Morality Policy: U.S. Death Penalty Reform, 1956–82." *Journal of Politics* 62 (1): 223–39.

Murphy, Dean. October 24, 2004. "California Rethinking '3-Strikes' Sentencing." *New York Times*.

Murr, Andrew. 2005. "Back on the Mean Streets: A Cop Shoots, A Black Kid Falls and L.A. Is on the Edge Again." Available at http://www.newsweek.com/id/48806 (accessed January 3, 2010).

Murty, Komanduri S., Julian B. Roebuck, and Joann D. Smith. 1990. "The Image of the Police in Black Atlanta Communities." *Journal of Police Science and Administration* 17: 250–7.

Mutz, Diana C. 1992. "Mass Media and the Depoliticization of Personal Experience." *American Journal of Political Science* 36: 483–508.

Mutz, Diana C., and Jeffery Mondak. 1997. "Dimensions of Sociotropic Behavior: Group-Based Judgments of Fairness and Well-Being." *American Journal of Political Science* 41: 284–308.

Myers, Martha A., and John Hagan. 1979. "Private and Public Trouble: Prosecutors and the Allocation of Court Resources." *Social Problems* 26: 439–51.

Myers, Martha A., and Susette M. Talarico. 1987. *The Social Contexts of Criminal Sentencing.* New York: Springer-Verlag.

Nelson, Thomas, and Donald R. Kinder. 1996. "Issue Frames and Group Centrism in American Public Opinion." *Journal of Politics* 58: 1055–78.

Nelson, Thomas E., and Zoe M. Oxley. 1999. "Issue Framing Effects on Belief Importance and Opinion." *Journal of Politics* 61: 1040–67.

Nelson, Thomas E., Rosalee A. Clawson, and Zoe M. Oxley. 1997. "Media Framing of a Civil Liberties Conflict and its Effect on Tolerance." *American Political Science Review* 91: 567–83.

Nelson, Thomas E., Kira Sanbonmatsu, and Harwood K. McClerking. 2007. "Playing a Different Race Card: Examining the Limits of Elite Influence on Perceptions of Racism." *The Journal of Politics* 69: 416–29.

Neville, Helen A., and Aalece O. Pugh. 1997. "General and Cultural-specific Factors Influencing African American Women's Reporting Patterns and Perceived Social Support following Sexual Assault: An Exploratory Investigation." *Violence against Women* 3: 361–81.

Nice, David C. 1992. "The States and the Death Penalty." *The Western Political Quarterly* 45: 1037–48.

Nicholson-Crotty, Sean, and Kenneth J. Meier. 2003. "Crime and Punishment: The Politics of Federal Criminal Justice Sanctions." *Political Research Quarterly* 56: 119–26.

———2000. "The Multi-Layered Impact of Public Opinion on Capital Punishment Implementation in the American States." *Political Research Quarterly* 53: 771–93.

Oliver, Eric J. 2010. *The Paradoxes of Segregation: Race, Neighborhood, and Civic Life in Multiethnic America.* Chicago: University of Chicago Press.

Oliver, Eric J., and Tali Mendelberg. 2000. "Reconsidering the Environmental Determinants of White Racial Attitudes." *American Journal of Political Science* 41 (3): 574–89.

Oliver, Wilford M. 1998. "Presidential Rhetoric on Crime and Public Opinion." *Criminal Justice Review* 23: 139–60.

Oskamp, Stuart. 1991. *Attitudes and Opinions.* 2nd ed. Englewood Cliffs, NJ: Prentice-Hall.

Page, Benjamin, and Robert Shapiro. 1992. *The Rational Public.* Chicago: University of Chicago Press.

Pager, Devah, and Hana Shepherd. 2008. "The Sociology of Discrimination: Racial Discrimination in Employment, Housing, Credit, and Consumer Markets." *Annual Review of Sociology* 34: 181–209.

Parker, Keith D., Anne B. Onyekwuluje, and Komanduri S. Murty. 1995. "African-Americans' Attitudes toward the Local Police: A Multivariate Analysis." *Journal of Black Studies* 25: 396–409.

Paternoster, Raymond. 1991. "Prosecutorial Discretion and Capital Sentencing in North and South Carolina," in *The Death Penalty in America: Current Research*, ed. R. M. Bohm. Cincinnati, OH: Anderson Publishing: 39–53.

Peek, Charles W., George D. Lowe, and Jon P. Alston. 1981. "Race and Attitudes toward Local Police." *Journal of Black Studies* 11: 361–74.

Peffley, Mark, and Jon Hurwitz. 1985. "A Hierarchical Model of Attitude Constraint." *American Journal of Political Science* 29: 871–90.

———1992. "International Events and Foreign Policy Beliefs: Public Response to Changing Soviet-American Relations." *American Journal of Political Science* 36 (2): 431–61.

———1993. "Models of Attitude Constraint in Foreign Affairs." *Political Behavior* 15: 61–90.

———2002. "The Racial Component of 'Race-Neutral' Crime Policy Attitudes." *Political Psychology* 23 (1): 59–75.

——— 2007. "Resistance and Persuasion to Arguments against the Death Penalty among Whites and Blacks." *American Journal of Political Science* 51: 996–1012.

Peffley, Mark, Jon Hurwitz, and Paul Sniderman. 1997. "Racial Stereotypes and Whites' Political Views of Blacks in the Context of Welfare and Crime." *American Journal of Political Science* 41 (1): 30–60.

Peffley, Mark, Todd Shields, and Bruce Williams. 1996. "The Intersection of Race and Crime in Television News: An Experimental Study." *Political Communication* 13: 309–27.

Perry, Ronald W. 1980. "Social Status and the Black Violence Hypothesis." *Journal of Social Psychology* 111: 131–7.

Petersilia, Joan. 1983. *Racial Disparities in the Criminal Justice System: A Summary.* Santa Monica, CA: Rand.

Petty, Richard E., and John T. Cacioppo. 1996. *Attitudes and Persuasion: Classic and Contemporary Approaches.* Boulder, CO: Westview Press.

Pfeiffer, Jeffrey E., and James R. P. Ogloff. 1991. "Ambiguity and Guilt Determinations: A Modern Racism Perspective." *Journal of Applied Social Psychology* 21: 1713–25.

Pierce, Glenn L. 1985. "Race and Prosecutorial Discretion in Homicide Cases." *Law and Society Review* 17: 587–621.

Piston, Spencer. 2010. "How Explicit Racial Prejudice Hurt Obama in the 2008 Presidential Election." *Political Behavior* 32 (in press).

Pomper, Gerald M. 1989. "The Nominations," in *The Election of 1988: Reports and Interpretations*, ed. G. M. Pomper, R. K. Baker, W. D. Burnham, B. G. Farah, M. R. Hershey, E. Klein, and W. C. McWilliams. Chatham, NJ: Chatham House: 33–72.

Pratt, John. 2000. "Emotive and Ostentatious Punishment." *Punishment and Society* 2: 417–39.

Prior, Markus. 2007. *Post-Broadcast Democracy: How Media Choice Increases Inequality in Political Involvement and Polarizes Elections.* New York: Cambridge University Press.

Provine, Doris Marie. 2007. *Unequal under Law: Race in the War on Drugs.* Chicago: University of Chicago Press.

Radelet, M. and G. Pierce. 1985. "Race and Prosecutorial Discretion in Homicide Cases." *Law and Society Review* 17: 587–621.

Rahn, Wendy M. 1993. "The Role of Partisan Stereotypes in Information Processing about Political Candidates." *American Journal of Political Science* 37: 472–96.

Rasinski, Kenneth A. 1987. "What's Fair Is Fair – Or Is It? Value Differences Underlying Public Views about Social Justice." *Journal of Peraonality and Social Psychology* 53: 201–11.

Rector, Neil, Michael Bagby, and Robert Nicholson. 1993. "The Effect of Prejudice and Judicial Ambiguity on Defendant Guilt Ratings." *Journal of Social Psychology* 133: 651–9.

Riedel, Marc. 2003. "Homicide in Los Angeles County: A Study of Latino Victimization," in *Violent Crime: Assessing Race and Ethnic Differences*, ed. Darnell F. Hawkins. Cambridge: Cambridge University Press: 44–66.

Richburg, Keith B. July 13, 2009. "States Seek Less Costly Substitutes for Prison." *Washington Post.*

Roberts, Julian V. 1992. "Public Opinion, Crime, and Criminal Justice," *Crime and Justice 16:* 99–180.

Roberts, Julian V., and Loretta J. Stalans. 1997. *Public Opinion, Crime and Criminal Justice.* Boulder, CO: Westview Press.

Rokeach, Milton. 1968. *Beliefs, Attitudes and Values: A Theory of Organization and Change.* San Francisco: Josey-Bass.

———1973. *The Nature of Human Values.* New York: Free Press.

Romer, Daniel, Kathleen Hall Jamieson, and Sean Aday. 2003. "Television News and the Cultivation of Fear of Crime." *The Journal of Communication* 53 (1): 88–104.

Rossi, Peter H., and Andy B. Anderson. 1982. "The Factorial Survey Approach: An Introduction," in *Measuring Social Judgments: The Factorial Survey Approach*, ed. P. H. Rossi and S. L. Nock. Beverly Hills, CA: Sage Publications: 15–67.

Rubin, Zick, and Letitia Anne Peplau. 1975. "Who Believes in a Just World?" *Journal of Social Issues* 31: 65–89.

Sampson, Robert J., and Dawn Jeglum Bartusch. 1998. "Legal Cynicism and (Subculture?) Tolerance of Deviance: The Neighborhood Context of Racial Differences." *Law and Society Review* 32: 777–804.

Sasson, Theodore. 1995. *Crime Talk: How Citizens Construct a Social Problem*. New York: Aldine de Gruyter.

Sattler, David N., Mary G. Adams, and Barrett Watts. 1995. "Personal Experience on Judgments about Natural Disasters." *Journal of Social Behavior and Personality* 10: 891–8.

Scaglion, Richard, and Richard G. Condon. 1980. "Determinants of Attitudes toward City Police." *Criminology* 17: 485–94.

Schlozman, Kay, and Sidney Verba. 1979. *Injury to Insult: Unemployment, Class and Political Response*. Cambridge, MA: Harvard University Press.

Schuman, Howard, Charlotte Steeh, Lawrence Bobo, and Maria Krysan. 1998. *Racial Attitudes in America: Trends and Interpretations*. Rev. ed. Cambridge, MA: Harvard University Press.

Schwartz, Shalom H., and Wolfgang Bilsky. 1987. "Toward a Psychological Structure of Human Values." *Journal of Personality and Social Psychology* 53: 550–62.

———1990. "Toward a Theory of the Universal Content and Structure of Values: Extensions and Cross-Cultural Replications." *Journal of Personality and Social Psychology* 58: 878–91.

Sears, David, and John B. McConahay. 1982. *The Politics of Violence: The New Urban Blacks and the Watts Riots*. Lanham, MD: University Press of America.

Sears, David O. 1986. "College Sophomores in the Laboratory: Influences of a Narrow Data Base on Social Psychology's View of Human Nature." *Journal of Personality and Social Psychology* 51: 515–30.

Sears, David O., Leonie Huddy, and Robert Jervis. 2003. *Oxford Handbook of Political Psychology*. Oxford and New York: Oxford University Press.

Sears, David O., Jim Sinadius, and Lawrence Bobo. 2000. *Racialized Politics: The Debate about Racism in America*. Chicago: University of Chicago Press.

Sears, David O., Colette Van Laar, Mary Carrillo, and Rick Kosterman. 1997. "Is It Really Racism? The Origins of White Americans' Opposition to Race-Targeted Policies." *The Public Opinion Quarterly* 61 (1): 16–53.

Seligman, Clive, and Albert N. Katz. 1996. "The Dynamics of Value Systems," in *The Psychology of Values*, ed. C. Seligman, J. M. Olson, and M. P. Zanna. Mahwah, NJ: Lawrence Erlbaum: 53–75.

Sheng, Shing-Yuan. 1995. "ANES Measurement of Values and Predispositions, 1984–1992," in *Technical Report Series No. neso10168*: American National Election Studies. Ann Arbor, MI: American National Election Studies: 1–32.

Sidanius, James. 1993. "The Psychology of Group Conflict and the Dynamics of Oppression: A Social Dominance Perspective," in *Explorations in Political Psychology*, ed. S. Iyengar and W. J. McGuire. Durham, NC: Duke University Press.

Sigelman, Lee, and Emmett H. Buell Jr. 2004. "Avoidance or Engagement? Issue Convergence in U.S. Presidential Campaigns, 1960–2000." *American Journal of Political Science* 48: 650–61.

Sigelman, Lee, and Susan Welch. 1991. *Black Americans' Views of Racial Inequality: The Dream Deferred*. Cambridge, MA: Cambridge University Press.

Sigelman, Lee, Susan Welch, Timothy Bledsoe, and Michael Coombs. 1997. "Police Brutality and Public Perceptions of Racial Discrimination: A Tale of Two Beatings." *Political Research Quarterly* 50: 777–91.

Sims, Barbara, and Eric Johnston. 2004. "Examining Public Opinion about Crime and Justice: A Statewide Study." *Criminal Justice Policy Review* 15: 260–93.

Skitka, Linda J., and Philip E. Tetlock. 1992. "Allocation of Scarce Resources: A Contingency Model of Distributive Justice." *Journal of Experimental Psychology* 28: 491–522.

Skolnick, Jerome H. 1966. *Justice without Trial: Law Enforcement in Democratic Society*. New York: John Wiley and Sons.

Smith, Douglas A. 1986. "The Neighborhood Context of Police Behavior," in *Communities and Crime*, ed. J. Albert J. Reiss and M. Tonry. Chicago: University of Chicago Press.

Smith, Douglas A., Christy A. Visher, and Laura A. Davidson. 1984. "Equity and Discretionary Justice: The Influence of Race on Police Arrest Decisions." *Journal of Criminal Law and Criminology* 75: 234–49.

Smith, Kevin B. 2004. "The Politics of Punishment: Evaluating Political Explanations of Incarceration Rates." *Journal of Politics* 66: 925–38.

Snell, Tracy L. 2001. "Capital Punishment 2000 NCJ 190598." Washington, D.C.: Bureau of Justice Statistics.

Sniderman, Paul M., and Richard A. Brody. 1977. "Coping: The Ethic of Self-Reliance." *American Journal of Political Science* 21: 501–21.

Sniderman, Paul M., and Edward G. Carmines. 1997. *Reaching Beyond Race*. Cambridge, MA: Harvard University Press.

Sniderman, Paul M., and Douglas B. Grob. 1996. "Innovations in Experimental Design in Attitude Surveys." *Annual Review of Sociology* 22: 377–99.

Sniderman, Paul M., and Thomas Piazza. 1993. *The Scar of Race*. Cambridge, MA: Harvard University Press.

Sniderman, Paul M., Richard A. Brody, and Phillip E. Tetlock. 1993. *Reasoning and Choice: Explorations in Political Psychology*. Cambridge, MA: Cambridge University Press.

Soss, Joe. 1999. "Lessons of Welfare: Policy Design, Political Learning and Political Action." *American Political Science Review* 93: 363–80.

Soss, Joe, and Sanford F. Schram. 2007. "A Public Transformed? Welfare Reform as Policy Feedback." *American Political Science Review* 101 (1): 111–27.

Soss, Joe, Laura Langbein, and Alan R. Metelko. 2003. "Why Do White Americans Support the Death Penalty?" *Journal of Politics* 65: 397–421.

Spohn, Cassia. 2002. *How Do Judges Decide: The Search for Fairness and Justice in Punishment*. Thousand Oaks, CA: Sage Publications.

Spohn, Cassia. 2009. *How Do Judges Decide: The Search for Fairness and Justice in Punishment*. 2nd ed. Los Angeles: Sage Publications.

Spohn, Cassia C. 2000. "Thirty Years of Sentencing Reform: The Quest for a Racially Neutral Sentencing Process." *Criminal Justice* 3: 427–501.

Stinchcombe, Arthur, Rebecca Adams, Carol A. Heimer, Kim Lane Schepple, Tom W. Smith, and D. Garth Taylor. 1980. *Crime and Punishment – Changing Attitudes in America*. San Francisco: Jossey-Bass.

Stuntz, William J. 1998. "Race, Class, and Drugs." *Columbia Law Review* 98: 1795–842.

Sunnafrank, M., and N. E. Fontes. 1983. "General Crime Related Racial Stereotypes and Influence on Juridicial Decisions." *Cornell Journal of Social Relations* 17: 1–15.

Taber, Charles S., and Milton Lodge. 2006. "Motivated Skepticism in the Evaluation of Political Beliefs." *American Journal of Political Science* 50 (3): 755–69.

Taber, Charles S., Damon Cann, and Simona Kucsova. 2009. "The Motivated Processing of Political Arguments." *Political Behavior* 31: 137–55.

Tate, Katherine. 1993. *From Protest to Politics: The New Black Voters in American Elections*. Cambridge, MA: Harvard University Press.

———2003. *Black Faces in the Mirror: African Americans and their Representatives in the U.S. Congress*. Princeton, NJ: Princeton University Press.

Taylor, Marylee C. 1998. "How White Attitudes Vary with the Racial Composition of Local Populations: Numbers Count." *American Sociological Review* 63 (4): 512–35.

Tesler, Michael, and David Sears. 2009. "Barack Obama and the Two Sides of Symbolic Racism: Explaining the Effects of Racial Resentment in the Primaries and Beyond." Paper presented at the Midwest Political Science Association 67th Annual National Conference, April 2–5, Chicago.

Tetlock, Philip E. 1986. "A Value Pluralism Model of Ideological Reasoning." *Journal of Personality and Social Psychology* 50: 819–27.

Thaler, Richard H. 1987. "The Psychology and Economics Conference Handbook: Comments on Simon, on Einhorn and Hogarth, and on Tversky and Kahneman," in *Rational Choice: The Contrast between Economics and Psychology*, ed. R. M. Hogarth and M. W. Reder. Chicago: University of Chicago Press: 95–100.

Thibaut, John, and Lauren S. Walker. 1975. *Procedural Justice: A Psychological Analysis*. Hillsdale, NJ: Lawrence Erlbaum.

Thomas, W. John, and Dorothy E. Stubbe. 1996. "A Comparison of Correctional and Mental Health Referrals in the Juvenile Court." *Journal of Psychiatry and Law* 24: 379–400.

Tonry, Michael. 1995. *Malign Neglect: Race, Crime, and Punishment in America*. New York: Oxford University Press.

Tuch, Steven A., and Ronald Weitzer. 1997. "Racial Differences in Attitudes toward the Police." *Public Opinion Quarterly* 61: 642–63.

Tyler, Tom R. 1988. "What Is Procedural Justice? Criteria Used by Citizens to Assess the Fairness of Legal Procedures." *Law and Society Review* 22: 103–35.

———1990. *Why People Obey the Law*. New Haven, CT: Yale University Press.

———2000. "Social Justice: Outcome and Procedure." *International Journal of Psychology* 35: 117–25.

———2001. "A Psychological Perspective on the Legitimacy of Institutions and Authorities," in *The Psychology of Legitimacy: Emerging Perspectives on Ideology, Justice and Intergroup Relations*, ed. J. T. Jost and B. Major. New York: Cambridge University Press.

Tyler, Tom R., and Robert J. Boeckmann. 1997. "Three Strikes and You Are Out, But Why? The Psychology of Public Support for Punishing Rule Breakers." *Law and Society Review* 31 (2): 237–65.

Tyler, Tom R., and Robert Folger. 1980. "Distributional and Procedural Aspects of Satisfaction with Citizen-Police Encounters." *Basic and Applied Social Psychology* 1: 281–92.

Tyler, Tom R., Peter Degoey, and Heather Smith. 1996. "Understanding Why the Justice of Group Procedures Matters: A Test of the Psychological Dynamics of the Group-Value Model." *Journal of Personality and Social Psychology* 70: 913–30.

Tyler, Tom R., Robert J. Boeckmann, Heather J. Smith, and Yuen J. Huo. 1997. *Social Justice in a Diverse Society*. Boulder, CO: Westview.

Tyler, T. R., and R. Weber. 1982. "Support for the Death Penalty: Instrumental Response to Crime or Symbolic Attitude?" *Law and Society Review* 17 (1): 121–45.

U.S. National Advisory Commission on Civil Disorders. 1968. "Report of the National Advisory Commission on Civil Disorders." Washington, D.C.: U.S. Government Printing Office.

Valentino, Nicholas A. 1999. "Crime News and the Priming of Racial Attitudes during Evaluations of the President." *Public Opinion Quarterly* 63: 293–320.

Valentino, Nicholas A., Vincent L. Hutchings, and Ismael K. White. 2002. "Cues that Matter: How Political Ads Prime Racial Attitudes during Campaigns." *American Political Science Review* 96: 75–90.

Van den Bos, Kees, E. Allan Lind, and Henk A. M. Wilke. 2001. "The Psychology of Procedural and Distributive Justice Viewed from the Perspective of Fairness Heuristic Theory," in *Justice in the Workplace: From Theory to Practice*, ed. R. Cropanzano. Mahwah, NJ: Lawrence Erlbaum: 49–66.

Van den Bos, Kees, E. Allan Lind, Riel Vermunt, and Henk A. M. Wilke. 1997. "How Do I Judge My Outcome When I Do Not Know the Outcome of Others? The Psychology of the Fair Process Effect." *Journal of Personality and Social Psychology* 72: 1034–46.

Vermunt, Riel, and Herman Steensma. 2003. "Physiological Relaxation: Stress Reduction through Fair Treatment." *Social Justice Research* 16: 135–49.

Walker, Samuel, Cassia Spohn, and Miriam DeLone. 2004. *The Color of Justice: Race, Ethnicity, and Crime in America*. 3rd ed. Belmont, CA: Thomson Learning.

Walker, W. Laurens, and E. Allan Lind. 1984. "Psychological Studies of Procedural Models," in *Progress in Applied Social Psychology*, vol. 2, ed. G. M. Stephenson and J. H. Davis. New York: John Wiley and Sons: 293–313.

Weitzer, Ronald, and Steven Tuch. 2002. "Perceptions of Racial Profiling: Race, Class, and Personal Experience." *Criminology* 40: 435–56.

———2004. "Race and Perceptions of Police Misconduct." *Social Problems* 51: 305–25.

Weitzer, Ronald, and Steven A. Tuch. 2006. *Race and Policing in America: Conflict and Reform*. Cambridge: Cambridge University Press.

Welch, Susan, Michael Combs, and John Gruhl. 1988. "Do Black Judges Make a Difference?" *American Journal of Political Science* 32 (1): 126–36.

Welch, Susan, Lee Sigelman, Tim Bledsoe, and Michael Combs. 2001. *Race and Place: Residence and Race Relations in an American City*. Cambridge: Cambridge University Press.

Western, Bruce. 2006. *Punishment and Inequality in America*. New York: Russell Sage Foundation.

White, Ismail K. 2007. "When Race Matters and When It Doesn't: Racial Group Differences in Response to Racial Cues." *American Political Science Review* 101: 339–54.

Wilbanks, William. 1987. *The Myth of a Racist Criminal Justice System*. Monterey, CA: Brooks/Cole.

Wilber, Del Quentin. June 29, 2009. "Two Judges Target Cocaine Penalties: Disparity for Crack Crimes Criticized," *The Washington Power.*

Williams, Kirk R., and Susan Drake. 1980. "Social Structure, Crimes, and Criminalization: An Empirical Examination of the Conflict Perspective." *Sociological Quarterly* 21 (4): 563–75.

Williams, Linda Meyer, and Ronald A. Farrell. 1990. "Legal Responses to Child Sexual Abuse in Day Care." *Criminal Justice and Behavior* 17: 284–302.

Wilson, James Q. 1968. *Varieties of Police Behavior: The Management of Law and Order in Eight Communities.* Cambridge, MA: Harvard University Press.

Wordes, Madeline, and Timothy S. Bynum. 1995. "Policing Juveniles: Is There Bias against Youths of Color?" in *Minorities in Juvenile Justice*, ed. K. K. Leonard, C. E. Pope, and W. Feyerherm. Thousand Oaks, CA: Sage Publications: 47–65.

Wordes, Madeline, Timothy S. Bynum, and Charles J. Corley. 1994. "Locking up Youth: The Impact of Race on Detention Decisions." *Journal of Research in Crime and Delinquency* 31: 149–65.

Yates, Jeff, and Richard Fording. 2005. "Politics and State Punitiveness in Black and White." *Journal of Politics* 67 (4): 1099–121.

Young, Robert L. 1991. "Race, Conceptions of Crime and Justice, and Support for the Death Penalty." *Social Psychology Quarterly* 54 (1): 67–75.

Zaller, John. 1992. *The Nature and Origins of Mass Opinion.* Cambridge, MA: Cambridge University Press.

Zimring, Franklin E. 2007. *The Great American Crime Decline.* Oxford and New York: Oxford University Press.

Index

Page numbers in italics refer to tables or figures in the text.

Books in the Series

Asher Arian, *Security Threatened: Surveying Israeli Opinion on Peace and War*

James DeNardo, *The Amateur Strategist: Intuitive Deterrence Theories and the Politics of the Nuclear Arms Race*

Robert S. Erikson, Michael B. Mackeun, and James A. Stimson, *The Macro Polity*

James L. Gibson, *Overcoming Historical Injustices: Land Reconciliation in South Africa*

James L. Gibson and Amanda Gouws, *Overcoming Intolerance in South Africa: Experiments in Democratic Persuasion*

John R. Hibbing and Elizabeth Theiss-Morse, *Congress As Public Enemy: Public Attitudes Toward American Political Institutions*

John R. Hibbing and Elizabeth Theiss-Morse, *Stealth Democracy: Americans' Beliefs about How Government Should Work*

John R. Hibbing and Elizabeth Theiss-Morse, *What Is It about Government That Americans Dislike?*

Robert Huckfeldt and John Sprague, *Citizens, Politics, and Social Communication*

Robert Huckfeldt, Paul E. Johnson, and John Sprague, *Political Disagreement: The Survival of Diverse Opinions within Communication Networks*

James H. Kuklinski, *Citizens and Politics: Perspectives from Political Psychology*

James H. Kuklinski, *Thinking about Political Psychology*

Richard R. Lau and David P. Redlawsk, *How Voters Decide: Information Processing in Election Campaigns*

Arthur Lupia, Mathew McCubbins, and Samuel Popkin, *Elements of Reason: Cognition, Choice, and the Bounds of Rationality*

George E. Marcus, John L. Sullivan, Elizabeth Theiss-Morse, and Sandra L. Wood, *With Malice Toward Some: How People Make Civil Liberties Judgments*

Diana C. Mutz, *Impersonal Influence: How Perceptions of Mass Collectives Affect Political Attitudes*

Markus Prior, *Post-Broadcast Democracy: How Media Choice Increases Inequality in Political Involvement and Polarizes Elections*

Paul M. Sniderman, Richard A. Brody, and Philip E. Tetlock, *Reasoning and Choice: Explorations in Political Psychology*

Karen Stenner, *The Authoritarian Dynamic*

Susan Welch, Timothy Bledsoe, Lee Sigelman, and Michael Combs, *Race and Place*

John Zaller, *The Nature and Origins of Mass Opinion*

Alan S. Zuckerman, Josip Dasovic, and Jennifer Fitzgerald, *Partisan Families: The Social Logic of Bounded Partisanship in Germany and Britain*